✳ ✳ ✳ ✳ ✳ ✳ ✳

"Thank you for making Mrs. Wearmouth's volumes (*Abstracts*) available to me. They are excellent and contain so much helpful data on making...Edelen, Gardiner, Bowling, Jameson, Dyer, Harris and Forbes ancestry "come alive" as to their participation in civic and social affairs. The manuscripts I compiled for our three children contain what I knew from Bible records, obituaries, tombstones, portraits, and scrapbooks here, but many of the 'news' items I did not have. The *Times* and *Advertiser* items are enlightening."

Vivian B. Edelen

✳ ✳ ✳ ✳ ✳ ✳ ✳

"I read it (*Abstracts*) from cover to cover and you get a real feeling for what 19th century Charles Countians were like in addition to the valuable statistical information such as marriages...I never knew my great-great-grandfather was Postmaster at Bryantown until I saw your book...You have done an outstanding service to Charles County and to the much wider genealogical community -- keep up the good work.

Timothy A. Colchord

✳ ✳ ✳ ✳ ✳ ✳ ✳

ABSTRACTS FROM THE

PORT TOBACCO TIMES

AND

CHARLES COUNTY ADVERTISER

VOLUME THREE: 1870-1875

Compiled by Roberta J. Wearmouth

Courthouse Main Entrance.

HERITAGE BOOKS, INC.

Also available from Heritage Books, Inc.
by Roberta J. Wearmouth:

*Abstracts from the **Port Tobacco Times and
Charles County Advertiser***
Volume I: 1844-1854
Volume II: 1855-1869

Published 1993 By

HERITAGE BOOKS, INC.
1540-E Pointer Ridge Place,
Bowie, Maryland 20716
(301) 390-7709

ISBN 1-55613-878-4

A Complete Catalog Listing Hundreds of Titles on
Genealogy, History, and Americana
Available Free on Request

Contents

A Note from the Author

A lady from Indiana wrote to say that all her life she had heard a story related about a black family retainer in an earlier generation. He had been taken in by her grandparents or great grandparents and raised with the family children. At the death of each family member, he insisted on being the one to dig the grave. The lady never knew whether the story was a myth or based on fact. She read the *Abstracts* and found the obituary of this man and in it the same facts were recounted which she had heard all her life.

It was so kind of these people to write to me sharing their interest in history and their appreciation for what I have done, I cannot thank them enough. I hope that Volume Three will serve the same useful purpose the other two volumes seem to have.

Roberta J. Wearmouth

About the Author

Roberta Wearmouth was born in Battle Creek, Michigan and she and her husband, John, moved to Charles County, Maryland in 1958, the year the county observed its tercentenary celebration. Their interest in history was piqued then and became a passion which has not diminished.

Through the years the author has observed that the microfilmed copies of the *Port Tobacco Times and Charles County Advertiser* should be read and abstracted since they provide the most sensitive and accurate reflection of the times and temper of Charles County people during its period of publication, 1844-1897. In 1990 the first volume was published, and the author hopes to complete the project with the issuance of the volume including the newspaper of 1897.

ABSTRACTS FROM THE PORT TOBACCO TIMES AND CHARLES COUNTY ADVERTISER NEWSPAPER PUBLISHED IN PORT TOBACCO, MARYLAND FROM 1844 UNTIL 1898 WHEN IT MERGED WITH THE CRESCENT TO BECOME THE TIMES-CRESCENT.

May 6, 1870, Vol. XXVII, No. 1

(Published every Friday, E. Wells, editor and proprietor.)

J.H.Roberts asks all credit customers to pay their accounts. As of May 1st only cash transactions.
The grading of the Baltimore and Potomac Railroad is completed from Collington (junction) to Marlboro.
Mrs. M.A.Scott, milliner, Port Tobacco, has just returned from Baltimore with new spring and summer millinery.

Following commissions received from Government office

Justices of the Peace

Edward D.R. Bean
W.Boswell
Earnest Hanson
W.P.Flowers
Thomas C. Wilkerson
Benjamin F. Bowling
J. Reverdy Carlin
James H.M.Dutton

G.C.Burch
George N. Rowe
George W. Carpenter
Allen B. Milstead
Richard W. Bryan
Francis D. Gardiner
J. Thomas Colton
J.B.Sheriff

Officers of Registration

James A. Franklin
William C. Brent
Marcellus Thompson
Charles C. Perry
Rufus Robey

William H. Gray
Henry M. Hannon
James B. Latimer
Townley Robey

George A. Huntt, Clerk of County Commission for Charles County

Luke W.B.Hawkins died Wednesday, April 27, 58 years "...the gentle and devoted husband, the affectionate father..."
Albert Milstead, Collector, 1st district, asks all taxpayers who have not settled their bills to do so immediately.

1

Mrs. John Murdoch, Nanjemoy, reports she set a
goose on 12 eggs, 2 eggs spoiled, out of the re-
maining 10, 11 goslings hatched. "This is a very
remarkable incubation, we are told." (Ed.)

Rev. Presley B. Smith will preach at the 1st quarterly meeting of the Methodist Episcopal Church,
to be held at Pisgah "Lovefeast Sunday 9½ A.M."

William H. Moore, Bryantown, advertises "Wanted!!!
By two young men of prepossessing personal appearance, permanent homes as sons-in-law in the
bosom of a respectable family. Blood no object,
being already supplied..."

Thomas A. Millar, 1st and 2nd districts and Pere
Wilmer, 3rd and 4th districts, appointed as assistant Marshals to take the 9th Census. [We
suppose the districts referred to are those which
were known before our county was divided into
nine districts. Ed.]

Dr. Thomas A. Carrico appointed State School Commissioner. These four commissioners with principal State Normal School constitute the Board of
State School Commissioners and have supervision
of public school interests of the State.

Richard B. Posey vs Henry E. Smith and Almira, his
wife.

John F. Dunnington, deceased, property "Stingham"
in Nanjemoy near the Cross Roads will be sold by
trustees, 105 acres and a 30 acre piece nearby.

Leonard C. Edelen vs C.M.Edelen, C.D.Edelen,
R.W.Edelen equity court. Daniel W. Hawkins,
trustee. Minor children L.C.Edelen.

Leonard Adams, former owner of 370 acres - several
tracts, "Double Trouble," "Double Trouble Enlarged." "Morning Work," and "Smallwood's Plains;"
also two lots in village of Beantown, 4 acres;
48 acres near village. Dwelling house on lots
in Beantown, tavern and dwelling house.

J.D.Hanson sells "Greenland" 3 miles from Port Tobacco on the road to Newtown, 200 acres, dwelling house. "Terms made known on application to me
at Salem, near Port Tobacco."

Bennett Neale lost "in the streets of Port Tobacco..."
gold spectacles in red morocco case.

William Coomes, deceased, sale of property. George
D. Mudd and William H. Moore vs Richard H. Edelen,
executor Coomes and heirs. Daniel W. Hawkins,
trustee. Richard Barnes, Stouten W. Dent, and
Robert Digges, Orphans' Court.

William L. Sheirburn property to be sold at suit of
George W. Webb & Co., storehouse and lot in Newtown. John R. Murray, sheriff.

2

Peregrine Davis vs E. Harriet Matthews. Equity Court. George A. Huntt, Clerk.

E. Griswold's stallion, Young Star, will be let to mares -- at stables of A.W.Neale; at "Mexico," Cobb Neck; Dr. Smoot's, Piccawaxen; and the stables of Townley Robey.

Miss Bettie A. Higdon has just opened a millinery shop in Bryantown.

Samuel Hanson's stallion, Black Hawk, will stand at Mr. Hamilton's "Milton Hill"; Mr. Mollyhorn's Cobb Neck; Dr. A.J.Smoot's, Piccawaxen; Mr. Thomas Matthews' near Port Tobacco; Benjamin Stonestreet's; Mr. McDaniel's "Independence"; W.E.W.Rowe's; and Mr. Rennoe's.

Robert E. Rison's stallion, Bell Founder, will stand at W. Bowie's (Trappe); Barnes Compton's barn; C.H.Wills' barn.

E.W.Dent, S.Cox, H.C.Page, Commissioners, will alter and change public road through lands of Dr. Francis R. Wills "...at a place called Gilpin's Hill..."

Dr. Cobey, graduate of Baltimore College of Dental Surgery, offers his services to Charles County. "...He will do both Operative and Mechanical work; correct Irregularity in Teeth; will insert Artificial Teeth by all the different methods deemed practicable; will mount teeth upon Rubber, Gold, Silver, Platinum or Aluminum. He will wait upon persons wishing to have Dental Operations at their homes. Cross Roads."

E.S.Chipley has taken rooms at Norris' Hotel, Port Tobacco, to execute ambrotypes, ferrotypes and porcelaine pictures.

Ralph Way is selling pumps which will force water to the top of the highest house in Charles County. May be seen on the premises of John Hamilton near the store of William Boswell in Port Tobacco.

Thomas H. Scott, Port Tobacco, advertises all kinds of carpentering.

R.S.Corry, undertaker in Newport.

May 20, 1870, Vol. XXVII, No. 3

Circuit Court Convened

Hon. Robert Ford, associate judge; Eugene Digges, State's Attorney; George A. Huntt, Clerk; John R. Murray, Sheriff; Hon. George Brent, Chief Judge.

John W. Spencer (colored) indicted for stealing a horse, property of Thomas B. Berry, Esq. at Troy. V. Brent, prisoner's counsel.

Henry G. Robertson, Secretary, St. Columba Lodge
annual meeting at Masonic Hall, Port Tobacco.
William L. McDaniel announces candidacy for office
of Sheriffalty.
Walter Mitchell, deceased, executors Hugh Mitchell,
John H. Mitchell and Bettie F. Mitchell told to
exhibit claims.
P.H.Muschett's store accounts told to come forward
and pay or be taken to court to obtain payment.
J.H.Mitchell and S.Cox, Jr., assignees.
Ten miles of the Baltimore and Potomac Railroad
construction below Marlboro have been placed
under contract.
John C. Bush, negro, Allen's Fresh, has been appointed postmaster of that place.
Mrs. Ann Key Speake, deceased, land "Harwood" to be
sold, 350 acres. on Port Tobacco Creek, has
dwelling house. R.H.Edelen, trustee.
N. Stonestreet and Eugene Digges, attorneys, have
office in Port Tobacco.
J.T.Mudd, Gallant Green, announces that he has new
goods at his store.

Circuit court cases

State vs Frank Kendrick - assault and battery
against William Sutherland - guilty, $10 fine.
State vs Alfred Nalley -- assault and battery
against Charles Garner (colored) - not guilty.
State vs Thomas Frederick (colored) indicted
larceny of piece of beef - guilty, sentenced
to county jail for one month.
State vs Richard Hall alias John W. Spencer (colored) for stealing bay horse the property of
Thomas B. Berry -- case to Anne Arundel County.
State vs Robert Calvert (colored) breaking and en-
tering meat house of John W. McPherson, stealing
and carrying off bacon - guilty, penitentiary
for five years.
State vs Thomas Calvert (colored) indicted for same-
not guilty.
State vs Matthew Scott (colored) for murder of Rufus
Dade. Not guilty of murder; guilty of manslaughter-
county jail one month, $50.00 fine.
State vs Jane Dade (colored) larceny. Not guilty,
confessed by State.
State vs William Johnson (colored) larceny. Not
guilty.
State vs Julius Quenzel for working on the Sabbath
day. Not guilty, confessed by State.

4

Walter H. Barkley died at his residence in Pomonkey. Leaves a wife and seven children. He was
46 years old.
        "His languishing head is at rest,
        Its thinking and aching is o'er,
        His quiet, immovable breast,
        Is heaved by affliction no more."
Mary F. Edelen, deceased, Orphans' Court. John W.
Mitchell, administrator.

                    Pension Law
(Authorized annual pension of $80 to be paid in
 four quarterly installments during the natural
 life of soldiers and widows of soldiers of the
 War of 1812)

J.H.Downing   Catharine Huntt
William Johnson   Mary A. Marr
Ellen O'Bryan   Floyd Johnson
Sarah Smith   Ellen H. Morton
Sallie Moore   Eleanor Marshall
Mariah Bailey   Amelia Scoot
Jane H. Miller   Ann S. Waters
Innocenes B. Shaw   John F. Lucas
Catharine Allen   Elizabeth Allen
Louisa Edelen   Hezekiah Franklin
Charles Farroll   Elizabeth Farroll
Jane Farroll   Asa Jenkins
Charles Kinnamon   Sally McDaniel
Juliana Montgomery   Mary E. Pickerell
Wady Posey   Eleanor A. Roby
Cecilia Reeves   Mary Robertson
Rachel Shannon   Ann S. Ware
Phebe Welsh   Catharine Mudd
Elizabeth Osbourne   Eliza Williams
Francis E. Dunnington

          June 3, 1870, Vol. XXVII, No. 5

John C. Bush (colored) who was appointed postmaster
   at Allen's Fresh has declined the appointment,
   having failed to obtain the usual bond.
J. Hubert Roberts, Esq. married Miss Lilla L.
   Padgett Tuesday May 31st at the residence of
   Rev. Dr. Lewin, both of Port Tobacco.
B.W.B.McPherson, Esq. married Miss Nannie Turner,
   daughter of the late Aquila Turner, Esq., both
   of Charles County on Thursday, June 2nd at St.
   Paul's Chapel, Port Tobacco Parish by Rev.
   Dr. Lewin.

George T. Simpson, Esq. of Charles County married
Miss Lizzie Mattingley of St. Mary's County at
the residence of R.T.Barber, Esq. near Chaptico,
St. Mary's County by Rev. Bennett Smith.
Lucinda Dent, deceased, property sold for taxes -
Charles L. Burch, Collector of Taxes, Charles
County.

June 17, 1870, Vol. XXVII, No. 7

Robert L. Burch, deceased, property to be sold -
store house, dwelling house and lot in Bryantown -
lot, 4 acres - store house nearly new.
Hon. Frederick Stone, M.C., married Mrs. Jennie
Fergusson, daughter of the late Colonel Nicholas
Stonestreet, 7 p.m. on Wednesday June 15th at
Christ Church, Port Tobacco by Rev. Dr. Lewin
assisted by Rev. John M. Todd.
Mrs. Sigismunda M. Chapman, wife of Pearson Chapman
died at the residence of her son in Alexandria,
Virginia on June 8, age 63 years, of this county.
William C. Brent house and lot in Port Tobacco for
sale, formerly occupied by Dr. H.R.Scott. "The
Lot attached to this House is very desirable, be-
ing sufficiently large for a good Garden and is
very fertile."

St. Columba Lodge Elects Officers

Edgar Griswold - Worshipful Master
John S. Button - Senior Warden
Henry G. Robertson - Junior Warden
Samuel Cox, Jr. - Secretary
William Wolfe - Tiler

James Willis (colored) was shot by John Plater (col-
ored) - later died. Willis was a hand employed on
board the steamer "Planter."
Oliver N. Bryan of Marshall Hall post office sells
Buckeye mower, tobacco prize and two pair white
Chester pigs.
William B. Matthews, executor John Matthews vs
Joseph Stewart, administrator Michael Farrall.
William A. Wills, deceased, Orphans' Court.
James A. Wills, administrator.

July 1, 1870, Volume XXVII, No. 9

John F. Boswell married Matilda O. Dent of Charles
County at parsonage of the Second Baptist Church,
Washington, D.C. June 23rd by Rev. P. Warren.

George Pearson, son of Marshall and Ellen Chapman
   died Wednesday, June 22, 5 months, 22 days. "God
   took thee, in His mercy, A lamb, untasked,
   untried..."
Mary M. Moran, deceased, personal property to be
   sold. Ellen F. Moran, R.H.Edelen, administrators.
John Thompson (colored) died in the harvest field
   of Dr. A.H.Robertson of heat prostration.
Richard Payne appointed postmaster at Allen's
   Fresh.

Governor Appointments

George W. Carpenter, Officer of Registration, 3rd
   Election District, vice W.H.Gray who declined to
   serve.
John H. Freeman, Officer of Registration, 4th Elec-
   tion District, vice James B. Latimer who declined
   to serve.
Marcellus Thompson, Officer of Registration, 6th
   Election District, vice self, failing to qualify.
Thomas M. Posey, Justice of the Peace, 3rd Election
   District, vice George W. Carpenter, failing to
   qualify.
Richard W. Bryan, Justice of the Peace, 7th Election
   District, vice self, failing to qualify.
Francis D. Gardiner, Justice of the Peace, 8th
   Election District, vice self, failing to qualify.

July 22, 1870, Vol. XXVII, No. 12

Ann Elizabeth Gough mortgage from Henry S. Mitchell -
   will sell 350 acres "Six Chimnies" or "Deep Point"
   on the north side of Mattawoman Creek at its junction with Potomac River - located on Potomac River,
   four miles below Glymont. B.A.Jamison, attorney,
   mortgagee.
John W. Mitchell, trustee, sells "Woodbury Harbor"
   generally known as "Nanjemoy Stores" 175 acres on
   Potomac River below Maryland Point - has comfortable dwelling - long known as one of regular steam
   boat landings on Potomac River.
John Hamilton sells thrashing machine and three pair
   of cartwheels.
William J. Scott, son of Joseph Scott died after hogshead of tobacco, between 800 and 900 pounds, rolled
   over him from head to toe. Accident happened at
   warehouse near Port Tobacco.
Major John T. Stoddert died at his residence "Wicomico
   House" Tuesday morning July 19th at 6 a.m. He was
   born at Smith's Point, Nanjemoy 28 October 1791. He

7

was a nephew of William Smallwood. Educated at
Princeton University, he studied law in Annapolis
under Judge Alexander O. Magruder. He was on the
staff of General Philip Steuart of Eutaw memory
in the War of 1812. He resided in Charles County
until a year ago when he moved to Baltimore. He
was on a visit to his country residence in Charles
County when he died. He had been a member of the
State Legislature and National Congress in 1833.
He was a member of the State Constitutional Con-
vention in 1867. He practiced law early in life
but in later years followed literary pursuits.
He was 79 years old.
Hillery Heard near Hill-Top has lost a small light
bay mare.
J. Richard Cox, teacher at School #2 in Election
District #4 will have examination of students.
Dr. F.M.Lancaster, Harris' Lot, sells 200 acre
farm, convenient to steamboat wharf, church,
school and post office.
George M. Lloyd, Secretary, announces that the
Board of School Commissioners will meet.
John D. Bowling vs Catharine D. Burch - Equity
Court.
Susan A. Goodwin, deceased, property to be sold
"Parnham's Amendment" - 520 acres now occupied by
George Dent, Esq. near Newport. Comfortable dwell-
ing and out buildings. Also "Calvert's Hope" -
273 acres between Centreville and Newport - good
barn, no dwelling - R.H.Edelen, John W. Mitchell
and Vivian Brent, Trustees.

July 29, 1870, Vol. XXVII, No. 13

Baltimore and Potomac Railroad - clearing way for con-
tractors from Brandywine to Potomac River. Grading
proceeding between Marlboro and Charles County line.
45 white and 60 colored men shipped to work on extension of B & P RR from Marlboro to Potomac River -
to expedite completion of that work to allow construction of Alexandria to Fredericksburg, Va. Line.
Kate M. Golden, wife of Robert A. Golden,died in Washington, D.C. on July 20th, only daughter of Rev.
W.I.Chiles. 25 years old. Born at Wade's Bay.
"...She sleeps her last sleep by the beautiful home
of her childhood..."
William J. Scott died on Saturday, July 16, 1870,
21 years. "...How touchingly and sadly true were
the remarks of a brother sailor, when standing on
the deck of the vessel a day or two after the death
of the deceased, 'I miss somebody!'..."

8

Mark L. Simmes, deceased, administrator notice -
Louisa E. Simmes and James E. Higdon, administrators.
Thomas Posey vs Mary P. Bailey - Equity Court.
Francis D. Gardiner - Equity Court.
John R. Turner vs Hy. A. Burch - James W. Burch,
deceased.

August 5, 1870, Vol. XXVII, No. 14

Francis H. Edelen, deceased, Sarah H.R.Edelen and
Joseph S. Boarman, administrators.
Thomas Groves, deceased, Samuel Posey, administrator.
Captain Leonard Marbury's property "Glymont" on the
Potomac River including the pavilion and farm attached has been sold for $28,000.00.

August 19, 1870, Vol. XXVII, No. 16

ANNUAL STATEMENT BY THE COMMISSIONERS OF CHARLES
COUNTY, MD.
Year Ending June 30th, 1870

(Summary of Accounts shows the single second largest
expenditure to be $11,354.93 for Public Roads. The
largest expenditure is Incidental Charges,
$15,177.03.)

Judges of Orphans' Court

Robert Digges, Stouten W. Dent and Richard Barnes

County Commissioners

James H. Neale, Mason L. McPherson, F.L.Dent, Thomas
Y. Robey, Joseph E. Sanders, George Taylor, Thomas R.
Halley, John H. Cox, A. Jackson Smoot, Josias Hawkins.

Judges of Election

George P. Jenkins, Thomas L. Speake, Richard B. Posey,
Washington A. Posey, Thomas Posey, Thomas B. Berry,
John W. McPherson, Benjamin D. Tubman, Zachariah Swann,
William Hamilton, Bennett Neale, George H. Simpson,
Thomas A. Jones, Jere W. Burch, James A. Mudd, Alexander H. Robertson, Charles E. Hannon, Noel B. Hannon,
John L. Johnson, Henry S. Dent, James T. Thomas,
Richard P. Wall, William L. McDaniel, George F. Beall,
John H.D.Wingate, John Hammersley, Joseph Price.

Clerks of Election

J.F.S.Middleton, William H. Williams, Peter W. Robey,
C. Claude Digges, Frederick L. Dent, William M.
Burch, W.E.W.Rowe, James A. Franklin, William H. Cox,
George W. Tubman, Richard Price, William P. Flowers,
Joshua B. Sheriff, Benjamin F. Blandford, John H.
Ward, J.H.M.Dutton, John T. Dutton, F.J.Wiley, use
E.D.R.Bean.

Grand Jurors (1869 November Term)

William Boswell, B. Leonard Higdon, John R. Murray,
Charles L. Burch, Thomas Y. Robey, Edward L. Huntt,
Wm. L. Harding, W.F.McGarner, Sylvester Mudd, G.H.
Gardiner, Ed. D. Boone, F.W.Weems, B.M.Edelen,
T.J.Gardiner, S.W.Adams, J.H.Freeman, use C.H.Wood,
Thos. Latimer, B.F.Burch, T.M.Posey, J.W.Burch,
L. Wilmer, use W.W.Padgett.

(1870 May Term)

F.L.Dent, C.L.Lancaster, G.C.Burch, Wm. H. Moore,
J.R.Carlin, Edmund Perry, Geo. P. Jenkins, M.L.
McPherson, Wm. H. Berry, M. Thompson, W.H.Williams,
John B. Lyon, Rufus Robey, Wm. M. Jamison, William
H. Gray, T.E.Gardiner, Samuel Hawkins, Francis Price,
Jos. S. Boarman, C.C.Digges, Benj. Welch.

Petit Jurors (1869 November Term)

Jos. C. Gray, William L. Sheirbourn, B.W.Gardiner,
John Hamersley, use T.Y.Robey, J.W.McPherson, Wm.
Turner, Geo. W. Berry, J.H.D.Wingate, E.D.R.Bean,
Rich. Farrall, Edwin Adams, Richard Payne, use
Dorsey,Miller &°Co.,W.E.W.Rowe, R.P.Wall, J.T.Ward,
John E. Bailey, M.P.Gardiner, Henry S. Dent, Regan
Deakens, Jas. M. Morgan, W.L.McDaniel, use W.L.Hicks,
F.P.Hamilton, P.H.Muschett, J.B.Lyon, J.T.Johnson,
use E.D.R.Bean

Talismen

Chas. S. Williams, use T.Y.Robey, Thomas B. Delozier,
J.W.Miller, use W.Boswell & Co., William Hamilton,
William L. Cook, Thomas L. Speake, William J.Boarman.

(1870 May Term)

Joseph Price, J.E.Wingate, T.K.Ching, G.W.Tubman,
Sam'l H. Cox, W.A.Posey, Thos. J. Speake, Geo. D.
Alvey, D.I.Sanders, J.M.Burch, M.Chapman, Peter
Wheeler, Geo. H. Muschett, Geo. F. Beall, Wm. F.

Dement, John T. Dutton, J.H.Montgomery, The. Smoot,
H.A.Neale, Peter Williams, Jere. T. Mudd, B.W.Bland-
ford, J.H.Roberts, Joseph Padgett.

Witnesses to Grand Inquest (1869 November Term)

Wilfred Jackson, George J. Chappelear, Samuel Smoot,
Alfred P. Willett, George Dent, Dennis Brooks, Thomas
B. Delozier, Benjamin F. Blandford, John S. Long,
William Southerland, George A. Huntt, W.G.Oliver,
Richard T. Halley, J.H.Roberts, Walter Southerland,
Elizabeth Adams, William A. Boarman, Thomas F.
Darnell, Albin Price, W.A.Posey, Len. Dunnington use
W.Hamilton, Lemuel Smoot, H.Clagett Page, George A.
Huntt, Benjamin G. Stonestreet, Luther Martin, Henry
G. Robertson, William A. Fowke, Zach. Swann, Susan
Mudd, Peter Connelly use H.C.Page, William Boarman,
(colored), Napoleon Jameson, Joseph Murphy, Eliza
Brown, (col'd), Chs. E. Garner, Thomas K. Moran,
R.A.Rennoe, Adelene Fendall, Edward Smoot, Henry
Marshall, Henry Hill, Wesley Franklin, Walter M.
Barnes, Robert Curry, Patrick Duffey, Joseph F.
Thomas, George H. Adams, John H. Downing, Harriet
Matthews, Geo. Butler use W. Boswell & Co., W.R.
Smoot use J.T.Mudd, Wm. H. Boswell use J.T.Mudd,
Alexander Edelen, Caroline Luckett use George A.
Huntt, Gerard W. Hungerford, J.C.Smallwood use
A.Smoot, Richard Harbin, Clem Ford use Wm. Boswell
& Co., Aloysius Robey, Patrick Duffy, Henry Swann
use Wm. Boswell & Co., Thomas Winters use Wm.
Boswell & Co., Stephen Penn use Wm. Boswell & Co.,
Elizabeth Duffy, Th. Dodson use Wm. Boswell & Co.,
Chs. Higdon use Wm. Boswell & Co., John Ware (col-
ored), Robert Duckett use Wm. Boswell & Co., Geo.
A. Huntt, Edwin A. Smith, George Dent, jr., W.T.
Hicks, Bernard Matthews.

(1870 May Term)

Thomas B. Berry, jr., William Barber (colored),
Francis Tennison, J.B.Sheriff, Samuel T. Berry,
John Farran, Thomas B. Delozier, Thomas I. Speake,
Benjamin F. Blandford, Sylvester A. Mudd, Samuel
Smoot, Geo. J. Chappalear, Geo. D. Mudd, Peter
Wheeler, Chs. H. Sheirbourn, William C. Jones,
William J. Boarman, James T. Bateman, William A.
Boarman, James T. Bateman, William A. Boarman, L.A.
M rtin, James Dorsey, Addison Gill, Jos. L. Murray,
R.T.Halley, Maria Yates, John Bean, G,W.Hungerford,
Hanson Beally, Charles Brawner, Sarah Blair,
Josephine Wallis, John F. Bradley, Thos. K. Ching,
John Chappalear, George S. Willett, Charles Dade,
John W. Posey, Henry Chapman, George H. Adams,

11

Rich'd Adams, Lem. Smoot, Henry A. Neale, Edward
Lloyd, J.B.Sheriff, E.C.Reeves, Vivian Brent, George
S.Willett, Luther A. Martin, W.H.Welch, E.M.Mudd,
Hugh Clements, Joseph Wheeler, B.Slye, Robert Semmes,
John H. Chunn, J.E.Higdon, Alfred Swann, J.A.Wills,
John Penny, Millard Edelen, Albin Price,

Witnesses in State Cases (1869 November Term)

Vernon Jackson, George R. Posey, Anthony Carroll,
Alonzo Simpson, Peter Trotter, W.G.Richardson, Har-
rison Edelen, John H. Robey, Richard J. Montgomery,
R. Williams use Joseph Stewart, C. Wedding, J.C.Swann,
W.H.Cooksey use J.M.Latimore & Son, Thomas K. Moran,
J.C.Flowers, John Leland, A.P.Willett, Augustus
Langley, Henry H. Bowie, Eugene Maddox, Charles
Queen, G.C.Swann use T.A.Carrico, William H. Cooksey
use J.M.Latimer & Son, Samuel T. Swann use T.A.
Carrico, Thomas A. Carrico, Thomas K. Moran, use T.A.
Carrico, George Gray, A.W.Clagett, B.W.B.McPherson,
B.D.Tubman, Thomas R. Halley, B.F.Blandford, A.P.
Willett, John S. Long, William A. Fowke, J.W.Newbury,
George P. Jenkins, George P. Oliver, Frank Bridgett,
Olivia Floyd, William Hill, use J.H.Roberts, Frank
Brown, use J.H.Roberts, Elizabeth Adams, Henry Roberts,
James Moore, colored, Miranda Moore, colored, Josey
Brawner, colored, William H. Moore, N.Jamison, use
William H. Moore, Augustus Langley, Jere W. Burch,
L.Dunnington, use Wm. Hamilton, H.C.Page, Peter
Connelly, Robert Corry, James L. Corry, Lucien Robey,
Richard Harbin, J.C.Smallwood, use A. Smoot, Edward
V. Edelen, George Dent, jr., Joseph T. Ward, J.
Hamersley, use J.T.Ward, Caroline Luckett, use G.A.Huntt

(1870 May Term)

William A. Boarman, H. Butler use J.H.Roberts, Samuel
T. Berry, Dr. A.L.Middleton, Thomas K. Moran, Samuel
T. Swann, G.C.Swann, Thomas A. Carrico, Wm. H. Cooksey,
Chapman Swann use Joseph I. Lacey, John H. Kinnamon,
Dr. Stouton W. Dent, Samuel Smoot, Robert J. Lloyd,
W.Duckett use Joseph I. Lacey, Edward Smith, James L.
Brawner, J.W.McPherson, Thomas Berry, jr., Sarah
Blair use J.H.Roberts, E.C.Reeves use A.J.Norris,
M.Butler use J.H.Roberts, William L. Harding, George
Thomas, colored, A. Wade, colored, Mary Washington
use J.I.Lacey, C.A.Wade, Eliza Bloice, use George A.
Huntt, H.Edelen, John A. Wood, Benjamin D. Tubman,
Thomas R. Halley, J.C.Fendall use T.B.Farrall, Dr.
George D. Mudd, G.L.Mudd use P.A.Sasscer, William A.
Mudd, J.R.Tompkins, J.T.S.Tennison, James D. Milstead.

Baillifs and Messengers (1869 November Term)

Joseph H. Mattingley, John D. Covell, William
Flowers, Asa Jenkins.

(January Term)

Joseph H. Mattingley, John D. Covell.

(1870 February Term)

Joseph H. Mattingley, John D. Covell, Asa Jenkins.

(May Term)

Joseph H. Mattingley, John D. Covell, Asa Jenkins,
Nicholas B. Crangle, use J.R.Robertson, Asa Jenkins,
messenger to county commissioners.

Crow Bill Certificates

George N. Rowe, R.D.P.Ratcliffe, Thomas Skinner,
Thomas S. Dent, Peter Wheeler, Peter Williams,
William B. Carpenter, Timothy A. Smith, William
Boswell & Co., Joseph I. Lacey, J.H.Roberts, Peter
W. Robey, J.F.Thompson, R.T.Farrall, C.C.Perry,
John M. Latimer & Son, Francis R. Wills, Sasscer &
Warring, George S. Gardiner, John L. Robey,Townley
Robey, Wilfred B. Moore, Samuel Smoot, E.D.R.Bean,
John T. Colton, William Simmons, Jere T. Mudd,
Thomas Y. Robey.

Registration

William H. Gray, James A. Franklin, Charles C. Perry,
James B. Latimer, use M. Latimer & Son, William C.
Brent, use G.A.Huntt, Marcellus Thompson, use J.T.
Ward, Henry M. Hannon, Rufus Robey, Townley Robey,
John T. Johnson (rent of room), Elizabeth Duffy
(rent of room).

Election Rooms

Timothy A. Smith, John A. Price, Richard Payne,
Charles C. Perry, Elizabeth Duffy, Samuel W. McPherson,
G.C.Burch, E.D.R.Bean.

Coffins for Paupers

W.J.A.Thompson, A.R.A.Murray, R.T.Tubman, Richard
Garner, Leonard Marbury, Sylvester Mudd, Charles
H. Pye.

Coroner Inquests

Dr. Charles H. Pye, post mortem examination
Allowance of 50 cents to each of the following per-
sons as Jurors of Inquest:
J.W.Warring, B.F.Blandford, P. Chapman, R.Wade,
W.Mitchell, William Carrington, Lee Southerland,
H.Maddox, T.L.Hannon, J.C.Cox, F.Richardson, B.W.
Hardy, W.H.Barkley, Southerland, William H. Cox,
D.D.Horton, J.T.Halley, J.H.Boswell, J.C.Cox, Oscar
Wade, J.T.Boswell, J.F.Richardson, Frank Werramont,
John W. Halley, J.L.Hicks, J.F.Wedding, H.Wilkerson,
R.Hicks, W.T.Hicks, C.A.Bowling, C.L.Gardiner, T.C.
Wilkerson, F.A.Gardiner, A.N.Gates, Job Cliff,
James E. Hamilton.

Collectors for Assessments and Insolvents

Albert Milstead, Joseph T. Ward, D. Ignatius Sanders,
Charles L. Burch, William H. Cox.

Incidental Charges

Geo. A. Huntt, Clerk, Circuit Court	$1,153.81
John R. Murray, Sheriff, use M.E.Higdon	1,193.00
William M. Morris, Sheriff, use J.H.Roberts	98.78
Eugene Digges, States' Attorney	1,052.67
George N. Rowe, Crier, use S.H.Cox	211.90
Joseph Stewart, Register of Wills	530.51
Elijah Wells, for Printing	858.32
J.W.Mitchell, Defending Criminals	16.67
Samuel Cox, Jr. Defending Criminals	10.00
Daniel W. Hawkins, Defending Criminals	35.00
A.G.Chapman, Defending Criminals	10.00
R.H.Edelen, Defending Criminals	113.33
R.H.Gardiner and R.H.Edelen, Defending Criminals	10.00
Board School Commissioners	2,000.00
Trustees of the Poor	1,600.00
Vivian Brent, Attorney to County Com- missioners, use J.H.Cox	100.00
John R. Robertson, Clerk to County Com- missioners 250.00, extra services 150.00	400.00
Dr. George D. Mudd, Medical Services to Prisoners	25.00
Dr. Bennett Neal, Medical Services to Prisoners	18.00
Dr. Robert Digges, Medical Services to Prisoners	4.00
J.H.Roberts, clothing furnished prisoners	9.00

Mrs. Caroline Jones, Error in Taxes   7.05
A.J.Norris, Boarding Jurors, per order
   Circuit Court   70.00
J.C.Middleton, Boarding Jurors, per order
   Circuit Court   7.70
William Boswell & Co., Stationery, etc.   42.29
Warren O. Willett, Support of Martha Dent,
   colored, Insane Pauper   125.00
John R. Murray, Support of Andrew Bruce,
   colored, Insane Pauper   150.00
John D. Covell, Keeper of Court House   20.00
Mount Hope Hospital, for support of two
   Insane Paupers   600.00
Maryland Hospital, for support of one
   Insane Pauper   200.00

County Commissioners for the following Purposes

Bonds issued in 1868   2,750.00
Interest on same   255.00
Interest on bonds of 1870   600.00
Fees for Magistrates & Constables   200.00
Court Fees in removed cases to St. Mary's
   and Anne Arundel counties   200.00
Contingent   500.00 -- 4,505.00

Public Roads

R.A.Murray, Supervisor, use J.H.Roberts, William
H.Moore, Charles Semmes, colored, Henry Millar & Co.,
Dr. Francis R. Wills, Dr. Robert Fergusson, Alfred
Nalley, J.H.Maddox, Clem Butler, colored, John G.
Chapman, Luke W.B.Hawkins, B.L.Higdon, John W.
Allbrittain, Francis W. Weems, T.R.Farrall, John
Hamilton, Marshall Chapman, Andrew G. Chapman,
William Cox, W.W. & T.T.Owen, H.Hawkins, colored,
William M. Morris, C. Digges, Moses Slye, colored,
Andrew Thomas, John R. Robertson, Samuel Cox,
J.C.Wenk, Samuel Hawkins, William Ford, colored,
Charles H. Wood, William Boswell & Co., George H.
Muschett, Supervisor, use Dr. Sanders, William T.
Hindle, Alexander Ross, E.J.Sanders, Edwin A. Smith,
John T. Davis, Supervisor, Andrew G. Chapman,
Marshall Chapman, William H. Matthews, Walter
Mitchell, Amanda Matthews, J.H. Roberts, William M.
Morris, Supervisor, Samuel Hanson, Supervisor,
Samuel W. Adams, William T. Hindle, Estate of O Dean,
Heirs of W. Millar, Edmund Perry, Ethelbert Bowie,
Mrs. James Gray, Joseph C. Gray, Heirs of Robert W.
Hanson, Barnes Compton, William B. Fergusson, John
A. Golden, Edward Lloyd, William Owens heirs, George
Taylor, Dr. Alexander H. Robertson, Hezekiah Franklin,

J.A.Price, J.Beall, Edmund Perry, William H. Gray,
J.H.Roberts, William Cox, Supervisor, Samuel W.
Adams, William Penny, Mason & Green, Mrs. M.Maddox,
Joseph E. Cox, Lydia Milstead, James Willis, James
B. Cox, Albert Milstead, Peter Wheeler, John Padgett,
Alexander Rison, William Simmons, William B.
Carpenter, Thornton Beall, H. Scroggins, Alexander
Franklin, John Grinder, Gerrard Rison, William J.
Bowie, Charles H. Wills, John W. Jenkins, William B.
Maddox, F.F.Garret, John H. Carpenter, Joseph C.
Gray, E.F.Mason, Ernest Hanson, Supervisor, use S.W.
Adams, Samuel W. Adams, Thomas A. Millar, Albert
Milstead, Joseph Price, Thomas S. Dent, Henry H.
Posey, Uzzial Nalley's heirs, Francis R. Speake,
Robert Prout, John Hancock, William H. Mitchell,
Mrs. C. Cobey, Francis Price, Henry H. Posey,
A. Haislip, Supervisor, use J.W. Mitchell, Samuel
W. Adams, M.Dunnington, Jane H. Millar, William H.
Gray, Reverdy A. Rennoe, F.Hancock, Cyrus Wheeler,
Thomas Skinner, W.W.Milstead, John Burgess, Alex-
ander Haislip, Francis E. Dunnington, William H.
Price, Peter Williams, John Murdock, William P.
Flowers, George Wheeler, Peter Wheeler, Thomas S.
Dent, Thomas A. Jones, Supervisor, William H. Moore,
James H. Neale, George D. Alvey, William H. Higges
& Co., Charles H. Wood, John T. Colton, Jere T.
Herbert, Thomas D. Stone, Mrs. Eleanore Robertson,
George Dent, James Taylor, J.F.Thompson, Margaret
Smoot, William B. Matthews, Richard Taylor, use W.B.
Matthews, Luke W.B.Hawkins, Frank Swann, colored,
Clem Rozier, colored, Samuel Cox, John R. Robertson,
J.R.Tompkins, William H. Moore, Charles H. Wood,
Robert J. Lloyd, John M. Latimer & Son, Mary Crain,
George H. Shannon, Washington A. Posey, John T. Colton,
Thomas D. Simpson, Supervisor, William H. Moore,
William H. Higges & Co., Charles H. Wood, John H.
Reeder, R. Danson, John E. Tennison, E.P.Maddox,
John H.D.Wingate, Mary E. Kearns, Charles H. Sheir-
bourn, John T. Colton, John E. Bailey, Supervixor,
Charles C. Perry, B.W.Blandford, use Sam'l Cox, Jr.,
B.W.Blandford, Henry E. Mudd, George H. Lucas, R.H.
Willett, Charles Stewart, Samuel T. Berry, James S.
Moore, William E. Dement, L.M.Moore, Mrs. E.Stewart,
William Tippet, Sandy Middleton, George L. Moore,
Thomas Carrico, L.C.Wilkerson, Nicholas Stonestreet,
Charles H. Willett, George Wilkerson, H.W.Hamilton,
J.B.Konklin, Charles C. Hardy, Maria Berry, William
L. Berry, E.L.Huntt, Dominic Mudd, Joseph R. Huntt,
J.L.Hamilton, P.A.Sasscer, Richard McDaniel, Elkanah
Lyon, Supervisor, B.W.Spalding, Isaiah Acton, Samuel
C.Robey, William Garner, colored, Edgar Griswold,
D.R.McDaniel, Francis Robey, F.O.Medley, Thomas S.
Martin, J.B.Sheriff, Judson Clements, Thomas R. Halley,
16

Heirs of J.H.Monroe, Richard W. Bryan, G.W.Under-
wood, George R. McDaniel, Jenifer Proctor, Enoch
E. Downs, James Maddox, R.T.Boswell, Supervisor, use
William Boswell & Co., Same, use Sasscer & Warring,
Mrs. E.M.Pye, William H. Cox, Benjamin D. Tubman,
Sasscer & Warring, Mrs. J.A.Hannon, James Lomax,
Supervisor, use J.M.Latimer & Son, Thomas A. Carrico,
E.D.R.Bean, J.M.Latimer & Son, George H. Simpson,
Marshall Moran, J.H.Freeman, James Keech, William
A. Lyon, George Dent, Thomas K. Moran, J.R.Turner,
G.B.Shannon, J.T.S.Tennison, Supervisor, Joseph S.
Boarman, J.T.Simpson, Peregrine Davis, Joseph T. Ward,
John W. Boarman, J.B.Latimer, Lucinda Gough, J.T.
Higdon, J.T.S.Tennison, Thomas A. Carrico, E.D.R.
Bean, J.M.Latimer & Son, George C. Davis, William A.
Boarman, Supervisor, Thomas Carrico, George W.
Carrico's heirs, Richard Farrall, George J. Chappa-
lear, Frederick L. Dent, Hosea Burch, B.F.Burch,
William Farrall, Henry A. Canter, Levi Dent, Thomas
A. Carrico, Mrs. M.R.Matthews, Mason L. McPherson,
Thomas I. Boarman, Thomas Carrico, William H.Moore,
B.M.Edelen, F.T.S.Dent, J.S.Gibbons, Supervisor,
William J. Boarman, Caleb Reeves, M.L.McPherson,
E.D.R.Bean, William H. Moore, B.M.Edelen, George A.
Goldsmith, Jere T. Mudd, Elizabeth E. Smoot, T.I.
Jamison, Supervisor, use Wm. H. Moore, Clinton Dent,
Alexander Smoot, Nicholas Miles, Jane Jamison,
Cincinnatus Murphy, H.H.Bean, J.R.Lawson, E.B.Edelen,
J.H.Freeman, George Oliver, Peter Trotter, George
Chappalier, John B. Dent, William B. Dent, T.A.
Carrico, George R. Chappalear, Mason L. McPherson,
John M. Latimer & Son, A.M.Freeman, C.L.Burch, John
H.Robey, Supervisor, J.T.Turner, J.L.Hamilton, Philip
A.Sasscer, J.A.Turner, Mason L. McPherson, William H.
Moore, Peter W. Hawkins, Charles L. Burch, Jere T.
Mudd, H.C.Robey, Philip A. Sasscer, C.S.Turner, John
N. Robey, Francis Montgomery, Lewis Shadrick, John H.
Robey, Ann A. Borling, C.S.Turner, Thomas Turner,
John N. Turner, A.R.A.Murray, Ann Murray, Martha
Davis, George W. Berry, Andrew G. Chapman, Henry A.
Thompson, Josias H. Hawkins, Josias Hawkins, John H.
Turner, John F. Gardiner, Henry Hamilton, Walter
Clarke, Washington Marlow, Benjamin D. Willett,
Stanislaus Farrall, Supervisor, John M. Latimer,
George B. Lancaster, W.A.Posey, Robert Oliver, John
R. Murray, Supervisor, use W.B.Moore, James H.
Montgomery,A. Thompson, Zachariah Swann, Supervisor,
use Alice Canter, George A. Huntt, Zachariah Swann,
John D. Bowling, R.C.Swann, Thomas C. Lyon, Levi
Woodruff, George Chappalear, J.T.Turner, J.H.Mont-
gomery, Frederick L. Dent, Thomas A. Carrico, E.D.R.
Bean, J.H.Padgett, Supervisor, use M.L.McPherson,

17

Mason L. McPherson, Townly Robey, George Chappalear,
J.T.Turner, E.D.R.Bean, William H. Moore, Jere T.
Mudd.

Sundry Accounts Omitted in 1869

F.T.C.Dent, John A. Hindle, Zepheniah Semmes, col-
ored, George B. Shannon, Alfred Swann, Leonard
Marbury, Joseph Wallace, colored, J.R.Turner,
E.B.Semmes use T.A.Smith.

Material used by Permanent Corps

William B. Stone, Sarah Floyd, William N. Sanders,
Marcellus Thompson, Joseph Lowe, Hugh Mitchell, Mrs.
E.A.Middleton, Charles H. Wills, E.F.Mason, William
M. Morris, William Cox, James Swann, colored,
William H. Williams, use William N. Sanders, use
William H. Cox, George P. Jenkins, R. Fergusson for
R.C.Fergusson, H.C.Page, E.Lyon, Walter Mitchell,
George Dent, John F. Gardiner, Henry Howard, George
Digges.

Extra Hired Team on Port Tobacco Canal

George P. Jenkins, William Hamilton, Richard Barnes,
use W. Mitchell, Caroline Farrall, Dr. Robert Fergusson, E. Wells, B.L.Higdon, Hamilton Williams,
George C. Davis, William H. Matthews, William Boswell.

New Road to Budd's Landing

Carpenter & Lyon, J.M.Latimer & Son, George H.
Shannon, John B. Lyon, John L. Budd.

William Samuel, only child of J.N. & Ellen L. Lomax,
died August 3rd at Middleville in Charles County.
One year, 8 months, 7 days old. "It died to sin, it
died to cares, But for a moment felt the rod;..."
John Middleton, youngest son of James and Sarah J.
  Garrett, died in Washington, D.C. on August 3rd.
  One year, 10 months, 12 days old. "Weep not dear
  parents and friends, thy Johnnie is at rest,..."
Mrs. Violetta G. Turner, deceased, property "Yatten"
  to be sold, 225 acres, on Wicomico River adjoining
  farms of Major Stoddert, Dr. A.J.Smoot, J.A.Bur-
  roughs, Esq. To be sold at court house door to
  satisfy complainant, G.W.Hungerford. F.W.Cox and
  wife, H. Ernest Hanson and wife defendants. Dwelling house, kitchen, barn stables, and other out-
  houses. Enquiries may be made of E. Dudley Turner
  at W.W.Padgett's store, Port Tobacco. A.G.Chapman,
  trustee.

18

B.W.B.McPherson brings suit against property of
Charles H. Pye and B.G.Stonestreet. Tract called
"Tranquility" or "Pye's Wharf" 420 acres. William
E. Dement, late sheriff.
William H. Mitchell rents "Thainston" or part of
"Friendly Hall"¨also two farms on Potomac River
opposite Aquia Creek Depot known as "Smith's
Point."

August 26, 1870, Vol. XXVII, No. 17

William C. Brent, Register, Election District #1,
Port Tobacco
James A. Franklin, Register, Election District #2,
Hill-Top
George W. Carpenter, Register, Election District
#3, Nanjemoy
John H. Freeman, Register, Election District #4,
Allen's Fresh
Charles C. Perry, Register, Election District #5,
Harris Lot
Marcellus Thompson, Register, Election District
#6, Middletown
Henry M. Hannon, Register, Election District #7,
Pomonkey
Townley Robey, Register, Election District #8,
Bryantown
Rufus Robey, Register, Election District #9,
Patuxent City

William H. Mitchell, delinquent taxpayer - "Smith's
Point" 278 acres. Part of Smith's Point, 299acres.
Gerrard W. Crain, delinquent taxpayer, house and lot.
Thomas A. Hancock has estray black ox - on farm
owned by J.D.Hanson.
W.N.Cobey has Cotswold buck lambs for sale at
"Efton Hills," Cross Roads Post office.

September 2, 1870, Vol. XXVII, No. 18

Col. Thomas A. Millar and Dr. William R. Wilmer
(whites) and John C. Bush (colored) attended Republican Nominating Convention for this Congres-
sional District at Bladensburg.
Francis, son of Francis P. and Priscilla Hamilton
died on August 27th at his parent's residence.
He was 5 years old. "...He was smiling as we laid
him beneath the coffin lid, as if the spirit in
parting had stamped its triumph, on the cold lips,
over the dominion of Death..."

19

Thomas A. Whitty advertises a 14' sailboat for sale.
"...If not previously sold, it will be raffled...
at Chapel Point..."
William Queen, executor Edward Edelen - Leonard B.
Edelen - F.T.C.Dent and John A. Price and Eliza-
beth Edelen involved in Sheriff's sale of "Part of
Assington," "Edelen's Discovery," "Molly's Choice,"
"Ford's Amendment" 280 acres.
Henry S. Mitchell mortgage to Ann E. Gough - Equity
Court.

September 9, 1870, Vol. XXVII, No. 19

Democratic and Conservative County Convention

Judge George P. Jenkins moved to call Hon. Barnes
Compton to the chair. J.A.Price appointed secretary. George W. Carpenter, Esq. moved to endorse
present Rep. Fred. Stone. Delegates to convention
in Ellicott City will be A.G.Chapman, R.P.Wall,
J.A.Price. Alternates will be J.W.Mitchell, George
W. Carpenter, Dr. George D. Mudd.

Bryantown Primary Meeting

Judge J. H. Hawkins was called to the chair. Townley
Robey was appointed secretary. Delegates to County
meeting in Port Tobacco were D.P.Haviland, William M.
Queen, Dr. P.W.Hawkins, Dr. G.D.Mudd, Josias Hawkins,
R.H.Gardiner, J.F.Gardiner, F.L.Dent, C.L.Burch,
Jere T. Mudd. Alternates - M.L.McPherson, D.W.Hawkins
Josias H. Hawkins, Alexander Smoot, Thomas I. Boarman,
G.C.Burch, F.D.Gardiner, William H. Berry, John R.
Murray, Richard Farrall.

Grand Jurors
John G. Chapman, foreman

William H. Cox, Francis W. Weems, Benjamin D. Tubman,
Francis O. Medley, Richard Price, Samuel T. Berry,
William A. Boarman, B.W.B.McPherson, William Wolfe,
John T. Davis, James A. Keech, E.D.R.Bean, Philip A.
Sasscer, William H. Higges, William B. Fergusson,
George H. Simpson, Pearson Chapman, Thomas I. Boarman,
B.L.Higdon, John H. Cox, Sam. Cox. W.E.W.Rowe

Petit Jurors

Townley Robey, Samuel T. Swann, John F. Hardy, Thomas
A. Millar, Thomas Carrico, Richard Barnes, Jr.,
Francis B. Green, Samuel Hanson, Francis P. Hamilton,
Alex. H. Robertson, E.N.Stonestreet, William L. Harding,

Robert J. Lloyd, John W. McPherson, James A. Mudd,
Richard B. Posey, Regan Deakens, Joseph E. Sanders,
John L. Budd, Charles C. Hardy, Jere W. Burch,
Richard Farrall, E.F.Mason, John H. Freeman,
James L. Brawner.

Radical Nominating Convention

Dr. W.R.Wilmer, John Bush, colored and Lemuel Wilmer
named delegates to Charles County Convention. Dr.
W.R.Wilmer was appointed Secretary.

Gustavus Brown executor of John T. Stoddert estate.
George M. Lloyd executor of Benjamin W. Jameson
    estate.
R.A.Rennoe, William H. Price and U. Wright trustees
    to school #4, 3rd Election District advertise for
    teacher.
James W. Burch, deceased, Equity Court.
John H. Freeman property - small tract on Gilbert
    Swamp composed of "Mount Morris," "Forest Hill,"
    "Partnership," "Dent's Resurvey" - 679 acres to
    be sold at suit of W.N.Bean, R.H.Edelen and
    J.R.Carlin and Sarah E. Carlin.
E.Reed, rector Trinity Parish, expresses thanks to
    many friends in Charles County for kindnesses
    shown him in his three years' residence in county.

September 23, 1870, Vol. XXVII, No. 21

Samuel Cox, Jr. advertises for sale a pair of old
    horses and a pair of work mules.
Thomas H. Scott and Ralph H. Way will do wheelwriting,
    blacksmithing and carpentering in Port Tobacco
    "...in the rear of Middleton's Hotel..."
James H. Shreve, Sr., died in Washington, D.C. Sept.
    16th. He was 67 years old.
A.H.Robertson advertises 20 head of cattle and a pair
    of young mules for sale.
Lemuel Wilmer advertises that he wants to rent a farm
    no more than 300 acres with good improvements near
    navigable water "...with the privilege of buying."
Leonard S. Adams' real estate to be divided.
George N. Rowe administrator for John S. Skinner est-
    claims to be presented.

September 30, 1870, Vol. XXVII, No. 22

J.G.Chapman sells Morgan colt "...would make a pleas-
    ant saddle horse."

Hon. William T. Merrick will address Charles County
voters at Port Tobacco and Bryantown.

October 14, 1870, Vol. XXVII, No. 24

John H. Mitchell of Baltimore marries Lillie T.C.,
daughter of Daniel Jenifer, Esq. of Baltimore
County October 11th at the residence of the bride's
father. Rev. A.P.Stryker performed the ceremony.
Mrs. Lucy B. Walker died at the home of her son-in-
law, Col. Samuel Cox at Rich Hill on October 7th.
She was 70 years old.
William M.D.Stone died of congestive fever. He was
the son of Walter H. Stone. He was 19 years, 7
months and 21 days old. He died on Sept. 25th.
F. Stone wants to purchase "good work horse."
William F. Berry will sell property at a public
sale at "St. John's, near Port Tobacco."

Tournament, ball and supper for St. Peter's church
at Bryantown
_____

Dr. George D. Mudd - Chief Marshal
Daniel W. Hawkins - Orator of the Day
Richard H. Gardiner - Orator of the Evening
Joseph B. Gardiner and E.M.Mudd - Aids to Chief
Marshal
Philip Sasscer, John E. Hamilton, Jr., Dr. William
Waring, Samuel Turner - Heralds
Col. J.D.Bowling, J.G.Chapman, R.P.Wall, George H.
Gardiner, Judge Josias H. Hawkins, William Guynn,
Sr., Eugene Digges - Judges
William Queen, Henry A. Turner, E.M.Mudd - Commit-
tee of Knights
M.P.Gardiner, Sylvester Mudd, Dominic Gardiner,
George L. Mudd - Committee of Arrangements
Mrs. Francis Hardy, Mrs. Samuel A. Mudd, Mrs. Mary
Jane Semmes, Miss Marian Mudd - Managers of the
Supper

C.E.Wade has closed his business in Port Tobacco.

Democratic-Conservative Club #1, Port Tobacco -
John G. Chapman - chair. A.W.Neale - Secretary.
Vivian Brent moved that a committee of five be ap-
pointed - Vivian Brent, George P. Jenkins, George
A. Huntt, B.L.Higdon, B.G.Stonestreet. Following
officers elected -
Major William B. Matthews - President
William Boswell and Thomas R. Farrall - Vice
Presidents

J. Hubert Roberts - Treasurer
E.A.Smith - Recording Secretary
George A. Huntt - Corresponding Secretary
E. Wells, John G. Chapman, Joseph I Lacey, Executive Committee
V. Brent - Delegate to Central Committee
J.C.Middleton - Sergeant at Arms

William A. Padgett and wife - defendants - property
will be sold - 1½ mile of Harris' Lot - adjoins
farms of Dr. Matthews Lancaster and Thomas Posey -
400 acres - lies on navigable creek - 1-2 mile
from Potomac - near Lancaster's Wharf. Peter W.
Crain, trustee.
E.F.Franklin, deceased, property to be divided.
Commissioners Edmund Perry, Samuel Hanson, Thomas
B. Delozier, George M. Barnes, John B. Carpenter.

October 21, 1870, Vol. XXVII, No. 25

REGISTRATION OF VOTERS
Names of Persons Registered in the several Election
Districts of Charles County at the Registration made
in October, 1870

FIRST DISTRICT

Names of Persons Stricken from the Lists of Qualified Voters and Books of Registration of the First
Election District of Charles County, at the Registration in October, 1870:--

William Burch, Thomas Frederick, Thomas A. Jenkins,
Hanson Johnson, Benjamin Johnson, Charles H. Lacey,
Charles Miles, John Davy Simmes, Joseph Lemuel Welch.

Corrected List of Registered Voters in the First
Election District of Charles County, made at the
Registration in October, 1870:--

John Quincy Adams, James Adams, Charles Henry Adams,
Hazekiah Adams, Henry Berry, Hillery Barnes, Richard
Butler, Henry Brown, Francis Bean, Dennis Bond,
Andrew Bond, John Bean, Hanson Barnes, Madison Butler,
William Brown, George H. Brown, Samuel Burch, Anthony
Brown, Thomas Brown, Charles Butler, Fitzjames Butler,
John Blair, Richard Barber, John Blair, Charles Barnes,
George Bailey, Thomas Butler, Jacob Butler, Washington
Burch, John Beal, John Brooks, John Brawner, George W.
Boarman, William Boarman, Charles Francis Brown, John
Banks, George Henry Butler, Harrison Brown,Benjamin F.
Burch, Benedict Boarman, J. Washington Cross, Basil

Clark, Charles Henry Cross, Moses Cameron, Aubin
Contee, James Cary, John Henry Ches, John Lee Contee,
George Wilson Combs, Josiah Cooper, Phil. Francis
Chisley, Gusty Chase, George Densmore, Thomas Dorsey,
Thomas Dotson, William Durrington, Frank Digges,
Robert Duckett, Joseph S. Dyson, Leonard Durrington,
Frank Dyson, Jas. Madison Dyer, Theodore Dent, Alex-
ander Dent, Alfred Dent, Edward Dent, Samuel Dotson,
Wm. Henry Day, Samuel Dotson, Dory Douglas, Paul
Edelin, John Henry Edelin, Geo. Othos M. Fendell,
Clem Ford, Joseph Farrall, Walter Fendell, John
Richard Ford, William Ford, John Finick,John W.
Fowler,Oscar Levi Fendell, Francis G.S.Franklin,
Hanson Farmer, Alfred Frederick, Louis Finick,
Chapelier Fendell, Washington Fenwick, Nathaniel
Fendell, William Finick, Samuel Freeman, Nathan Henry
Farrall, Charles Henry Gray, Benton Garner, Alfred
Green, William Gilham, Dennis Green, George J.R.Huntt,
William Hill, Richard Hawkins, Joseph Holmes, Henry
Hill, William Edward Hill, Fr. Hollin Hawkins, Fr.
Thomas Hawkins, Samuel J. Hawkins, Horace Henneken,
James Hanson, Henry H. Hall, Ignatius Hanson, John
Daniel Hawkins, Jacob Hungerford, John Hawkins, John
Paptist Hemisly, Thomas Hawkins, John Holt, Charles
Higdon, Oscar Hoe, Dennis Hawkins, John Francis Holt,
Wm. Henry Holt, Geo. Henry Hawkins, James Henry
Johnson, Isaih Jones, Thomas Jones, William Johns,
Robert Johnson, Edward Johnson, James Jackson,
Zachariah Johnson, Luke Jameson, William Johnson,
Alfred Jenifer, William M. Jones, Vincent Jacks,
Wilford Jackson, John Jackson, James Kelly, Bernard
Key, Philip Key, Robert Kelly, jr., Jefferson Kelly,
Robert Kelly, sr., Samuel Kelly, Benjamin Kelly,
Michael Kaanan,Henry Luckett, Walter Lyles, Joseph
Lee, Bap Lyles, Joseph Linkins, James Luckett, Meyer
Lewin, Thomas Marshall, John Henry Mason, King
Matthews, Madison Mason, Benjamin Millard, John
Middleton, George Henry Milburn, Frank Miles, John A.
Milburn, Basil Matthews, Stephen Morris, Thomas Morris,
Humphrey Miller, Jerry Miner, Louis Miles, Charles
Mankin, Richard Mitchell, Ignatius Millard, James A.
Mason, John W. Maddox, John Miles, Nicholas Matthews,
Michael Martin, James Perry Murdoch, P.H.Muschett,
Henry Miles, James Norris, Ferdinand Plowden, Henry
Pierce, Washington Pye, Oscar Penn, Charles Henry Pye,
Ignatius Patterson, T.Yates Robey, jr., John Henry
Ross, Jerry Ross, Henry Roberts, Robert Reed, Clem
Rozier, William Riley, Isham Richards, George S.
Richards, John Francis Richards, John Richard Stewart,
James G. Stuart, Hillery Smallwood, Stoddert Smallwood,
Patrick Smallwood, Charles H. Simms, James Henry Scott,
Thomas Swann, Walter Smith, James H. Swann, Alexius

Sweetny, William Smith, Henry Smallwood, Jesse
Stuart, Charles Henry Simms, Alexander Simms, Thomas
Simmes, Willliam Henry Simms, Frank Stuart, Daniel
Stuart, George Sewell, Richard M. Smoot, Richard
Small, Harrison Sewell, Peter Smith, William Short,
Frank Sewell, Philip Smoot, John Edward Sly,
Charles Sweetny, James A. Swann, Joseph Norris
Sanders, William V. Smith, George Robert Slye, Chs.
Henry Thomas, William Tubman, John Thomas, Richard
Thomas, William Thompson, Jesse Thomas, Samuel
Thomas, Andrew Thomas, John Vincent Thomas, Madison
Thomas, Henry Thomas, Chandler Thompson, Philip
Tolson, John Taylor, James Thomas, William Vincent,
Albert Williams, John Wallace, Horace Wallace,
Charles Henry Watts, Washington Willis, Jas. Thomas
Winters, Wilson Wallace, John Francis Watts, Noble
Wallace, Lemuel Wheeler, Francis Wallace, Wesley
Wills, John Washington, John Alex. Ware, Frank
Wheeler, Joseph Wallace, Edward Wallace, John Wood,
Henry Washington, Joseph Waters, Harrison Williams,
Richard Washington, Samuel J. Young, John Was'n
Yates, Samuel Young.

SECOND DISTRICT

Names of Persons Stricken from the Lists of Qualified Voters:--

John Henry Bell, Wesley Bell, Wm. P. Barker, Francis
L. Higdon, Frederick Johnson, James F. Mattingley,
James L. Powers.

Corrected List of Registered Voters:--

Solomon Angell, Nelson Adams, John Bannister, John
H. Barnes, John H. Boarman, Alexius Butler, Basil
Brown, Henry Brown, George Brown, Alfred Bell,
Francis Briscoe, Leonard Butler, John Barnes, Wm.
Joseph Butler, Henry Butler, Basil Brooks, James
Brown, John S. Baxter, Thornton Beall, Thomas Beall,
William J. Bowie, John H. Beatley, John A. Clements,
Walter H. Clements, Hugh Clements, George Carpenter,
Edward Chunn, Samuel Cooper, George Craig, Jas. Wm.
Campbell, Washington Chapman, John H. of Ed. Chunn,
John H. of D. Chunn, Edward Chase, Gerard Cofer,
Andrew W. Cridlin, Ignatius Dyson, Lewis Dogan,
William Dye, John Digges, John Dent, Henry Dotson,
Francis Dyson, Ignatius Dorsey, Samuel Dunbar,
Stephen Dorsey, Moses Dorsey, William Dulaney,
Richard Datcher, Henry Delozier, Ignatius Farmer,
Frederick Frederick, Joseph A. Gray, John Thos.
Gainer, Thomas Gray, Charles Henry Gray, John Gray,

25

Samuel F. Gray, Frederick Gray, John Arch Gray,
Joseph Gray, John F. Hughes, Richard T. Hardesty,
Thomas Higdon, Hillary Hurd, Henry Hanson, George
Hawkins, George Hall, Israel Hanson, Hendly Hemsley,
Seigh Hackerson, Samuel Henson, Grandison Hall,
Charles Wm. Hurd, John Henry Hurd, Daniel Hender-
son, Delvey Hawkins, James Howard, sr., Harry Hawkins,
Wm. Henry Howard, James Howard, jr., William H.
Jenkins, Samuel Johnson, Ignatius Jenifer, Hanson
Jordan, Thomas Jones, Alfred Jones, sr., Alfred
Jones, jr., John Jones, Horton Jackson, Edward
Jackson, Charles Jones, Levi Jones, Grandison Johnson,
Thomas Jacks, Washington Johnson, Robert Johnson,
Alfred Johnson, Thomas A. Jenkins, Fred Jackson,
Ed. Jackson of Butler, Horace Key, Edward Lemon, jr.,
Nicholas Lancaster, Edward Lemon, sr., Charles H.
Lacey, George Litrall, John T. Mattingley, Josias H.
Milstead, James Montgomery, Ambrose Miles, Edward
Mundle, George Mankins, sr., George Marshall, Samuel
Manuel, Robert Miller, John Montgomery, Wm. B.
Matthews, James Matthews, Jere Marbury, Alexius Mason,
Francis McPherson, Matthew Matthews, Joseph Marbury,
George W. Mankins, George Monroe, James Newman,
Richard A. Oliver, Lemuel B. Owen, William Perry,
Thomas Penny, William Penny, James Price, George
Passage, Samuel Queen, Henry Queen, John Queen, Alex.
H. Robertson, jr., Stephen Richardson, Vincent
Richardson, James H. Ransom, William Ross, Grandison
Reeder, L.M.Southerland, Henry Shiveral, James
Spaulding, Joseph Small, Clem Smith, John Thomas
Short, Charles Short, Marcellus Short, Noble Snowden,
William Smith, Timothy Smith, James Short, Alonzo
Shelton, Adam Smith, Philip Spriggs, John Spriggs,
Wm. Smith of Wm., Charles Simmons, Wm. Smith of Adam,
W. Francis Scroggin, James Simmons, Thomas Thomas,
Congey Thompson, Hanson Tinker, Robert Thomas, Joseph
Thomas, Joseph Wm. Thomas, Sydney Thompson, George
Travis, John Travis, George Thomas, Thomas West,
Henry Willis, Walter Wheeler, Francis Warren, Steward
Walker, Thomas Ward, Wallace Ward, Henry Winter,
John Ward, James L. Willis, George Waller, Hanson
Willis, William Washington, Wm. B. Washington, Walter
Waites, Lemuel Welch, James R.W.Willis, John H.
Washington, Jacob Young.

THIRD DISTRICT

Names of Persons Stricken from the Lists of Qualified
Voters:--

Ignatius Dent, Sandy Turner

Corrected List of Registered Voters in the Third
Election District:--

Thomas Bratton, Pearson Bastin, Lorenzo Bastin,
William Butler, Wm. Butler of H., James Butler,
James Barns, Henry Butler, Charles Brown, John S.
Butler, John Barns, Sandy Branch, Henry Barns, Isaac
Brown, Truman Barns, William Butler, Ben Barbour,
Walter Butler, Robert Barbour, Henley Barns, Ferdinand
Barns, Jacob Barbour, Dennis Brown, William Branch,
Thomas Briscoe, Wesley Bowie, Joseph Bowie,
B. Franklin Beall, Lewis Coates, William Carroll,
James Cunningham, Nace Craig, Anthony Carroll,
Moses Carter, Edward Coby, Moses Coats, Claudius
Cook, Francis Cater, Basil Dorsey, Frederick Dorsey,
Basil Digges, John Datcher, Joseph Dogan, Henry
Dorsey, Henry Dulaney, James Dent, Jeremiah Davis,
Samuel Dent, Stephen Dorsey, Horatio Day, Francis
Digges, John Dunnington, Lewis Dickerson, John W.
Dickerson, Leonard O. Dean, Henry Ford, Joseph
Flowers, William Gibson, Jesse Gibson, Ben Gutrick,
James Garner, John Gray, John Gough, Daniel Hanson,
John Hart, Jas. R.A.Henderson, Peter Hil, Thomas
Henson, C.H.Hart, George Harrison, F.P.Hollister, Ned
Jones, David Johnson, William Jordan, Moses
Johnson, Joseph Jenkins, Charles Jordan, Columbus
Jackson, Phil Jenifer, Bailey Jackson, Robert Jackson,
Vernon Jackson, James H. Key, Alexander Kelton,
Joseph Kelton, Edward Lawson, Saul Lawson, George
Lawson, John Lawson, Nathan Linkins, Baley Lemmon,
William C. Long, J.D.Moore, William Mudd, Marcus
Moore, Walter Mudd, Hillery Middleton, Henry
Montgomery, Joseph Mitchell, Lenn Montgomery, Wm. W.
Murdock, Hannibal Milstead, Martin Montgomery, Benson
Marbury, Henry Manden, Cook Manden, Frederick Manden,
James Montgomery, Hillery Milstead, Grandison Morris,
Austin Marbury, Theophilus Mudd, Jesse Newman, Francis
Newman, William N. O'Brien, John E. Owens, William H.
Posey, Joseph Posey, Clements Perry, Edward Perry,
Lemuel Posey, Sandy Posey, Frank Posey, Ignatius
Posey, John Penny, Valentine Price, Frank Queen,
Hezekiah Robey, Wesley Richardson, Jesse Ross, John
Redgit, Joseph Ross, Wm. Richardson, James Riley,
Robert Scott, Ananias Savoy, James Simpson, Jesse Short,
John F. Simmons, John Smallwood, Josias Swann, Jas. H.
Smallwood, Alonzo Simpson, Richard Shiveral, James
Saunders, Isaac Scott, James Smith, Frank Simmons,
J.B.Smart, Wm. Smallwood, George W. Skinner, James R.
Smart, J.A.Sandy, Silas Scott, John Sutherland, John
Shelton, Linsey Tolson, Pad Turner, Walter Tolson,
Daniel Thomas, Joseph I. Taylor, Dennis Toyer, James
Tibbs, Jesse Thompson, Adam Tolson, Mitchell Thomas,

27

Nathan Turner, James Tyler, Joseph Tolson,
Valentine Toyer, Isaac Thomas, James H. Turner,
Peter Tubman, Sampson Thompson, Wesley Tolson, James
Thompson, Alexander Vincent, Michael West, John
Washington, Robert Williams, John Walters, Ralph Ward,
Henry Williams, Robert Ward, Daily Ward, Alex.
Washington, William West, Ben Winter, Wesley
Washington, Alexander Ward, Lemuel Wills, Jesse
Wallace, Grason Willis, Patrick Willis, Frank Wedge,
Frank Waters, Frank Wheeler, William Young.

FOURTH DISTRICT

Names of Persons Stricken from the Lists of
Qualified Voters:--

Matthias A. Cooksey, Mitchell Higdon, Andrew
Jackson, Thomas Mitchell, George S. Richards,
John F. Richards.

Corrected List of Registered Voters:--

John A. Burch, John I.B.Barnes, James O. Brook,
John T. Briscoe, Christopher C. Blair, John C. Bush,
Henry Bush, Washington Butler, Washington Barber,
John Blackiston, Josias Bush, Ignatius Boarman, Henry
Boarman, William Butler, William Bush, Henry Butler,
Henry Briscoe, John T. Butler, James H. Blackiston,
Francis Bush, John Brown, Richard Briscoe, Washington
Brown, William Butler, Charles G. Burch, Charles
Boarman, Josias Banks, William Brawner, Louis Barnes,
Francis Banks, John R. Brown, Francis H. Beans,
Christopher C. Biscoe, Philip T. Briscoe, John E.
Cart wright, William H. Cooksey, Samuel Countee,
Nicholas Countee, Thomas Carter, George F. Campbell,
Alexius Campbell, jr., Edward Cooper, Alexius Campbell,
sr., George H. Cole, Jacob Campbell, John I. Campbell,
Charles Campbell, sr., William Campbell, Wash'ton
Campbell, Charles Campbell, jr., Earnest Campbell,
William Countee, Osborne Chisley, Charles Chisley,
Luke Countee, Abraham Calvert, Joseph A. Calvert,
Creed Callwell, Marcellus Chapman, Joseph Clark, James
Carter, Joseph Campbell, Francis Clark, Alexander
Clark, Lawrence Cawood, Ignatius Chase, Philip
Collins, Gerard W. Crain, Edward C. Dutton, Mathias
Dyson, Michael Digges, John Dorsey, Math Dyson,
William Dyson, William H. Dyson, Thomas H. Day,
Stephen Dent, Henry Dent, Solomon Dorsey, Francis
Doraty, Samuel Mc. Dent, Charles Digges, James
Dorsey, Charles H. Dorsey, Joseph W. Digges, Richard
Dorsey, Richard D. Day, Wm. H. Dunmore, John S. Dyson,
William W. Dyson, Alexander Edelen, Lawrence Edelen,

John Edelen, Thomas L. Farrall, Samuel Farmer,
Hillery Fenwick, Dallas Ford, Richard Frederick,
Moses Ford, James C. Fenwick, John M. Ford, William
M. Gardiner, James Green, Charles H. Gray, James
Garner, Richard Goldring, Washington Garner, William
Garner, George Gray, Louis M. Hayden, William
Hawkins, sr., Jere Hanson, Warren Hawkins, Nathan
Hungerford, William B. Hawkins, Hillery Hawkins,
Matthew Hawkins, Andrew Hawkins, William Hawkins,
jr., John H. Hawkins, John Hanson, sr., John Hanson,
jr., John W. Hanson, Hugh Hawkins, John A. Hawkins,
Robert Hawkins, Benjamin Higdon, James L. Hill,
Francis L. Higdon, Spencer Hutt, John C. Irwin,
Andrew Jones, William H. Jenifer, Francis L. Jones,
Joseph Johnson, Charles H. Jones, William P. Jameson,
John B. Kinnaman,Albert Knott, Philip King, John N.
Lomax, Thomas Luckett, Peter Linkins, Wesley Lee,
James Lancaster, Ignatius Lancaster, Francis Lloyd,
Raphael Lee, George Lancas, Boyd R. Livous, Philip
Livous, James R. Lawson, John B. Lawson, Michael
McMahon, Jas. H.A.Middleton, John Matthews, Henry
Matthews, William Matthews, Francis Middleton,
Benjamin Middleton, Francis Middleton, sr., George
Miles, Anthony Middleton, James F. Mahorney, Francis
Mahorney, Francis Matthews, James H. Matthews,
William I. Matthews, Thomas Murry, Nicholas Matthews,
John Moulden, John P. Nevitt, George Norris, Henry
Norris, Henry Pye, George C. Payne, William T. Payne,
James H. Payne, William N. Proctor, James L. Pye,
Louis Plater, George W. Proctor, Sylvester Pye,
William Pye, James W. Proctor, James H. Plater, Peter
Proctor, John Queen, Henry Queenan, William L. Queenan,
Andrew Queenan, Isaac Queenan, James Queenan, Aloysius
Rollings, William R. Rollings, Henry Ross, George
Rustin, Samuel J. Railey, Richard T. Simpson, John
Short, Henry Short, Robert Short, James Short, Joseph
Short, John F. Swann, James W. Swann, Henry Shade,
John F. Smoot, John Smoot, Josias Smallwood, Moses
Slye, Edward Slye, Thomas H. Shade, Benedict Simms,
William S. Short, Philip Smith, Edward Short, Thomas
P. Turner, Thomas S. Turner, Francis Tennison, Daniel
Thomas, Lorenzo Thomas, Hillery Thomas, Washington
Thomas, Thomas Turner, Thomas B. Thompson, Francis H.
Thomas, John E. Thomas, Henry Thompson, Charles
Thompson, William Thomas, Miley Toy, John H. Thomas,
Francis Thomas, Thomas Thomas, William H. Thomas,
John Thomas, Gerard B. Turner, Richard Turner,
Littleton Turner, Thomas L. Turner, James A. Thompson,
Rezin I. Thompson, John C. Thompson, Wm. H. Thompson,
James H. Taylor, John Thomas, sr., Edward Thomas,
William Taylor, William Thompson, John Thomas, jr.,
Orlando Thomas, George Thomas, Samuel Thomas, Charles
A. Turner. Wm. Henry Thomas, Chapman Weems,

Benjamin Washington, Walter Weems, Henry Weems, Eli
Waters, Lemuel Ware, Henry Williams, William
Williams, Francis Wheeler, Keleon White, Peter Wills,
Francis Yates, Rezin Yates, John Young, Wesley Young,
Stephen Young, Thomas Young, James H. Yates, Joseph
Yates, Calvert Young.

FIFTH DISTRICT

Names of Persons Stricken from the Lists of
Qualified Voters:--

Ples. Coombe, Edward Green, William Martin.

Corrected List of Registered Voters:--

Hillery Bell, Washington Burgess, James R. Brown,
James H. Brown, Cato Bell, Philip Bell, Henry Brown,
James Brown, Addison Briscoe, Austin Butler, James E.
Barnes, Jerry Beaufort, Beal T. Barnes, Richard
Banks, Thomas Butler, Richard C. Butler, James W.
Butler, John H. Butler, Joseph E. Barnes, Walbert
Bell, Charles H. Brown, Hillery Bell, Dominic Brown,
Lewis Burroughs, Robert Burroughs, John H. Blair,
Edward Burroughs, George A. Butler, Thomas Butler,
Gusty Brown, John Bell, John H. Butler, Francis
Brown, John R. Brown, Gusty T. Brown, Hanson Barber,
James H. Boarman, Ignatius Butler, John W. Burroughs,
George W. Berry, William J. Blair, Hanson Barber,
Charles Blair, Hanson Bell, Robert J. Bailie, Francis
Brawner, John R. Brawner, John Cooper, Edward Chapman,
William Calvert, William Clark, John T. Calvert,
Math Campbell, Samuel Contee, Richard Contee, John
Clark, Charles Coats, Thomas Craig, Hanson Calvert,
Charles Coleman, John Cooper, Rufus Calvert, John L.
Chisley, George F. Chisley, Warring Chapman, Thomas
R. Coombe, Robert L. Cash, Samuel W. Dyson, Henry
Digges, George W. Dyson, John W. Dyson, Novel W.
Dyson, James Dyson, Moses Duckell, S.A.Davis, John
T. Digges, William Donley, William H. Dyson, A.M.Dyer,
Henry Easton, Calvin Ford, Richard T. Fowler, Charles
H. Fowler, Thomas Fowler, Zach. Ford, Stephen H. Ford,
Philip Ford, Joseph H. Fowler, H.P.Freeman, L.D.
Freeman, Lewis Green, Nathan Gainer, John Green,
Maddison Green, Gerard Grayer, George W. Green,
James W. Green, George Grayer, James Gardiner, Z.T.
Hayden, James Harris, Samuel Hughes, Carrol Hughes,
Wm. Holly, John Holton, Daniel Hawkins, Joseph
Hamesly, William J. Hamesly, John E. Hopp, Cornelius
Hill, John W. Hill, Contee Higdon, A. Hayden, T.D.
Hayden, John S. Higdon, James Harty, Francis E.

Herbert, Charles Hayden, Luke Hayden, Zachariah
Hayden, Daniel Hagan, Henry Jones, Charles Jones,
Robert Jupiter, John Jackson, Lewis Jupiter, J.H.
Jupiter, George L. Jerdon, Richard Johnson, Charles
C. Jackson, John W. Jenifer, William H. Jackson,
John R. Jenkins, Benjamin Johnson, C.C.Jupiter,
George A. Jenkins,
Benjamin Jenkins, Charles Key, Grandison Keltson,
James J. Lancaster, Philip Lyles, Richard Lee,
Leonard Love, John D. Lyles, Isaiah Lyles, Charles
Leeper, George Lyles, A.T.Lloyd, Hanson Marshall,
Frederick Marshall, James Marks, J.B.Maddox, George
Murry, R.H.Mahorney, Henry Marshall, John H.
Marshall, John W. Marshall, David Miller, Francis
Middleton, James Marshall, Richard H. Middleton,
Joseph G. Marshall, Luke W. Mankins, F.J.Maddox,
M. Newman, H. Newman, George W. Norris, Francis T.
Neale, Charles Ofellow, Washington Page, J.R.Perry,
Henry Prior, John A. Proctor, John H. Plowden, Joseph
Plowden, Robert H. Plowden, Jerry Plowden, Hillery
Proctor, James M. Rozier, Henry Robertson, William
Sheirbourn, H.R.Scott, Hanson Smallwood, Lemuel
Shade, William H. Short, Wm. Sommerville, George H.
Short, John Smallwood, John H. Sly, Samuel Swann,
Wm. H. Smallwood, Clem. A. Simms, Humphrey Singfield,
Thomas H. Steward, John Steward, John Slivill,
Alton Sly, George Smith, George Shanks, William
Shanks, Samuel Singfield, J.W.Simpson, J.T.Stoddert,
David Smoot, James H. Swann, Henry Thomas, George H.
Taylor, Henry Thomas, Eugene Thomas, Alex. Tolson,
Moses Tolson, S.W.Thomas, John A. Thomas, R.H.Thomas,
Columbus Thomas, William W. Thomas, John W. Thomas,
William Tillman, Leck Tolton, James W. Thomas,
Benjamin Thompson, Barnes Taylor, J.T.S.Tennison,
Toney Tolson, David Tyler, William Vincent, James A.
Wills, Alex. Washington, George W. Worrick, Allen
Wells, Thomas Weems, Richard Wood, Ferd. Washington,
O. Wheeler, Benjamin Williams, Moses Wheeler, Sandy
A. Wheeler, F. Wheeler, Joseph Wheeler, William
Wheeler, Millard F. Wells, Henry Woodland, Francis
Yates, Washington Young, William Yates.

SIXTH DISTRICT

Names of Persons Stricken from the Lists of
Qualified Voters:--

Charles Henry Brown, William Dent, Wilson Duckett,
Richard Alfred Dent, James Duckett, Spencer
McPherson, John H. Robertson, Levi Waters

Corrected List of Registered Voters:--

Chs. Henry Adams, Thomas Amiger, Lewis Briscoe,
Wm. Henry Brown, Sam Beans, Aaron Butler, John R.
Bond, John Brooks, Frederick Belt, George Butler,
Swaney Brawner, Emanuel Butler, John Alex. Booth,
Henson Butler, Peter Beans, William Booth, Patrick
Brown, Shederick Bland, James Beans, Joseph Brawner,
John Thos. Boarman, Charles Brawner, Harrison
Butler, Joe Butler, Dennis Brooks, Jim Beans, Phil
Brown, Charles Brown, Henry Booth, William Briscoe,
Alfred Battle, Frederick Booth, Addison Coleman,
James H. Calbert, Nathan Chapman, Darby Chun, Wm.
Henry Chapman, Fairfax Clark, Caleb Chapman, Wilson
Coomes, Richard Calbert, Joe Conner, Matthew Cole,
John Godfrey Clark, John Hillary Coats, Samuel
Cole, E.L.Clagett, Levin Carr, Dory Douglass, Thomas
Delaney, Bernard Dent, Sandy Digges, Wellington
Delaney, Alfred Duckett, Sandy Duckett, Scott Dabbs,
Sandy Douglass, John Easton, Lewis Edwards, Richard
Farmer, Wm. Albert Fergusson, Jim Forest, jr., Harry
Forest, Nace Forbes, Jim Forest, Ross Ford, John H.
Fergusson, George Forbes, Robert Green, William
Guest, Thomas Gray, Alexander Gillam, Rogers
Grindford, Jas. Henry Garner, William Garner, John
Henry Gameby, Francis Gill, Henry Gray, Daniel
Hawkins, Lemuel Henson, Washington R. Heard, John
W. Humphries, Edmund Heard, Alfred Hemsly, Harrison
Hanson, Joseph Wm. Hawkins, Wm. Clinton Hardy,
Michael Heard, Hizzy Jenkins, Wm. Alfred Jones,
Harry Jones, John Henry Jackson, William Leigh,
William Lancaster, Jere Lancaster, John W. Lyon,
John Miller, George Matthews, Henson Matthews,
Joseph Murray, Henry Martin, Anthony Muschett,
Ralph Munson, George H. Matthews, Brooke Muschett,
Wm. M. Muschett, James B. Moore, Clem Mullikin,
Wm. T. Moore, Bruce M. Marshall, Nicholas Matthews,
Alexander Mason, Wilson McPherson, Hollis Matthews,
Benjamin Martin, Edward Miles, Dick Matthews, John
McPherson, Grandison McPherson, Wm. Francis Marshall,
Jas. Francis Matthews, Nicholas Marshall, James A.
Murray, Walter Marr, James Marr, Thomas Marr, Lewis
Neale, Columbus Norris, Benjamin F. Oliver, Stephen
Penn, Joseph I. Proctor, John Penny, Michael Plowden,
H.T.Padgett, John Queen, Franklin A. Robey, William
A. Short, Henry Speak, William Scott, John Smallwood,
George S. Speake, Patrick H. Shivel, John Henry Speak,
Ben Swann, John Swann, Alfred Stoddert, Henry Scott,
Jos. Henson Small, Alexius Speak, John Alex. Shorter,
Chapman Swann, Patrick Slattery, Philip Thomas, John
T. Thompson, John Tyler, Ch. Columbus Taylor, William
Thompson, John Taylor, Charles Thompson, Henry Thomas,

James Thompson, Tom Thomas, Allen Thomas, William
Taylor, William Thomas, Dennis Williams, Cornelius
Woodland, John Henry Wills, Jim Wood, Townley Way,
Edward Ware, John Ware, Henry Lewis Wood, Alfred
Williams, Anthony Washington, Linus P. Wilcox,
Joseph Young, Geo. Henry Young.

SEVENTH DISTRICT

Names of Persons Stricken from the Lists of
Qualified Voters:--

Joseph T. Boswell, Walter H. Barkley, B.F.Beall,
Joseph F. Bateman, J.S.Baxter, John Boarman, Hanson
Brown, James C. Cox, George C. Church, S.H.Cawood,
H.R.V.Cawood, E.L.Clagett, John W. Chapman, Levin
Carr, Benedict Foster, William L. Huntt, Judson
Jenkins, Henry Jenkins, jr., Louis H. Key, Nathan
Key, Thomas Marr, Walter M. Marr, James A. Marr,
Leigh M. Sutherland, Marcellus Swann, Philip Thomas,
G.W.Underwood

Corrected List of Registered Voters:--

William Abell, Grandison Alexander, James Bumbery,
George W. Brown, John Butler, Thomas Brisco, Henry
Boarman, Alfred Branson, George Brook, William Brown,
William H. Butler, Henry Butler, James Brown,
Thomas Brown, Jordan Brawner, Leon Barris, Wallace
Brown, Jub. Barber, Thomas Boston, G.R.Bryan, George
Brown, C.J.Butler, S.A.Butler, Louis Branston, Henry
Ball, Nathan Beall, John H. Boswell, William Bowers,
W.P.Barker, Cornelius Butler, Oswald Carroll, Matthew
Chapman, James H. Coats, Charles Chapman, David
Coats, Jesse Coats, John Chase, William Carter,
George Chase, Wm. J. Clements, Matthew Chapman,
John T.W.Clagett, Oswold Connell, Henry Carter, J.H.
Dotson, Augustus Digges, Henry Datcher, Samuel Day,
Dederick Ducker, J.H.Datcher, Washington Day, William
Day, Joseph W. Dixon, Joseph T. Downs, William B.
Dent, Middleton Day, William Dulany, P.D.Everett,
Henry Edison, W.L.Etcherson, Richard Foster, Francis
Ford, James Fletcher, Anthony Flarity, John Flarity,
John Green, David Greer, John H. Green, Peter Green,
Thomas Gray, William W. Gray, Richard Garner, Richard
Garner, jr., James Henry, Harrison Hanson, George
Hawkins, Charles B. Hawkins, J.H.Hawkins, Joseph
Hawkins, William Hagan, James Hungerford, Francis
Holt, Winfield Halley, Littleton Hawkins, Alex. E.
Howard, A.O.Horton, John Johnson, Joseph Jackson,
Rozier Jackson, W.F.Jenkins, Henry Jenkins, Joseph

Johnson, George Jackson, George Jenkins, Thomas G.
Jones, Peter Jenifer, Columbus King, Francis Key,
James King, Ignatius King, John King, James Lewis,
Joseph Lowe, J.H.Marr , Webster Marr , Wilson Moore,
Washington Macc, Hillery Matthews, Thomas Matthews,
B.F.Miles, Frederick Miles, Washington Marshall,
Ambrose Mudd, James Massey, J.F.S.Middleton, John
Marr, Eugene DeC. Mitchell, Richard S. Mitchell,
Hillery Neale, Lemuel Neale, Henry Offer, Joseph
Proctor, Robert Porter, Robert Pearson, Savanah
Payne William B. Proctor, Raphael Queen, Harrison
Reed, Richard Rozier, John Randolph, William Rozier,
William Ransom, Charles H. Rowe, George Robertson,
John Short, James Swann, Wiley Smith, Joseph H.
Small, W.B.Small, S.B.Scoot, Coats Slater, Samuel
Smith, Warren Swann, Bealle Swann, Walter J. Swann,
George W. Swann, Columbus Smith, Charles Smith,
William Thomas, H.A.Thomas, Henry Thomas, Edmund
Taylor, John W. Thomas, Reuben Wallace, John S.
Warren, J.J.White, Cyrus Washington, Matthew
Winters, Isaac Wright, Henry Wallace, John
Washington, Alexius Waters

EIGHTH DISTRICT

Names of Persons Stricken from the Lists of
Qualified Voters:--

Gusty Briscoe, James D. Cox, R.T.Farrall, Francis
Humphries, B.J.Montgomery, B.S.Smoot, William
Thomas, James T.S.Tennison, Joseph B. Wathen

Corrected List of Registered Voters:--

William Akin, James A. Acton, Charles H. Blois, Dury
Butler, T.Smith Butler, Harry Butler, Charles Boarman,
Charles Booth, James Thomas Bowen, Wm. Alex. Butler,
Patrick Briscoe, James Mad Butler, John F. Butler,
Stephen Butler, Miley Butler, George Briscoe, Thomas
H. Butler, John Butler, Peter Blackistone, John H.
Brown, Washington Brown, Frank Bloise, Richard Thos.
Butler, John H. Blackistone James R. Butler, John F.
Blackistone, James H. Brown, Thomas Brown, Edward
Brown, Henry Baxter, George Booth, Dony Baker,
C. Eugene Burch, Thomas A. Burch, Josea Burch, C.M.
Bond, Joseph H. Boswell, John Best, Andrew Buckner,
George F. Canter, Thomas Calvert, William Cope, Isaac
Contee, George Chapman, Harry Coats, Baptist Calvert,
Michael Chew, John W. Chapman, Baptist Chase, Francis
H. Carter, Alfred Coats, Henry Coats, Alexius Chapman,
Alexander Cooper, George Chesley, Sandy Cregg,

34

Stephen Cole, Hugh W. Clarke, Simon Chapman,
Mathias A. Cooksey, James Douglass, David Duckett,
William Duckett, Calvert Duckett, Samuel Dorsey,
William Dade, Jordan Dory, Peter Douglass, Edmund
Dyer, Thomas Duckett, Stephen Dent, Ignatius Diggs,
Frederick Dorsey, Henry Dorsey, Thomas Duckett, sr.,
Josias Duckett, Patrick Duckett, Charles H. Duckett,
Gusty Duckett, F.T.C.Dent, Rowland G. Devol, George
W. Downing, Clinton H. Dent, Alfred Edelen, Dominic
Edelen, Harrison Edelen, Geo. Richard Edelen, Wm.
Harrison Edelen, David Edelen, Wm. Joseph Edelen,
David Edelen, jr., Albert Farrall Adam Ford, Francis
Farmer, James Ford, Nathan Ford, Richard Forbes,
Joseph B. Gardiner, Charles Green, James Gross,
Joseph Gill, Richard Green, Henry Green, George Gwin,
Henry Grinfield, John F. Grinfield, John Gantt,
Richard Graham, Joseph Gardiner, Samuel Gross, Alfred
Gross, jr., James Robert Gross, George Gardiner,
A.A.Hancock, John A. Hindle, Henry H. Hawkins, Jas.
Sam'l Hawkins, Benjamin Hawkins, Samuel Hawkins,
William Hall, Charles Halley, Wm. Henry Hanson,
Francis Hawkins, Charles Hawkins, Samuel Hawkins,
Francis A. Jamison, Ben. Tho. Jenkins, Joseph Jenifer,
George W. Jenifer, Samuel Johnson, Stephen Johnson,
Edward Johnson, Geo. Wash. Johnson, Albert Jenifer,
John H. Jenifer, Alexander Johnson, John H. Jones,
Primus Johnson, Patrick Johnson, John Johnson,
W. Henry Jones, Charles A. Jones, Andrew Jackson,
David Jackson, Wm. J. Knott, Baptist Kimbo, Richard
Kingsley, Nelson Lee, George Lacey, Moses Lancaster,
John Lee, William Lyles, George P. Lee, Samuel A.
Mudd, Richard Edw. Miles, Thaddeus Mudd, John Ed.
Miller, Jordan Moore, George A. Miller, Richard
Mason, James H. Mason, Henry Miles, Benjamin
Marshall, Randolph Moore, Alfred Matthews, James
Matthews, Gusty Makle, John F. Middleton, John
Matthews, Caleb Mills, Ignatius Moore, Benj. L.
Moore, Thomas Marshall, Cope Marshall, Dennis
Marshall, George Mills, Richard E. Miles, James
Makle, jr., John H. Marshall, William Miles, James
Makle, sr., George F. Mudd, Thomas Morton, William
Murphy, Sylvester B. Mudd, Edward McC. Mudd, Henry
Nelson, George H. Oliver, Chs. Proctor of Gusty,
Henry Proctor, H. Thomas Proctor, John H. Proctor,
Miley Proctor, John Proctor, Chs. Proctor of Rob't,
Alexander Proctor, Willie Proctor, W.A.Penny, Edward
Proctor, W. Henry Proctor, Thomas Proctor, Joseph
Queen, Caleb Reeves, John Ross, Marion Reed, R.G.W.
Richardson, Samuel D. Reed, George H. Sewall, Walter
Stewart, Thomas S. Shorter, Neely Stewart, William
Simms, Alfred Swann, Benedict Stewart, Francis Simms,
Henry Slye , George R. Sembly, Robert Semmes, Charles

35

Savoy, John Savoy, John Sewell, Joseph Sweetney,
Rich. M. Smallwood, Cornelius Savoy, Miley Savoy,
Frank Speak, Lewis Shadrick, Dennis Smith, William
Shorter, Samuel Simms, Washington Shorts, Joseph
Spencer, George Sembly, James Sembly, Hillery Simms,
Henry Smallwood, George H. Smith, William Simms, sr.,
Arthur D. Smoot, John H. Smoot, George Smith, James
R. Shorter, Henry A. Turner, Frank Thomas, Alexius
Thomas, John Turner, Robert Thomas, Benjamin Tabb,
Miley Toy, Washington Thomas, Neely Thomas, Elzara
Thomas, James Vall, Dominic Wade, Anthony Ware,
James Wills, Richard Washington, George H. Woods,
Charles Whalen, Thomas Woodland, Hillery Wood,
R.H.Warrington, Baptist Washington, Frank Washington,
Alexander Walker, Henry Wearmett, P. Wilmer, William
Young, Frank Young, Hillery Young, William Yeats,
Henry Yeats, Abram Young, Aaron Young, Alexander Young

NINTH DISTRICT

Names of Persons Stricken from the Lists of
Qualified Voters:--

John R. Butler, Isaac Douglas, David Edelen, James
F. Garner, John H. Morgan

Corrected List of Registered Voters:--

Richard H. Acton, John Bond, Benjamin Butler, James
Burroughs, Charles Henry Butler, Mason Banks, Nace
Briscoe, James Bowling, George Butler, Moses Brooks,
John Henry Butler, James Brent, Joseph Butler,
Charles Brooks, William Butler, Caesar Boarman,
Col. Jacob Brooks, Washington Berry, George Blake,
David Contee, Abram Craig, John H. Craig, Robert
Craig, Leonard Craig, Josias Chase, Raymond Chase,
Francis Clagett, Wm. H. Chapman, William Curtis,
Sandy Craig, Washington Curtis, James Cole, John H.
Chappelear, Robert Duckett, Patrick Douglas, Peter
Duckett, Richard Douglas, Isaac Duckett, James Ford,
William Ford, Walter D. Fowler, Henry Ford, David
Ford, George Ford, John Ford, Thomas R. Farrall,
Joseph Gant, Philip V. Gilum, Leigh Garner, Zach.
Greenfield, Romulus Gross, Robert Greenfield, John
Greenfield, Albert Gardiner, John Hawkins, Richard
E. Hawkins, Hillery Hawkins, Samuel Hodge, Stephen
Hawkins, Smith Hawkins, Louis Hillery, Isaac Holt,
Hanson Hammersley, Wm. J. Horseman, James K.P.Hurley,
Isaac Jas. Horseman, John B. Insley, Peter Jones,
Philip Johnson, William Johnson, Baker Johnson, Henry
Johnson, Washington Key, Saulsbury Key, Hanson King,
William King, Alfred Lyles, John W. Lamar, Jere Lucas,

Washington Larkins, Alfred Lewis, David Livers,
George Livers, Benjamin Larks, James H. Love, David
Larkins, Stephen R. Livers, Jacob Leigh, James
Molison, Dory Middleton, George Medley, John Munroe,
Charles H. Marshall, Alexander Matthews, John Mack,
John McKee, Louis McWilliams, Theodore Mack, Ben-
jamin Marshall, James Meade, J.H.Montgomery, sr.,
Benjamin L. Messick, Frank Newton, George A. Newton,
Charles H. Proctor, Daniel Ransom, John Wesley Reeder,
Calvert Reeder, Richard E. Skinner, James Slater,
Richard Smallwood, Edward Skinner, Alexander Sembly,
Benjamin Spriggs, James E. Skinner, John A. Savoy,
John Simms, Peter Simms, Wm. B.T.Stafford, Thomas W.
Shorter, Benjamin I. Thomas, Jere Thomas, William
Thompson, Henry Thomas, John Walter Thomas, Richard
Thomas, Chas. Henry Thomas, George Thomas, William
Thomas, John Tarmin, Daniel Thomas, Miley Thomas,
Sylvester Thomas, Matthew Turner, Joshua C. Townshend,
Benjamin Wade, Hillery H. Wade, Thomas West, Peter
West, Fielder J. Wade, Frank Wade, John B. Wade,
Fielder J. Wade, Marcellus Wade [The following 17
names, Wade, Washington, Welch, Wall, Wilkerson
and Young, are impossible to read.]

J. Thomas Colton advertises for sale new stock at
Allen's Fresh.
B.W.Jameston, deceased, personal property to be sold
at Maryland Point, his late residence -- lists items
and ends "...with many articles too tedious to
mention."
                    Sheriff's sale
Suit Peregrine Davis, use Victorine R. Hughes against
Mary E. Bateman, Caroline Redmund and Notley H.
Bateman. "Decker's Delight" 116 acres.
Francis Thompson advertises for rent for the year 1871
house and lot at "Forest Grove" 15 acres.
W.A.Posey, near Allen's Fresh, advertises winter pippin
apples for sale.
J.T.Higdon wishes to employ miller for his mill near
Newport.
John Fearson warns trespassers.
James F. Maddox deceased, property to be sold -- 215
acres lying in Chickamuxen - small dwelling.
J.H.Roberts has removed his business to Hamilton's
new store house.
Mrs. Col. Millar has fall cherries on a tree at her
home "Holly Springs."

            November 11, 1870, Vol. XXVII, No. 28

Miss Jane S. Carrington died Oct. 28 of consumption

the residence of her uncle, John Newberry. She
was the daughter of Samuel Carrington, was 32
years of age. "Confirmed in 1863..."
Victorine R., 3rd daughter of J.J. & V.R.Hughes
died Oct. 29, 7 years, at the residence of her
parents.
Robert P. Giffon announces a Temperance meeting at
the home of L.T.Robey near Cricklintown. Dr. Dent
will speak.

November 18, 1870, Vol. XXVII, No. 29

Richard Bateman died at his home "Bromont" November
10th, 60 years of age. "...he was gathered to his
fathers, in the communion of the Catholic Church..."
William L. Cook, W.W. & T.T.Owen and J.D.Hanson warn
trespassers.

November 25, 1870, Vol. XXVII, No. 30

William Matthews deceased, property to be sold -
"Monastery" and "Pennies Point" on Cobb Neck,
250 acres - north side of the road from Port To-
bacco to Lancaster's Wharf - comfortable dwelling -
F. Stone, complainant and Joseph I. Wills and
Miles Dyer, defendants. S. Cox, Jr., trustee.
John H. Mitchell advertises - lawyer in Port Tobacco.
M.L.Semmes deceased, personal property sold.
L.E.Semmes and J.E.Higdon, administrators.

December 2, 1870, Vol. XXVII, No. 31

Lemuel Wilmer, Esq. resigned position as Assistant
Assessor for Internal Revenue for Charles County.
Rev. Dr. Lewin, rector, will move into newly acquired
rectory for the Vestry of Port Tobacco. "Brentwood"
formerly residence of Judge Brent "...about a mile
from this place [Port Tobacco]...modest sum $3500..."
Lemuel Wilmer sells 9 year old mule.
G.W.Hungerford advertises for rent for the year 1871
his farm "Sunnyside Farm."
Gerard W. Hungerford warns trespassers on "Waverley"
or "Sunnyside Farm."
J.H.Luckett advertises blacksmithing at Gallant Green.
Charles H. Rowe, Pomonkey, lost "two bags of material
for making a carpet, warp and filling..." in lane
near Dr. Robert Digges' mill near Mattawoman Swamp
on the road leading from Port Tobacco to Glymont.

Giles Dyer sells personal property at the residence
of Mrs. J.C.Dyer near Bryantown.

Delinquent taxpayers

Baker Edelen - "Part of Cornwallis' Neck, 500 acres.
Francis W. Rozier - Genfield" 550 acres.
Mary E. Bowling "Part of Fox's Race," "Four Brothers,"
"New Addition" 53 acres and "Store House Tract"
228 acres.

John T. Clagett, Esq. of Prince George's County
marries Jane Y. Hawkins, daughter of Josias H.
Hawkins, Esq. November 23rd at St. Paul's Church,
Piney, by Rev. Dr. Lewin.
Albert Farrall marries Mary E. Luckett at St. Thomas'
Church, November 24th, by Rev. Father McAtee.

December 9, 1870, Vol. XXVII, No. 32

Meeting to consider immigration to State

Judge George P. Jenkins - chair; E. Wells - secretary;
Hon. Barnes Compton moved to appoint committee of
five men to select nine delegates to the Baltimore
Convention. Delegates - Oliver N. Bryan, Esq.,
Judge George P. Jenkins, Major William B. Matthews,
Hon. Andres G. Chapman, Dr. H.H.Bean, Philip
Contee, Esq., Jere. T. Mudd, Esq., Col. Thomas A.
Millar and Capt. E. Wells.

Peter W. Crain and James R. Annan will sell "Clifton"
400 acres ½ mile below Pope's Creek - on Potomac
River - dwelling house. Equity Court - George R.
Gaither vs Johannes D. Storke.
Benjamin F. Bowling, Walter R. Franklin, Marcellus
Jameston, trustees of school #4, 8th Election
District advertises for teacher.
Violetta G. Turner, deceased, A.G.Chapman, trustee.
F.C.Burgess, agent for heirs of Thomas A. Burgess
will rent farm in Nanjemoy now occupied by Dr.
W.H.Bruce.
Frank Greenfield found stray bay mare colt near
Bryantown.
John H. Smoot marries Sarah J. Hancock December 5th
by Rev. Dr. Lewin.
George N. Row, administrator for James F. Maddox,
deceased vs. Columbus Maddox, Samuel Maddox.
S. Croft near Port Tobacco advertises for lost cattle.
Thomas D. Stone, Esq.'s farm scene of cave-in 25'
high bank burying three men - Victor W. Russell,

white, Joseph Banks, colored, formerly slave of
J.E.A.J.Howard, Esq. of Charles County - killed
outright. Jim Dent, colored, was freed and lived.
Justice J.R.Carlin called and held an inquest.
The men were working on the Baltimore and Potomac
Railroad construction.

December 16, 1870, Vol. XXVII, No. 33

St. Columba Lodge Holds Election in Port Tobacco

John S. Button - Worshipful Master
H. Gerard Robertson - Senior Warden
S. Cox, Jr. - Junior Warden
Edwin A. Smith - Secretary
J. Hubert Roberts - Treasurer
William Wolf - Tiler

William Worrall, purchasing agent for Baltimore and
  Potomac Railroad advertises 50,000 cross-ties
  wanted - "white oak, box oak, and chestnut oak...
  in quantities of 2,300 per mile...8½' long, 7"
  thick, hewn smoothly on two sides...stripped of
  the bark." Price 50¢ each.
$500 reward for the arrest and conviction of arson-
  ists at Budd's Creek Store House on 8 Nov. 1870 -
  Daniel J. Payne, occupant.
Capt. Thomas Stackpole - Steamer Arrow leaves
  Washington, D.C. daily at 10 a.m. from the 7th
  Street wharf), touches Alexandria, Virginia,
  Forts Foote and Washington, Maryland, Mount Vernon,
  White House and Iona, Virginia, arriving at
  Marshall Hall at 12 noon. Leaves Marshall Hall at
  1 p.m. and arrives at Washington, D.C. at 4 p.m.
  "Accommodations for passengers and stabling for
  horses, etc. at Marshall Hall."
Mrs. Scott, milliner in Port Tobacco advertises
  "Pinking done at the shortest notice."

December 23, 1870, Vol. XXVII, No. 34

Internation Immigration Union

Met in Baltimore "...for the purpose of taking action
  on the subject of immigration and the introduction
  of white labor in the State." Delegates from
  Charles County, George P. Jenkins, William B. Matthews
  Dr. H.H.Bean, O.N.Bryan, E. Wells, J.T.Mudd, Col.
  Samuel Cox. E. Wells serves on committee to prepare

and submit business to Convention. "...The possession of large tracts of land is an empty honor
unless the same are tilled and made productive..."
William B. Matthews, Charles County, appointed to
committee to ask the Legislature for $200,000 to
pay the passage of immigrants from Europe.

County committee favorable to immigration held in
Port Tobacco at Courthouse. O.N.Bryan, Esq. -
president; Dr. Robert Fergusson - Vice president
from 1st Election District; Samuel Hanson - Vice
president from 2nd Election District; Richard B.
Posey - Vice president from 3rd Election District;
Dr. S.W. Dent - Vice president from 4th Election
District; Dr. F.M.Lancaster - Vice president from
5th Election District; Hugh Mitchell - Vice presi-
dent from 6th Election Distric; Dr. J.W.Thomas -
Vice president from 7th Election District; Jere. T.
Mudd - Vice president from 8th Election District;
Richard P. Wall - Vice president from 9th Election
District;   Recording Secretary - E. Wells; Corres-
ponding Secretary - D.I.Sanders; Treasurer -
William Boswell; Committee on Bylaws - John W.
Mitchell, William Boswell and George M. Lloyd.

Henry Luckett, colored, died in Port Tobacco on
Saturday morning last - short illness - about
75 years. "...well known for his industrious,
steady and frugal habits."

December 30, 1870, Vol. XXVII, No. 35

Mrs. Mary E. Miles, while working in the kitchen,
"...took fire...and was so badly burned that she
died in a few hours..." She was the widow of
William Thomas Miles, daughter of Dr. Calistus
Lancaster and resided near Newport Catholic Church.

Census of Maryland, 1870

Charles County population was 15,751; 501 farms; 12
industrial establishments; 2512 dwellings. Only
Calvert, Caroline and Howard had fewer dwellings.
Charles County had the fewest number of farms in
the State. Only Calvert County had fewer industrial establishments. Change in statistics from
1860 to 1870 shows a decrease in population from
16,517 in 1860 to 15,751 in 1870. Only Dorchester,
Prince George's and Queen Anne's Counties had
higher decreases.

C.H.Hamilton's property "Milton Hill" was sold by
the Sheriff - at the suit of B.P.Donnelly -
500 acres.
Edward Bonegar vs William A. Padgett - Equity Court.
W.W.Dunnington, Esq., dwelling in lower Nanjemoy consumed by fire. Spark from chimney fell on roof.
"Almost all the furniture was saved."

January 6, 1871, Vol. XXVII, No. 36

F. McAtee offers $250 reward for the return of "...a gum coat, cap and leggings attached to a saddle pad." Lost between Hill-Top and Piscataway.

William R. Thompson marries Miss Clarinda V.H.Davis December 20th at the residence of the bride's father in Nanjemoy by Rev. W.W.Watts.

January 13, 1871, Vol. XXVII, No. 37

R. Payne, John H. Reeder, and J. Thomas Colton, trustees of school #1, 4th Election District, near Allen's Fresh, advertise for teacher.

William H. Gray, Tax Collector for the 1st Election District advises all to please, pay up.

St. Thomas' Church, Chapel Point, raffle a washing machine. All chance holders to be present for drawing.

John D. Bowling vs Catharine D. Burch - Equity Court.

Henry A. Turner marries Amelia Jameson on January 5th at Trinity Church in Washington, D.C. by Rev. Mr. Addison.

John T. Stoddert marries Laura Smith of St. Mary's County January 5th in St. Paul's Church, Baltimore by Rev. Mr. Hodges.

B.W.Spalding marries Bettie Dement January 10th at St. Joseph's Chapel, Pomfret, by Rev. C. Vicinanza, S.J.

Thomas Mattingley marries Mrs. Eleanor Hutton on January 10th by Rev. F. McAtee.

Marbury Carpenter marries Kate Golden on January 11th by Rev. W.W.Watts.

Lee Monument Association of Maryland

Barnes Compton writes letter to Editor about soliciting funds for a monument to Robert E. Lee. Contributions may be made to him for Hill-Top; Josias Hawkins for Bryantown; D. Ignatius Sanders for Middletown and Samuel Cox, Jr., for Allen's Fresh.

January 20, 1871, Vol. XXVII, No. 38

Samuel H. Robey marries Mary C. Davis January 12th at St. Paul's Chapel, Piney, by Rev. Dr. Lewin.

H. Bruce, Nanjemoy, has public sale of personal
property at the residence of Brent Pye.
Dr. Robert Neale died at "Westwood" the residence
of his son-in-law, John T. Crismond. 64 years old.
Col. Samuel Cox, contractor for the railroad at
Pope's Creek station has 140 hands employed in
the grading for the railroad bed - "...much more
required here than any other part of the line
within our county."

January 27, 1871, Vol. XXVII, No. 39

John W. Simpson marries Mary J.E.Barber of St.
Mary's County on January 13th in St. Mary's
County by Rev. Mr. Martin.
James O. Oliver died Wednesday last at his residence
in Cedar Point Neck. 54 years old.
Mrs. Boswell's home will be location of meeting of
the Ladies' Mite Society, Port Tobacco Parish.
Mrs. Elizabeth M. Hodges' kitchen near her dwelling
burned. "But for extraordinary exertions made by
persons who were near by, the dwelling would have
caught fire and burned down also."

February 3, 1871, Vol. XXVII, No. 40

Thomas W. Webster marries Eliza C. Burroughs of St.
Mary's County on January 18th in St. Mary's County
by Rev. Mr. Chesley.
Hannah O. Burgess died on February 2nd inst. - wife
of F.R.Burgess, Esq. She was 22 years old.
Francis E. Dunnington died at Arlington, residence
of his son, Francis. He was 90 years old.

February 10, 1871, Vol. XXVII, No. 41

George M. Lloyd, secretary to the School Board for
Charles County announces State scholarships available for Charles County students - one male to the
Agricultural College; 3 males to the St. John's
College, Annapolis; one female to the St. Mary's
Institute, St. Mary's County. (These scholarships
include board as well as tuition.)
Sister Stanislaus, Carmelite nun from Charles County
died at the Baltimore Convent. She was an original
member of the Carmelite Order. She was 70 years old.
When the Carmelites were permitted to teach, she was
an earnest and thorough instructor. A year ago she
celebrated fifty years as a nun.

February 17, 1871, Vol. XXVII, No. 42

J.R.Huntt, Esq. reports work progressing on the
    railroad.
John R. Turner, executor for Harriet B. Swann vs
    Henry A. Burch, Susan R. Burch, his wife.
    Equity Court.

February 24, 1871, Vol. XXVII, No. 43

Article lists signers of "The Declaration of Certain
    Fundamental Rights and Liberties of the P.E. Church
    in Maryland" issued August 13, 1783. A list of
    signers from Charles County include John McPherson
    of William and Mary Parish and Walter Harrison of
    Durham Parish. William Paca was Governor of Mary-
    land at that time.
Mrs. Sarah F. Blake, relict of the late Major James
    F. Blake died on February 7th inst at "Elmwood"
    in William and Mary Parish. A member of Holy
    Catholic Church. "...When her mortal remains were
    committed to the earth, the winter blast, which had
    prevailed for many days, were hushed, sombre clouds
    rolled away, and the sun, as if reflecting the
    Saviour's smile, shined out in all his glory..."
James D. Carpenter, Esq.'s dwelling house was con-
    sumed by fire - spark on the roof. Furniture and
    large library destroyed, in lower Nanjemoy. He was
    the former register of wills.
George F. Berry and William Shaw were arrested for
    robbing a bar-room in Beantown, run by Messrs Harbin
    and Hamilton. Stolen was demijohn and jug of whiskey,
    two boxes of cigars, small quantity of beeswax and
    $50 in cash. The robbers were followed and appre-
    hended in a barn 3½ miles away.

March 3, 1871, Vol. XXVII, No. 44

Capt. Hunter Davidson of the Maryland Oyster Police
    stopped at Chapel Point and paid a visit to Port
    Tobacco. He arrested several parties near Marshall
    Hall who were charged with using sink boxes, etc.
    in violation of the law - $10 fine in each case.
Letter to the Editor - August 13, 1788 List of Signers
    of Declaration of Rights shows Rev. Isaac Campbell
    as Rector of Trinity Church, Charles County, signing
    Declaration. Port Tobacco Parish was without a Rec-
    tor and continued to be until the 1787 ordination of
    Rev. John Weems, III. He appended a statement of his
    declaration to the original. On November 3, 1788

at a meeting of vestrymen, the Port Tobacco Parish met and adopted and ratified the Rules of Convention - G.B.Causin, Richard R. Reeder, Josias Hawkins, William McPherson and John Hanson, jr.

Mrs. Ann Frances Freeman died at "Bromont". Consort of Leonard D. Freeman, on 21st of February. She was 23 years old, left husband and two children, also an aged mother. Communicant Catholic Church.

Samuel Cox advertises 30 good cart horses or mules for work at Pope's Creek.

P.H.Hamilton estate to be divided - Commissioners H.R.Harris, J.H.Morgan, F.M.Lancaster, J.H.D. Wingate, P.A.S.Contee.

James A. Swann, deceased. Orphans' Court, William Boswell, administrator.

Grand Jurors
James H. Neale, foreman

William L. Berry, Charles L. Gardiner, William F. Dement, F.T.C.Dent, Jere. T. Mudd, Thos. Latimer, A.W.Neale, Rufus Robey, Mason L. McPherson, John Ware, Richard W. Bryan, John S. Gibbons, William M. Burch, Daniel P. Haviland, James H. Morgan, Samuel W. Adams, Joseph C. Gray, B.F.Burch, William L. McDaniel, George Dent, Sr., William L. Cook, George F. Beall.

Petit Jurors

Thomas Posey, G.C.Burch, John I. Jenkins, William P. Flowers, Francis D. Gardiner, Albert Milstead, George Digges, B.W.Blandford, Thomas F. Darnall, George H. Muschett, Edward D. Boone, Edward L. Huntt, Francis R. Speake, William B. Matthews, Joseph S. Boarman, John T. Colton, Oliver N. Bryan, Barnes Compton, Benjamin F. Bowling, J.A.Price, Lemuel Smoot, J.T.S. Tennison, Henry R. Harris, Edgar Griswold, Charles L. Carpenter.

March 10, 1871, Vol. XXVII, No. 45

J.G.Chapman, Esq., grew corncob in shape of human hand with thumb and four fingers being distinct and separately formed.

Mrs. Verlinda S. Robertson died on March 5th at "Gunston" residence of her husband, Dr. Alexander H. Robertson. She left a daughter and three sons. She was 58 years old and the daughter of Gerrard Fowke.

A.J.Norris asks patrons of his hotel to settle
their accounts.
Richard B. Posey vs Henry R. Smith - Court of
Equity sells property occupied by Smith, 350 acres
on Potomac River between Smith and Maryland Points.
Delinquent taxpayer - Joseph Parker's heirs - "Part
of Burch's Reserve" - 56 acres and "Part of Monmouth" 120 acres - 4th Collection District.
Alexander Franklin, near Grinder's Mill, found stray
red heifer.

March 17, 1871, Vol. XXVII, No. 46

Hon. Frederick Stone, late M.C., and lady reached
home from Washington, D.C. "Both are looking well."
John H. Cox, Esq., resigned as Commissioner of Tax.
No reason stated. He later reconsidered and took
back his seat.
Gerrard W. Hungerford died on 9th inst. in Baltimore.
He was 51 years old. "His remains were interred
at his late residence "Waverley."
One grey mare assessed to George Dent, trust. Mary
Stewart to be sold at Courthouse door.

March 24, 1871, Vol. XXVII, No. 47

Road supervisors appointed: Joseph Price for 1st
Election District; Richard Taylor for 2nd Election
District, William Wolfe for 3rd Election District;
William A. Boarman for 4th Election District.
Dr. George Mudd of Bryantown attempted to take his
life during fit of temporary insanity, superinduced
by mental prostration. Was prevented by friends
but not before he had inflicted ugly cut upon his
throat. Out of danger.

March 31, 1871, Vol. XXVII, No. 48

Amos O. Horton deceased, personal property to be
sold. D.D.Horton and George W. Berry, administra-
tors.
Frederick Stone vs Joseph I. Wills and Miles Dyer,
Equity Court.
Delinquent taxpayers - Henry B. Goodwin's heirs -
"Marsh Land" and "Part of Mount Pleasant" 10 acres.
G.C.Swann - Lot two division of Z.Swann's real
estate - 110 acres. William H. Smoot's heirs -
"Part of Calvert's Hope" and "Gray's Rest" 270 acres.

Richard Taylor and William A. Boarman declined their
appointments as Road Supervisors. In their place
the County Commissioners appointed George Dent, Jr.
in Allen's Fresh and Joseph H. Padgett in Bryantown - increase salary to $300 "...each to have a
permanent corps of laborers."

Gerard W. Hungerford's obituary appeared again in
this issue. "...He was a good husband, father,
brother, uncle, relation, master, neighbor,
friend...[he] avowed to ratify his baptismal vows
in the Apostolic Ordination of Confirmation at the
coming vernal visitation of the Bishop to his old
Parish Church..."

Henry A. Thompson, deceased, claims to estate to be
filed. William J. Boarman, Executor.

Hunter Davidson, Port Tobacco, Commanding State
Fishery Force announces Maryland Laws regarding
"Fish and Fisheries."

Charles County Library Association now incorporated.
Persons wishing to become members are to meet in
Port Tobacco.

George Taylor, Sr., died at "Cherry Grove," his residence. He was 72 years old. He engaged in merchandising in Newport - later pursued agricultural
interests. He was the President of the Board of
County Commissioners. "...The deceased was one of
our most estimable and exemplary citizens..." A
Tribute of Respect by the Vestry of Durham Parish
was printed.

Collectors of Tax appointed: William Gray for 1st
Election District; John T. Dutton for 2nd Election
District; John H. Hancock for 3rd Election Dis-
trict; William M. Burch for 4th Election District.
Collectors' pay goes from 5% to 6%.

Robert Dudley Digges, son of the late John H. Digges
has been nominated by Hon. William M. Merrick, M.C.
for appointment to the Naval Academy.

April 14, 1871, Vol. XXVII, No. 50

Mrs. Joseph H. Padgett has moved her confectionery
store "...to a room adjacent to her residence which
is on the street leading to the Postoffice. She has
a fine assortment of candies, cakes, oranges,
lemons, nuts, etc."

James A. Swann, deceased, property sold at his late
residence in Port Tobacco.

Rev. J.M.Todd of William and Mary Parish will deliver
funeral sermon for Gerard Hungerford "after Divine
Service at Christ Church..."

Iron rails for Baltimore and Potomac Railroad are
being unloaded at Annapolis. Rails are very long
and weigh 666 3/4# each.

April 21, 1871, Vol. XXVII, No. 51

Samuel Hanson appointed to Governor to fill the
position on Charles County's Board of County Com-
missioners made vacant by the death of George
Taylor.
J.H.Ryland is the real estate agent of County and
City properties. c/o William H. Moore, Bryantown.
J. Thomas Colton, Allen's Fresh, Charles County agent
for the State of Maryland Mutual Fire Insurance
Company.
Walter Barnes vs Charles Barnes, Equity Court.
Charles C. Robey, deceased, property to be sold -
"Broomfield" 200 acres adjacent to land of Col.
Samuel Cox and Dr. Francis R. Wills - has small
dwelling. Baltimore and Potomac Railroad is ¼
mile away - ½ mile to one of the Railroad stations.
Richard B. Posey vs Henry E. Smith - Equity Court.
Elizabeth J. Stone vs Charles V. Wills - sells land
in Middletown district, "Robey's Help" adjacent to
J.B.Conklin and W.O.Willett and the line of the
Baltimore and Potomac Railroad - 103 acres.

April 28, 1871, Vol. XXVII, No. 52

This volume of the Port Tobacco Times closes out 27
years of publishing "...we have labored steadily and
arduously...to make it...not only one of the in-
stitutions but one of the necessities of old
Charles..."
Dr. John Morris of Baltimore marries Mrs. Caroline C.
Jenkins of the "Wilderness" in Charles County on
the 20th by Rev. F. McAtee.
County Commissioners change dividing line between 2nd
and 3rd Election Districts: Line now runs direct
line from J.B.Carpenter's house in a northwesterly
direction to a walnut tree on the west side of
Thomas Delozier's house; northeast direction to a
cherry tree standing on the side of the public road
from J.B.Carpenter's to Sweetman's Point.
Quensel's store has large tomato plants, also sage
plants.
Land adjacent to John D. Bowling, T. Elzear Gardiner,
formerly owned by Dr. John H. Robertson and wife -
"Lot #44" and "Mount Pleasant" - 600 acres near
Patuxent City - has a fine dwelling.

Frederick Stone and Walter Mitchell, complainants
vs George H. Adams and Elizabeth Adams, defendants "Tryall," "Nottingham," "Carter's Inheritance," "Ware," and "Nonsuch" near Mount Pleasant
in Charles County - 450 acres - has dwelling.
J. Thomas Colton, Esq., Allen's Fresh grew wheat
4' in height - Tappahannock variety.

May 5, 1871, Vol. XXVIII, No. 1

James T. Chipley, formerly of Alexandria, marries
Mary Wheeler 27 April 1871 at the Rectory of the
Port Tobacco Parish by Rev. Dr. Lewin.

May 12, 1871, Vol. XXVIII, No. 2

Pearson Chapman and John S. Chapman write to editor
complaining of an earlier editorial directed at
them about their high fish prices to county people.
J.C.Middleton has taken the bakery and store room
adjoining Quensel's store in Port Tobacco - offers
confectionery, cakes, nuts, fruits, etc. "...Fresh
bread every day..."
Dr. A.D.Cobey, surgeon dentist at Brawner House during court.
C.M.Bond, undertaker, furnish coffins at Bryantown.
"...He will attend funerals and furnish all things
necessary -- such as Crepe, Gloves..."
Joseph B. Padgett marries S.A.Roberta Tucker on the
26th of April by Rev. L.G.Martin.
John W. Hawkins died at his residence on April 17th.
He was 46 years old.

May 19, 1871, Vol. XXVIII, No. 3

George B. Shannon marries Jane F.D.Corry on May 14th
in the village of Newport by Rev. L.G.Martin.
C.Vicinanza lost "small Latin book with black cover..."
between store at Harris' Lot and the turn of the
road to Allen's Fresh. Undersigned will leave
suitable return at Mr. Perry's and Mr. Higges'
Stores.
Samuel Swann and Stoddert Smallwood, ages 18 and 30,
and a boy Walter Thomas, age about 10, all colored,
were drowned when the steamer Vanderbilt, Capt.
Hollingshead of Aquia Creek Line ran over and sank
a gill-boat. Inquest held by Justice F.W.Bryan.

May 26, 1871, Vol. XXVIII, No. 4

Richard H. Gardiner , candidate State's Attorney.
Eugene Digges, candidate for State's Attorney.
Thomas Croft, late of Lincolnshire, England, will
    act as agent in offering real estate to English
    purchasers. Farms will be advertised in English
    newspapers.
Rt. Rev. William Pinckney, D.D., Assistant Bishop
    of Maryland, visited Charles County churches -
    Rev. Mr. Gallaudet, Rector, Trinity Parish;
    Rev. John M. Todd, Rector, William and Mary
    Parish (Piccawaxen); Rev. Robert Prout, Rector,
    Durham Parish. Not visited was Rev. Meyer Lewin,
    D.D., Rector, Port Tobacco Parish.

June 2, 1871, Vol. XXVIII, No. 5

John Fearson, Newburg, advertises farm "Persimmon
    Point" for sale, 205 acres.
Benjamin F. Bowling, near Hughesville, will petition
    County Commissioners to straighten road running
    through his lands - B.F.Bowling, J.H.Haviland and
    H.A.Canter.
Robert P. Gifford will petition County Commissioners
    to change road through Gifford's premises to east
    side of said farm. Robert P. Gifford, John H.
    Ward and B.F.Bowling.
G.C.Burch, candidate for sheriffalty.
William L. McDaniel, candidate for sheriffalty.
George Lloyd, secretary of School Board for Charles
    County announces that the school house on Mount
    Hill Road in Port Tobacco will be sold at public
    sale.
William McK. Burroughs marries Sallie Hayden of St.
    Mary's County on May 23rd at "Savvua" residence of
    bride's mother by Rev. J.B.Pedlupa.
Samuel E. Keech died May 27th. He was 34 years old.
Mrs. Elizabeth E. Dement died in Washington, D.C. on
    19th of May of typhoid fever - 60 years, 9 months.
Col. Frank Neale, formerly of Charles County, died in
    Bernard, Texas on April 12th. He was the second
    son of the late Dr. Francis Neale. He was 34 years
    old. He practiced law in Texas and in 1861 entered
    the Confederate Army. Late last fall he was married.

June 9, 1871, Vol. XXVIII, No. 6

Jere. T. Mudd, Gallant Green, has stray red bull
    yearling.

Joseph Parker, deceased, property to be sold for
division between sons James A. Parker of Prince
George's County, John F. Parker of Charles County,
George T. Parker of St. Mary's County and Peter
Henry Parker of Virginia.
Thomas F. Darnall property sold for taxes.
Henry B. Goodwin's heirs property sold for taxes.
Thomas D. Stone and wife vs Frederick Stone, trustee
benefit of creditors.
Mrs. Adelaide R. Padgett's residence will be scene
of meeting of the Ladies of Port Tobacco Parish
to make plans for the festival "for completing
the purchase of a Rectory..."
John H. Jenkins, undertaker in Port Tobacco. "...
Will also furnish hearse and attend funerals with-
out extra charge..."
St. Columba Lodge elects officers:
Henry G. Robertson - Worshipful Master
Samuel Cox, Jr. - Senior Warden
James L. Brawner, Jr. - Junior Warden
John S. Button - Secretary
J. Hubert Roberts - Treasurer
William M. Morris - Tiler

June 16, 1871, Vol. XXVIII, No. 7

William M. Morris and William Cox will petition
County Commissioners to change location of County
road leading from Salem and by Owensville where
the Baltimore and Potomac Railroad crosses said
road on lands of William N. Morris and Richard L.
Murdoch.
J.B.Conklin and George N. Rowe will petition County
Commissioners to change location of County road
where Baltimore and Potomac Railroad crosses said
road, on lands of J.B.Conklin, running from Middletown towards Beantown.
Thomas D. Stone and John Ware will petition County
Commissioners to change location of County road
where Baltimore and Potomac Railroad crosses on
lands of Thomas D. Stone at Pope's Creek.
Frederick Stone, complainant, vs Nannie G. Hungerford,
defendant, land sold "Part of Marshall Hall" 400
acres. ½ mile from one of the finest wharves.
Potomac River steamers from Washington and Alexandria touch there several times each day. 13 miles
below Alexandria. Marshall Hall Pavilion, one of
the most popular and frequented pavilions on the
Potomac River is on part of the original tract,
adjoining the farm being sold.

J. Walter Boarman's property to be sold "Boarman's Rest," "Calvert's Hope," and "Hardship" -
422 acres "...large and well arranged dwelling
in excellent condition..."
James T. Bateman who now resides at the Warehouse
is employed by Capt. Bradley's schooner "John
Samuel" "...The Warehouse and Cellar has been
rented for the use of shippers by the "John
Samuel" free of charge."
A. Hayden, Harris' Lot, advertises for a lost sorrel filly. "...She...was last seen...at Dr.
S.W.Dent's gate, near Centreville..."
Mrs. Adeline A. Murray died at the residence of
her husband, A.R.A.Murray on June 8, 1871. She
was 57 years, 8 months, 18 days old. "...as a
wife, mother, friend, she did her duty in that
state of life to which it pleased God to call
her..."
Hon. Barnes Compton sells "Rosemary Lawn" to Mr.
Dowse, also part of furniture, stock, agricultural implements, etc. $11,250 cash.

<u>June 23, 1871, Vol. XXVIII, No. 8</u>

Barnes Compton, chairman and F. Stone and J.W.
Mitchell, executive committee members advise
Voters of Conservative Democratic Party of
Charles County of meeting to be held.
C. Claude Digges lost "a bundle containing pair
of new pants and vest..." Reward given.
John I. Jenkins, occupant of "Locust Grove" and
heirs advertise for sale beautiful farm 441
acres formerly possessed by Mrs. E.G.Davis -
situated in Port Tobacco Valley, 3 miles from
village, convenient to several churches, all
steamboat landings, and Baltimore and Potomac
Railroad now under completion. 196 acre wood
land - large and convenient frame dwelling.
Contact George P. Jenkins or John T. Davis.
D.P.Haviland, President and Robert P. Gifford,
secretary of the Union Temperance Society announce meeting "...for the cause of Temperance..."
will be held in Grove near Bryantown.
Miss Mary A. Wells, of Port Tobacco received a
silver medal for excellence in Latin from the
Baltimore Female College at its 20th annual
commencement.
Dr. H.H.Bean near Centreville shot and killed
Thomas Proctor, "...literally tearing off the
entire upper portion of the skull..." Inquest

was held, jury ruled "...deceased came to his
death at the hands of H.H.Bean, while laboring
under a temporary fit of insanity..." Accused
admitted to bail.
Gaitley, an Irishman, laborer on the railroad was
stabbed in the groin near Whitty's store about
four miles from Port Tobacco on the main road
leading to Allen's Fresh. No information on
who did it or for what cause.

June 30, 1871 , Vol. XXVIII, No. 9

Drs. Edward Miles and John F. Price, two of the
county's oldest and most estimable citizens,
died within the past few days. Both had retired,
owing to bad health. Dr. Miles, 60 years old,
died on Tuesday and Dr. Price, about the same
age, died on Wednesday. "...Both were high beloved and respected and both leave behind a
large circle of sorrowing relatives and friends..."
G.H.Bryant, Harris' Lot, found a 20' canoe,adrift
on the Potomac River.
Charles C. Robey, deceased, Court of Equity.
F. Stone, trustee.
Alexander Bowling, formerly of Charles County, now
works for a new dry goods house, Mr. George
McAlpin, in Baltimore.
James F. Matthews, attorney at law, Port Tobacco.
William B. Stone has stray brindle buffalo cow and
one red calf.
John F. Gardiner, candidate for Orphans' Court.
J. Cocking who has purchased "Retreat" was presented
gifts by the village of Louth (England) upon his
and his family leaving for U.S.A. They lived in
Louth for fifty years. Articles presented was a
silver inkstand valued at 10 pounds, 10 shillings
to Mr. Cocking and a silver cream jug valued at
4 pounds, 17 shillings, 6 d to Mrs. Cocking.
Two hundred parishioners attended presentation.
There were intervals of speech making, enlivened
with music, toasts, etc. Mr. Cocking will shortly
be joined here by his family. "...He is undoubt-
edly of that class of immigrants we need most here."

July 7, 1871, Vol. XXVIII, No. 10

Charles W. Barnes, deceased, property to be sold –
house and lot in Port Tobacco adjoining lots where
Joseph I. Lacey and John D. Covall reside. S. Cox,

trustee.

George P. Jenkins sells brick house in Port Tobacco "...one of the most desirable residences in Port Tobacco "...now occupied by James Wingate.

Mrs. Nannie G. Hungerford's batteau lost from shore of her farm "Waverly." $5.00 reward.

Alexander Dent advertises for strayed or stolen bay colt. "...It was last seen by me on Whitsuntide..." James E. Wingate will receive information concerning whereabouts.

July 14, 1871, Vol. XXVIII, No. 11

John W. Mitchell, Esq. chosen by County Convention for choice of Attorney General.

Hamilton vs Chapman case being heard by Judges Ford and Magruder. "The case is an old one, and, we learn, has been in controversy since 1828.

Democratic Conservative County Convention

Dr. F.M.Lancaster - President
John T. Davis and Samuel N. Cox - Secretaries
Hon. F. Stone, Col. John W. Jenkins and John A. Price, Esq. - delegates to Gubernatorial Convention in Baltimore. A.G.Chapman, Esq. offered resolution- Barnes Compton for Governor of the State and John W. Mitchell for Attorney General for Maryland.

William Whitty advertises for grinding grain at his Chapel Point Mill - persons living near Lancaster's Wharf can send grain to him by steamers "Express" or "Georgeanna."

Census Statistics

Charles County - 5,796 white population, 1860 census
6,418 white population, 1870 census
6,466 population ages 5-20 - 1860
6,250 population ages 5-20 - 1870

W.W.Cobey details successful Cotswold sheep raising.
Dr. H.H.Bean bail set at $5,000.
Dr. William R. Wilmer was recently appointed to 1st class clerkship at the Post Office Department in Washington, D.C.

July 21, 1871, Vol. XXVIII, No. 12

Democratic State Convention

Hon. F. Stone, chair; Andrew G. Chapman - candidate for House of Delegates; James F. Matthews - candidate for State's Attorney

Miss Jennie Neale and sister advertise a boarding school for young ladies at "Mount Air."
Thomas O. Hodges, teacher at school #4 in the 7th Election District, announces examinations.

July 28, 1871, Vol. XXVIII, No. 13

Mr. Brawner, proprietor of the hotel "Brawner House" "...kindly surrendered his hotel for the Festival without charge; the Tableaux were exhibited in the Court House." Port Tobacco Parish ladies' Festival was to raise money to "...aid in the lifting of the debt upon the Rectory..."
Hon. John V.L.McMahon, deceased, will reads "I give...to the Protectors of the St. Mary's Orphan Female School, in...Baltimore, all the real and lease-hold estate and ground rents which were devised to me by the late Mrs. Elizabeth A. Mitchell of Charles County for the use and benefit of the said corporation."
Richard T. Tubman vs Robert Porter - sale of property "Market Overton" 70 acres in Pomonkey adjoining lands of Dr. J.W.Thomas, Howard Shaw, bought by R. Porter and Coates Slater from Richard B. Posey. Also, personal property to be sold.
R. Fergusson, Jr. "Poynton Manor" 6 miles from Port Tobacco advertises peaches for sale - 1.50 - 2.00 a bushel.
John W. Waring, Esq. Bumpy Oak Store advertises a pair of horses, carriage and harness for sale.
L. Allison Wilmer, valedictory oration at commencement exercises at St. John's College, Annapolis. Also "...distinguished by being the only one in the College who received a 1st grade certificate to which no one is entitled who has not deserved 9/10's both in conduct and scholarship for the last year..." The valedictory address was "... one of the very best discourses ever delivered by a Bachelor of Arts. It was full of beauty, power and pathos..."
Andrew G. Chapman candidate for the House of Delegates.
P.W.Robey, on road from Port Tobacco to Allen's Fresh, has several barrels of pure apple vinegar for sale - 33 1/3¢ per gallon or 50¢ for lesser amount.

STATEMENT OF THE EXPENSES OF CHARLES COUNTY FOR
THE YEAR ENDING JUNE 30th, 1871

Judges of Orphans' Court

Richard Barnes, F.P.Hamilton, P.Chapman, J.H.
Roberts, Robert Digges, Stouton Dent.

County Commissioners

George Taylor, Thomas B. Halley, John H. Cox,
A. Jackson Smoot, Josias Hawkins, Samuel Hanson.

Judges of Election

George P. Jenkins, Thomas L. Speake, Richard B.
Posey, W.A.Posey, Thomas Posey, Thomas B. Berry,
Benjamin D. Tubman, John W. McPherson, T. Elzear
Gardiner, William L. McDaniel, George F. Bealle,
George H. Simpson, William Nevitt, sr., William H.
Cox, John A. Wood, Charles E. Hannon, Samuel Hanson,
Jere W. Burch, James A. Mudd, Henry S. Dent, Joseph
Price, John T. Thomas, Richard P. Wall, William
Hamilton, Bennet Neale, John H.D.Wingate, George
T. Simpson.

Clerks of Election

J.B.Sheriff, B.F.Blandford, Peter W. Robey, C.
Claude Digges, Alfred T. Monroe, John W. Nevitt,
James A. Franklin, W.E.W.Rowe, Townley Robey, Richard
Price, William P. Flowers, Rufus Robey, Thomas E.
Webster, William H. Williams, John I. Jenkins,
James H.M.Dutton, John T. Dutton, Frederick L. Dent.

Guards at the Election

John W. Dyson, F.H.Turner, O.I.Lacey, J.R.Carlin,
Henry Thompson, Charles J. Butler, James Mollison,
William A. Boarman, L.A.Martin, George J. Chapalear.

Grand and Petit Jurors 1870 - November Term

J.G.Chapman, Benjamin D. Tubman, Francis O. Medley,
Richard Price, Samuel T. Berry, William A. Boarman,
B.W.B.McPherson, William Wolfe, John D. Davis, J.H.
Padgett, James A. Keech, Philip A. Sasscer, W.B.
Fergusson, George H. Simpson, Pearson Chapman,
Thomas J. Boarman, B.L.Higdon, John H. Cox, Samuel
Cox, W.E.W.Rowe, Samuel T. Swann, John F. Hardy,
Thomas A. Millar, Thomas Carrico, Richard Barnes,
Francis B. Green, Samuel Hanson, Francis P. Hamilton,
Alex. H. Robertson, E.N.Stonestreet, William L.

Harding, Townley Robey, Robert J. Lloyd, John W.
McPherson, James A. Mudd, Richard B. Posey, Joseph
E. Sanders, John L. Budd, Charles C. Hardy, Jere W.
Burch, Richard Farrall, E.F.Mason, John H. Freeman,
J.B.Lyon, J.L.Brawner, Ragan Deakens, James M.
Burch.

1871 - May Term

James H. Neale, William L. Berry, A.W.Neale, William
M.Burch, Benjamin F. Burch, Charles L. Gardiner,
Rufus Robey, William L. McDaniel, William E.
Dement, Mason L. McPherson, James H. Morgan, George
Dent, John Ware, Samuel W. Adams, William L. Cook,
Jere T. Mudd, Richard W. Bryan, Joseph C. Gray,
George F. Bealle, F.T.C.Dent, Thomas Latimer, J.S.
Gibbons, J.T.Mudd, Thomas Posey, George Digges,
Francis R. Speake, Benjamin F. Bowling, George C.
Burch, Benj. W. Blandford, William B. Matthews,
John A. Price, John I. Jenkins, Thomas F. Darnall,
J.T.Ward, J.S.Boarman, Lemuel Smoot, William P.
Flowers, Geo. H. Muschett, J.H.Roberts, John T.
Collins, J.T.S.Tennison, Francis D. Gardiner,
Edward D. Boone, Oliver N. Bryan, Henry R. Harris,
Albert Milstead, Edward L. Huntt, Barnes Compton,
Edgar Griswold, Charles L. Carpenter.

Talismen

Richard T. Boarman, R. Barnes, J.I.Lacey, B.F.
Robbins, Sylvester M. Mudd, Richard Payne, John T.
Crismond, Luther A. Martin, Henry G. Robertson,
William Boswell, J.E.A.J.Howard.

Witnesses in State Cases 1870 - July Term

C.C.Perry, Rufus Perry, Robert Semmes, F.M.Lancaster,
Web. Simpson, James E. Willet, James Taylor, J.W.
Dyson, William Sheirbourn, Theobold Briscoe, William
J. Mollyhorn, C.C.Higdon, A.Milstead, G.T.Higdon,
Ben Higdon, James Taylor, Ben Kelly, M. Chapman,
John Ford, Jeff Kelly, J. Hawkins, Wm. Johnson, Perry
Thomas, A. Milstead, Edward Lawson, Luther A. Martin,
Ellen McWilliams, D.M.Hawkins, Townly Robey, F.L.
Dent, Ann Bealle, Wm. C. Brent, Thomas H. Scott,
Lewis Edwards, Wm. Boswell & Co.,Thomas H. Scott,
Geo. A. Huntt, Richard Forbes, G.J.Carpenter,
William A. Boarman.

1870 - November Term

W.Thomas, F.L.Dent, John S. Gibbons, Wm.C.Brent,

J.H.Roberts, Dr. S.W.Dent, Thomas B. Delozier,
Vivian Brent, Thomas Posey, Charles B. Wade, Clem
Rozier, Marcellus Thompson, Samuel Swann, William
B. Matthews, John A. Price, Richard T. Halley,
Thomas J. Speake, Albin Price, Charles J. Sidler,
Robert Semmes, William Boswell, J.H.Roberts, S.M.
Mudd, C. Adams, J.H.Hancock, W.Hill, F.L.Dent,
Wesley Murdoch, James H. Morgan, H.Hill, J.H.
Hancock, George W. Carpenter, Joseph F. Thomas,
James A. Franklin, W.C.Acton, J.Hawkins, M.Chapman,
Lemuel Smoot, John Ford, Aloysius Hayden, Thomas
B. Berry, Rufus Robey, Margaret McDaniel, Thomas W.
Wright, B.G.Stonestreet, William P. Compton, David
Larkins, Marshall Chapman, F.C.Burgess, Dr. W.J.
Boarman, John T. Crismond, H.C.Page, J.R.Carlin,
Robert Jenkins, Mary E. Bond, Thomas H. Scott,
G.A, Huntt, Richard Burgess, Caroline Edelen, John
H. Ward, Zach. Swann, R. Calvert, Wm. Wolfe, Jacob
Brooks, Thomas A. Padgett, John W. Mitchell, J.T.S.
Tennison, Joseph H. Padgett, Richard Forbes, Richard
Thomas, Philip Stone, C.L.Padgett, J.H.Roberts, Ben
Kelly, M.Chapman, Thomas H. Scott, C.E.Wade, W.C.
Brent, Thomas H. Scott, Anthony Brown, Jane Brown,
Ben Kelly, M. Chapman, Ben Fendall, J.H.Roberts,
John Ford, A. Milstead, Jeff. Kelly, M. Chapman,
W. Jameson, A. Milstead, J. Hawkins, A. Milstead,
L. Mills, Frank Swann, Robert Jenkins, Penny Turner,
Edward Lawson, J.D.Hanson, John Maddox, E. Short,
Susannah Semmes, Francis R. Wills, R.L.Murdoch,
Charles H. Semmes, Wm. C. Brent, John H. Jenkins,
Luther A. Martin, George A. Huntt, W. Butler,
J.R.Johnson, Lewis McWilliams, D. Wade, J.R.Murray,
George Chapalear, David Larkins, Mary Plater,
G. Chapman, John R. Johnson, F. Nicholson, A.J.
Norris, William Roche, Stephen Hawkins, F.L.Dent,
H.Wilkerson, T.C.Wilkerson, E. Bloice, G.A.Huntt,
C.Adams, T.Y.Robey, Joseph I. Lacey, Tolison Thomas,
Chapman Swann, A. Bealle, W.A.Boarman, W.H.Cooksey,
John M. Latimer & Son, Dr. Thomas A. Carrico,
Thomas K. Moran, Samuel Smoot, William J. Boarman,
C.H.Sheirbourn, Madison Gill, Edward Lloyd, Joseph
Wheeler, James A. Willis, Jos. H. Hancock, J.H.
Hancock, Charles F. Lancaster, J.B.Bryan, C.J.
Chapalear, C.C.Perry, Rufus Perry, Robert Semmes,
R.G.Harris, James E. Higdon, F.M.Lancaster, James H.
Morgan, Web. Simpson, James E. Willet, John W. Dyson,
James B. Franklin, W. Murdoch, A. Milstead, Samuel
Keech, W.Boswell & Co.,Bettie Higdon, A. Milstead,
C.C.Higdon, George T. Higdon, Ben Higdon, James
Taylor, Charles E. Wade, William B. Matthews,
W. Thomas, F.L.Dent, C.Adams, R.H.Edelen, M.Reeder,

E.D.R.Bean, J.H.Freeman, George Sewall, G.C.Swann,
A.J.Norris, Tolison Thomas, James Taylor, Joseph
I. Lacey, Charles Adams, T.Y.Robey, M.J.Stone,
Fred. Stone.

1871 - May Term

Luther A. Martin, George A. Huntt, Sylvester M.
Mudd, Thomas C. Wilkerson, J.L.Hamilton, W.Harbin,
William T. Hicks, Elisha Padgett, Mrs. Waters,
A.G.Chapman, James Chipley, W.W.Padgett, Joseph H.
Padgett, W.Boswell & Co., Logan Padgett, Thomas
Newman, Michael Hunower, N.B.Crangle, J.H.Roberts,
William H. Elkins, James T. Bateman, Richard L.
Murdoch, Eugene Long, John H. Cox, G.C.Swann, Jere.
Gibbons, Thomas B. Delozier, Thomas W. Wright,
Benjamin P. Donnelly, Samuel Smoot, Lemuel Smoot,
C.C.Perry, William M. Lyon, Richard White, James F.
Ware, Frank Clements, J.T.S.Tennison, George B.
Bryan, George J. Chapalear, Luther A. Martin,
William A. Boarman, James Chipley, Joseph H. Padgett,
John Ware, Francis Clements, Thomas Newman, Reverdy
A. Rennoe, W.W.Milstead, Jane Fields, V.Matthews,
Thomas H. Scott, Sylvester M. Mudd, T.C.Wilkerson,
Francis P. Hamilton, Hanson Barber, R.A.Garner,
Anthony Flaherty, John W. Fowler, C.G.Brown, W.W.
Padgett, Ferdinand Koskosky, J. Nevitt, J. Jenkins,
Christopher Blair, Thomas L. Speake, Robert L.
Wedding, Uriah Bowie, James H. Bowie, Frank Waters,
James H. Montgomery, Francis Dunnington, F.L.Dent,
Logan Padgett, Peter Trotter, C.M.Bond, James Hill,
John I. Jenkins.

Bailiffs and Messengers

Joseph H. Mattingley, R.H.Edelen, Asa Jenkins,
Julius Quenzel, Nicholas B. Crangle, J.H.Roberts,
John D. Covall, Asa Jenkins, Messenger to County
Commissioners.

Crow Bill Certificates

R.D.P.Radcliff, Peter Williams, Thomas B. Delozier,
William Simmons, Thomas Skinner, William Cox,
Thomas S. Dent, John B. Carpenter, John A. Price,
T.A.Smith, George N. Rowe, Peter Wheeler, William
Boswell & Co., J.I.Lacey, J.R.Robertson, G.C.
Perry, F.R.Wills, J.T.Colton, James B. Latimer,
Albert Farrall, J.M.Latimer & Son, Joseph T. Ward,
J.H.Roberts, John H. Freeman, Sasscer & Warring,
John H. Cox, William H. Moore, Andrew J. Norris,

Richard T. Tubman, Philip A. Sasscer, Townley
Robey, Jere T. Mudd, William R. Acton, Samuel
Smoot, Thomas R. Farrall, E.D.R.Bean, Mason L.
McPherson, Henry C. Robey, T.A.Carrico, G.W.C.
Smoot, James E.C.Bailey.

Rent of Election Rooms

John A. Price, T.A.Smith, Jere Herbert, C.C.Perry,
Elizabeth Duffey, S.W.M.McPherson, G.C.Burch,
E.D.R.Bean.

Registration

William C. Brent, Dr. R. Digges, George W. Carpenter,
James A. Franklin, Charles C. Perry, John H.
Freeman, Marcellus Thompson, Henry M. Hannon, C.H.
Rowe, Townley Robey, Rufus Robey, Timothy A. Smith,
J.A.Price, Elizabeth Duffey, Wm. M. Sheirbourn,
G.C.Burch, E.D.R.Bean.

Collectors for Assessments and Insolvencies

William H. Gray, John T. Dutton, John H. Hancock,
William M. Burch, William Boswell, John T. Colton,
Richard W. Bryan, T.C.Wilkerson, T.W.Wright, Lemuel
Smoot, L.A.Martin, R.T.Bailey, S.M.Mudd.

Coroners' Inquests

Edward D. Boone, Coroner and acting Constable,
George W. Carpenter, Willis Rye, William Brown,
William O. Milstead, Oswald Connell, Isam Baxter,
William Murphy, William B. Murphy, Ignatius Boswell,
James Murphy, Nathan Murphy, George W. Carpenter,
Jr., William P. Flowers, Coroner, Thomas W. Wright,
Constable, Thomas P. Gray, A.W.Claggett, D.W.
Carpenter, R.Price, jr., James Haislip, Uzzial
Wright, M.W.Dunnington, Luther L. Leland, Ragan
Deakins, Richard Johnson, Joseph Johnson, William
Johnson, Richard W. Bryan, Coroner, in three cases,
George R. Bryan, Constable, Charles H. Wills, T.L.
Joins, S.A.Miles, T.A.Green, T.H.Johnson, J.W.Warring,
C.Welch, T.R.Hart, Thomas Maddox, Benjamin Hodges,
Benjamin Hardy, William H. Cox.

Coffins and Burying Paupers

James A. Franklin, Archey Gray, L.L.Leland, George W.
Carpenter, Joseph Clark, Eli Waters, Nicholas
Stonestreet, Sasscer & Warring, Warren O. Willet,

H.W.Clark, Charles M. Bond, William B. Moore,
James H. Montgomery, William H. Higges.

Public Roads

Thomas A. Jones, R.Payne, Samuel Cox, jr., James
Taylor, Wm. B. Matthews, Benjamin M. Edelen,
William E. Dement, A. Haislip, R.K.Posey, Thomas
S. Martin, Lucinda Gough, Peter D. Hatton, Joseph
H. Padgett, John Carrington, B.F.Montgomery, John
D. Bowling, Dr. Thomas A. Carrico, Edward D. Boone,
Benjamin D. Tubman, John E. Bailey, Thomas D.
Simpson, Thos. K. Ching, J.R.Robertson, James H.
Morgan, Henry R. Harris, Mrs. Laurence, H.Luckett,
John A. Burroughs, Mrs. C. Edelen, John Garner,
Benjamin Bateman, Robert Semmes, William M.
Gardiner, Thomas Semmes, J.E.Higdon, W.A.Padgett,
Walter Swann.

Road System of 1870

W.W.Padgett, F.A.Carpenter, J.M.Dudley, Levi
Woodruff, E.D.R.Bean, W.T.Edelen, B.W.B.McPherson,
William T. Hindle, Henry Howard, Joseph Gray, John
Hamilton, Edmund Perry, Wilson Compton, Edward J.
Sanders, Benton Burgess, W.A.Posey, William and
Mary Parish, Mrs. Lucretia Lancaster, Ambrose
Adams, John D. Bowling, George H. Gardiner, George
Gardiner, William L. Berry, Henry L. Mudd, Dr.
Samuel Mudd, John T. Crismond, B.H.Jameson's heirs,
Robert Young, Oliver N. Bryan, William Garner,
George Washington, John H. Mitchell, E.F.Mason,
Samuel Hanson, P.A.Murphy, H.Clagett Page, Rezin
Barnes, J.R.Robertson.

Road System of 1871

Highland Brawner, Benjamin D. Tubman, William N.
Sanders, E.A.Bowling, Patrick Dudley, John H. Cox,
B.W.Spalding, John D. Bowling, Mason L. McPherson,
B.F.Bowling, William H. Berry, A.R.A. Murray, J.F.
Gardiner, Frederick Stone, Theodore L. Robey,
Wilfred B. Moore, George Gardiner, E.D.R.Bean,
John H.D.Wingate, Henry R. Harris, Mrs. Elizab eth
J. Stone, George H. Simpson, Thomas Carrico, Mrs.
Lucinda Gough, Mrs. Sarah Edelen, John G. Chapman,
Mrs. E.A.Middleton, Mrs. Eleanor Robertson.

Miscellaneous Items

County Commissioners for the following purposes--

```
Clerk to the Circuit Court            $1,153.00
Sheriff                                1,200.00
Register of Wills                        630.00
State's Attorney                       1,050.00
Crier of the Circuit Court               212.00
County Bonds and Interest              2,400.45
Roads and Bridges                      6,000.00
Repair of Court House                    500.00
Contingent Expenses                      500,00
Insane Paupers                         1,635.00
Magistrates' and Constables' fees         80.00
Trustees of the Poor                   2,100.00
Board of School Commissioners          3,172.76
Elijah Wells, for Printing               700.00
Vivian Brent, Attorney to Co. Commrs.    100.00
John R. Robertson, Clerk to Co. Commrs. ⎫400.00
John R. Robertson, for Postage, etc. 2 yrs⎭
John D. Covall, Keeper of the Court House 20.00
William Boswell & Co., for Registration
  Books, Stationery, etc.                 90.39
Daniel W. Hawkins, fees for defending
  criminals                              108.50
John W. Mitchell, fees for defending
  criminals                               50.00
Andrew G. Chapman, fees for defending
  criminals                               15.00
Samuel Cox, jr., fees for defending
  criminals                                5.00
Richard H. Edelen, fees for defending
  criminals                               33.33
George W. Carpenter, hire of wagon and team
  for conveying Prisoners to Court        20.00
George W. Carpenter, for expense to
  Annapolis on Registration Account       20.00
Andrew J. Norris, for boarding criminals  10.00
Dr. Bennet Neale, for medical services at
  the Jail                                19.54
Dr. George D. Mudd, for medical services at
  the Jail                                18.00
John B. Murray, for clothing for Prisoners 9.00
```

The following for erroneous assessment -
Mrs. Caroline Jones, William H. Higgs, Jere. T.
Mudd, Warren O. Willett, Henrietta McWilliams,
John H. Cox, Thomas A. Davis, John L. Budd,
Edward D. Boone, John T. Dutton, John D. Covall.

T.T.Hancock, teacher at School #2, 1st Election District held Examination and Exhibition. R.H.
Gardiner was speaker. Ignatius Sanders made brief
but eloquent speech on behalf of the cause of
education.

J.R.Robertson, Clerk to County Commissioners
announces meeting for purpose of receiving
proposals for repairing the courthouse.
C.H.Gray advertises farm for rent near Nanjemoy
Church.
Hon. Fred. Stone, late M.C. and lady, departed on
a six week trip to Omaha, Salt Lake City and
San Francisco.

August 11, 1871, Vol. XXVIII, No. 15

Tickets for excursion to Acquia Creek may be pur-
chased at stores of J.I.Lacey, W.Bowwell & Co.,
and W.W.Padgett in Port Tobacco; T.A.Smith in
Cross Roads; J.T.Colton, Allen's Fresh; and
Thomas A. Whitty, Chapel Point.
John A. Gray announces that there will be "...a
Pic-nic and Public Speaking on the Glymont Road,
near Palmoine..."
"The Charles County Committee for Church Extension,
etc." will hold Divine Service at Trinity Chapel,
Old Fields, Wed.
Charles Farrall died Monday in Port Tobacco. He
served as a soldier in the War of 1812, old and
highly respected citizen. He was 83 years old.
Rev. C. Vicinanza, S.J. who has served in Charles
County for 19 years has been ordered to St.
Mary's County. "...His loss will be regretted,
outside of the fold of his church, by many, whose
affections he has won by his genial manners and
courteous demeanor."

August 18, 1871, Vol. XXVIII, No. 16

E. Wells, Times editor and members of the Maryland
Editorial Association left Baltimore on the
Baltimore and Ohio Railroad for Put-in-Bay, a
resort in Lake Erie.
Daniel P. Haviland, formerly of Poughkeepsie, New
York who has lived the last four years in Bryan-
town, died on August 12th. He was 60 years old.
Daniel W. Hawkins, candidate for State's Attorney.
Noble Thompson, near Newport, holds a party to bene-
fit the Newport Catholic Church.
Mrs. Camilla Edelen, in Cobb Neck, has a pic-nic to
benefit Cobb Neck Catholic Church. "...fish,
oysters, crabs and terrapins, in abundance."
A.H.Robertson, Benjamin Welch, R.V.Welch and Hugh
Mitchell apply "...to make the road leading from
Cedar Hill to where it intersects the road from

Hill-Top to Taylor's Landing, a Public Road."
Barnes Compton and John W. Mitchell ask the Democratic and Conservative Voters to assemble in
voting places to select ten delegates to the
County Convention at the Courthouse to nominate
candidates for the House of Delegates and County
officers.

August 25, 1871, Vol. XXVIII, No. 17

Richard F. Mattingley marries Rose Thompson of
Prince George's County on Wednesday morning by
Rev. John Towles.
Joseph Dixon marries Anna E. Garner on August 10th
by Rev. F. McAtee.
Thaddeus Beverly Middleton died August 23 at Fairfax
Courthouse of congestive chill. He was the only
son of J.C. and Anna L. Middleton of Port Tobacco.
He was 2 years, 6 months old.
Robert Digges, Sr., is candidate for Orphans' Court.
Margaret A. Padgett and W.E.W.Rowe, administrators
for estate of John E. Padgett, ask creditors to
submit claims.
Samuel Cox, Jr., "having finished his contract on
the Baltimore and Potomac Railroad in Charles
County..." will sell livestock, harness, wagons,
tools and also store goods usually kept in a
first class country store.
Thomas V. Robey, executor for Francis Robey asks
creditors to submit claims.
Thomas A. Millar of "Holly Springs" will rent
Nanjemoy Stores and Granaries, also farm attached. Persons wanting to gill from "Nanjemoy
Stores," "Woodbury Hope," "Walnut Landing," "Tea
Pot," or the "Sheds" will apply to him.
U.Nalley, deceased — persons indebted to his estate,
make settlement. Thomas A. Millar and S. Hanson,
executors.
Four scholarships are available to Charles County
students for St. John's College, Annapolis.

September 1, 1871, Vol. XXVIII, No. 18

Mail not available because key to the bag was broken!
Mrs. Joanna Harriet Tennison died at "Cedar Grove,"
Piccawaxen on July 15, 1871. She was 73 years old.
"Few could be more faithful than this good lady..."
W.C.Brent asks for payment of accounts due him.
Cecilia A. Miles, executrex for Edward Miles asks
creditors to submit claims.

Robert Oliver applies "to change that part of the
road leading from Port Tobacco to Cobb Neck, ly-
ing between Dr. B.Jameson's land and Robert
Oliver's lot,.."
R.H.Edelen, trustee, will sell "Crain's Low
Ground" and part of "Timber Neck" now in one
farm called "Laurel Grove" 370 acres where
Lawrence Posey and Ann Posey now reside. "...
one of the best dwelling houses in the county..."
2 miles from Allen's Fresh, convenient to Post
Office, school and mill - 50 yards from the line
of the Baltimore and Potomac Railroad.
Luther A. Martin is candidate for sheriffalty.
William L. Chiles and James M. Harvey, Nanjemoy,
have purchased the site and are building a wharf
at Liverpool Point, on Potomac River.

September 8, 1871, Vol. XXVIII, No. 19

Maryland State Agricultural and Mechanical Fair
now has committees of ladies "...to solicit
household and fancy articles for exhibition.
The committee for Charles County consists of
Mrs. Barnes Compton, Mrs. H.R.Harris, Mrs.
Frederick Stone, and Miss Helen M. Chapman.
John Hamilton advertises for rent his house in
Port Tobacco now occupied to John S. Button.
John H. Mitchell applies to change the road lead-
ing through "Hanson Hill."
William F. Brawner, Esq., teacher at primary school
#4 has Master T. Lawrence Martin of Charlotte Hall
School address the annual examination.
D.Ignatius Sanders, Late Collector, will sell "Part
of Cornwallis' Neck," assessed to Baker Edelin.
George H. Simpson died on Saturday at his residence
near Newport. He was 56 years old.
Nettie Ellen Long died 25 July of congestive fever.
She was the oldest daughter of J.H. and Mary V.
Long. She was 2 years, 9 months old.
Land in Charles County selling for $25-50 per acre,
3/4 cultivated, all fenced.

September 15, 1871, Vol. XXVIII, No. 20

Francis W. Weems, executor for Eleanor Marshall,
deceased, asks creditors to submit claims.
Henry A. Brawner marries Mattie Wagaman of Washington, D.C. on Sept. 6, 1871 at the Church of the
Incarnation, Washington, D.C. by Rev. Mr. Harris.

66

Margaret Harwood Chapman died at "La Plata" on
September 6th, daughter of Marshall and Ellen
Chapman. She was 10 days old.
Judge George P. Jenkins buys "Locust Grove" for-
merly owned by Mrs. Elizabeth G. Davis. $8,000.
L.L.Hamilton of Beantown, has lost an iron gray
horse.

Charles County Democratic and Conservative Convention

Hon. Barnes Compton, president; Samuel N. Cox,
secretary.
County commissioner candidates - Dr. A.J.Smoot,
Josias Hawkins, John H. Cox, Thomas R. Halley,
Samuel Hanson, William Turner, Thomas M. Posey,
James H. Neale and Charles H. Wills.
Smoot, Hawkins, Cox, Halley and Posey received
the five highes number of votes - declared the
nominees.
List of delegates to County Convention;
No. 1 - Port Tobacco - George A. Huntt, John C.
Wenk, Elijah Wells, F.W.Weems, John W. Mitchell,
John G. Chapman, James L. Brawner, N. Stonestreet,
John H. Jenkins, George Digges.
No. 2 - Hill-Top - R.H.Edelen, Barnes Compton,
J.B.Carpenter, J.A.Price, A.Milstead, H.H.Bowie,
C.H.Wills, F.C.Burgess, R.E.Rison, William
Milstead.
No. 3 - Nanjemoy - George W. Carpenter, Dr. Thomas
C. Price, William S. Chiles, Albin Price, Francis
Dunnington, Joseph Price, Edwin Adams, William H.
Gray, John Murdoch, S.W.Adams.
No. 4 - Allen's Fresh - James H. Neale, John T.
Crismond, Samuel Cox, Dr. J.H.Reeder, J.H.Freeman,
Samuel Cox, Jr., J.H.Kinnamon, T.K.Ching, R.Payne,
Joseph R. Harrison.
No. 5 - Harris' Lot - Dr. A.J.Smoot, H.R.Harris,
J.T.F.Wingate, R.Simms, P.A.L.Contee, J.H.D.Wingate,
J.F.Matthews, J.T.Dutton, L.Smoot, F.McWilliams.
No. 6 - Middletown - D.I.Sanders, Samuel N. Cox,
Dr. William N. Sanders, John R. Murray, William F.
Dement, B.W.Spalding, J.B.Sheriff, T. Yates Robey,
J.H.Hancock, John H. Cox.
No. 7 - Pomonkey - Thomas R. Halley, John W.
Jenkins, William H. Cox, O.N.Bryan, Dr. John W.
Thomas, R.T.Tubman, John A. Wood, R.O.Wade, T.L.
Hannon, J.F.S.Middleton.
No. 8 - Bryantown - Peter Trotter, Townly Robey,
Dr. T.A.Carrico, F.L.Dent, William Berry, F.D.
Murphy, R.Farrall, H.Murray, M.P.Gardiner
Dr. P.W.Hawkins.

No. 9 - Patuxent City - R.P.Wall, William
Turner, Rufus Robey, George J. Chapalear, Jere
Dudley, Henry A. Burch, Richard Adams, John R.
Johnson, Z. Swann, William F. Edelen.

September 22, 1871, Vol. XXVIII, No. 21

Mrs. Mary Sanders died on Sept. 13, 1871 at "Cedar
Grove." She was the wife of Joseph E. Sanders
and was 48 years old. "Death has visited a happy
household, now sad and mourning, and taken from
it a loving wife and affectionate mother..."
Thomas O. Bean, deceased, property sold - the homeplace on Gilbert Swamp, 500 acres - 2 story brick
dwelling - adjoining place "Uncle Peter's" 150-
200 acres - small tenement house. A farm in the
Piney Church neighborhood - 200 acres - dwelling.
John H. Mitchell and Frederick Stone, trustees.

September 29, 1871, Vol. XXVIII, No. 22

John H.D.Wingate warns trespassers on "Poppleton."
Maynard N. Millar and Samuel O. Wells awarded schol-
ships to St. John's College.
Joseph C. Gray was awarded a scholarship to the
Maryland State Agricultural College.
Dr. B.Neale's house was entered by two men intent
on robbing it. The doctor found them and the en-
suing scuffle wakened the rest of the family and
the two men fled. "...This is the first attempt
at burglary that we remember to have taken place
in this village..."

October 6, 1871, Vol. XXVIII, No. 23

Amanda C. Simpson and Thomas Carrico, executors for
George H. Simpson, deceased, ask creditors to
submit claims.
J.F.S.Middleton announces a meeting of candidates
at Pye's Wharf.
J.G.Chapman advertises livestock for sale.
Leonard C. Edelen vs C.M.Edelen - Court of Equity.
P.A.Sasscer & J.W.Waring partnership dissolved -
J.W.Waring now.
Samuel Cox, Jr. marries Ella Magruder of Montgomery
County at the Church of the Epiphany in Washington,
D.C. on Oct. 4, 1871 by Rt. Rev. William Pinckney,
Assistant Bishop of Maryland.

Wilson Compton marries Kate Carpenter, eldest
   daughter of William B. Carpenter at the residence of the bride's father on Sept. 20th by
   Rev. William J. Chiles.
Capt. H.C.Page appoin ted assistant engineer of
   the Baltimore and Potomac Railroad, for laying
   track.

Grand Jurors
George P. Jenkins, foreman

Townley Robey, William M. Jameson, R.P.Wall, F.L.
Higdon, John W. Boarman, Joseph B. Gardiner, B.L.
Higdon, Francis Price, John B. Carpenter, Joseph A.
Gray, S.W.H.McPherson, William B. Fergusson, Thomas
A. Millar, Ragan Deakens, Joseph T. Ward, William
Wolfe, Henry L. Budd, sr., W.A.Posey, William L.
Sheirburn, John R. Turner, James A. Mudd, James M.
Burch,.

Petit Jurors

William P. Compton, Joseph E. Sanders, P.A.Sasscer,
T. Yates Robey, Hugh Mitchell, Francis W. Weems,
John E. Bailey, Alexander A. Robertson, Samuel
Hanson, Thomas P. Turner, Samuel Cox, Samuel
Carrington, Charles H. Wills, Benjamin Welch,
Thomas J. Boarman, William H. Berry, E.D.R.Bean,
Clinton H. Dent, Charles F. Lancaster, Benton Barnes,
James A. Franklin, John T. Davis, B.W.Hardy, John
F. Cobey, John Hamersly.

October 13, 1871, Vol. XXVIII, No. 23

(There is no explanation why this issue and that of
   October 6, 1871 carry the same number.)

B. Compton, chair; J.W.Mitchell and Frederick Stone,
   executive committee for the Democratic and Conservative County Convention.
Samuel Carrington's property "Part of Mount Rose"
   110 acres to be sold at suit of Marshall Chapman.
   John R. Murray, sheriff.
State Comptroller's office publishes list of account-
   ing officers in default to the State of Maryland
   and the principal and interest due by each:

	Principal	Interest	Total
R.W.Mitchell, late Clerk	$ 46.01	53.37	99.38
Thomas S. Stewart, late Sheriff	1,958.00	438.35	1,496.35

William M. Morris, late Sheriff	565.00	90.43	655.43
John R. Murray, late Sheriff	190.00	16.08	206.08
Eugene Digges, State's Attorney for money recovered of John R. Murray, late Collector of State Taxes	929.11	160.27	1,089.38

William B. Matthews warns trespassers on farms "Plenty" and "Laidler's Ferry"

J. Cocking warns trespassers on farm "Retreat."

Republican Convention Nominates Candidates

Delegates to Legislature - Dr. William R. Wilmer and Edward W. Gardiner.

Judges of the Orphans' Court - John F. Gardiner, Edmund Perry and George P. Jenkins.

County Commissioners - John R. Turner, Levi Hicks, William P. Flowers, Egbert Carey, William H. Brawner.

Sheriff - William H. Welch.

William P. Flowers announces that the use of his name on the Republican ticket is "...unauthorized and without my consent...am a Democrat and will remain one..."

James L. Brawner announces candidacy for re-election as County Surveyor.

R.L.Mathany announces candidacy for the House of Delegates as an independent Republican.

Capt. D.J.Thomas announces candidacy for the House of Delegates as a Republican.

W.T.Fearson found "gunning skift [sic]" in Wicomico River.

October 20, 1871, Vol. XXVIII, No. 24

(The following article was taken from the Editor of the Virginia State Journal.)

Glymont

Along the whole Potomac front there is no richer, or more charming spot than Glymont. Winding through a beautiful valley, overhung with grand trees, the roadway rises from the water's edge to a magnificent plateau nearly two hundred feet above the river, and

commanding a view unsurpassed in beauty and mag-
nificence. Here is the residence of our friend,
Captain Leonard Marbury, embowered in fruit trees
and surrounded with rare and beautiful flowers,
the evidence of his refined and gentle taste.
Captain Marbury is now nearly eighty, but hale and
hearty, and his mind clear and strong, as when he
proudly trod the deck of his favorite ship on the
seas. He was for thirty years a companion of old
Neptune, and recounts now tales of the stormy sea
with zest. He is one of the most remarkable and
noteworthy men we have ever met. He was a sturdy
Unionist during the war. He uses neither liquors
of any kind nor tobacco, reads and follows <u>Hall's
Journal of Health</u>, and an enlightened experience,
and enjoys very good health. His fine estate was
somewhat run down during the war, but is still
very beautiful. It abounds in valuable beds of
marl, easily made available both for his own fields
and for shipment. Fine springs of pure, healthful
water gush out of the banks.--One of these not far
from the river would furnish a supply of water suf-
ficient to run the boilers of a 200 horsepower engine
for a mill or factory. We wish a bright future to
Glymont, and long life and prosperity to its noble
and hospitable proprietor.

Democratic and Conservative State Ticket

House of Delegates - Hon. Frederick Stone and
    Andrew G. Chapman, Esq.
County Commissioners - Dr. A.J.Smoot, Josias
    Hawkins, Esq., John H. Cox, Esq., Thomas R.
    Halley, Esq., Samuel Hanson, Esq.
Judges of the Orphans' Court - Dr. Stouten W. Dent,
    Richard Barnes, Sr., Robert Digges, Sr.
Sheriff - Luther A. Martin

John Queen announces Candidates' meeting "...at the
    'Relay' near Gilpin's Hill..."
Clarisa Dunnington announces "...Pic-nic and Public
    Speaking on the Pompfret [sic] Road near Mr.
    William Hamilton's..."
F.McWilliams and Co. announce three days of Racing
    over the Plainfield Course, Cobb Neck.
Chappelear & Smoot announce three day's racing over
    Bryantown Course.
William Dows warns trespassers on "Rosemary Lawn."
Joseph H. Haviland and Samuel R. Neave are partners
    in real estate business.

R.A.Rennoe, William J. Chiles, Thomas Wright,
William P. Harvey and Frank Dunnington appeal
"...to close road leading past Cross Roads to
the Blue Banks, on Potomac River, and to open and
make public a Road to Liverpool Point."
Samuel Lunt, late of Alexandria, deceased, property
sold Fishery on Potomac River known as "Thorn's
Gut." The Fishery, as reserved in the sale of
the farm heretofore made, comprises a lot of land
of several acres at the lower end of the farm,
embracing the HOUSES attached to the Shore, and
the Beach the entire extent of said farm up the
river..."
W.W.Cobey, J.W.Wheeler, T.E.Speake warn trespassers
on farm known as "Tayloe's Neck."
William Boswell warns trespassers on "Chandler's
Hope."
Joseph H. Haviland warns trespassers on "Oakland."
L. DeBarth Gardiner formerly of Charles County
marries Emma, daughter of Richard Wilson of
Baltimore at St. Ignatius Church, Baltimore on
October 12th by Rev. Father W.F.Clark.

Democratic and Conservative County Convention

J.W.Mitchell, Esq. proposed an official resolution
that three persons in each election district be
nominated to serve as County Executive Committee:

#1 - George Digges, Thomas R. Farrall, John T.
     Davis
#2 - Robert E. Rison, H.H.Bowie, J.A.Price
#3 - William H. Gray, Albin Price, Edwin Adams
#4 - Samuel Cox, Sr., J.H.Freeman, J.T.Crismond
#5 - Robert Simms, J.H.D.Wingate, Dr. A.J.Smoot
#6 - Capt. W.F.Dement, John H. Cox, J.B.Sheriff
#7 - John W. Jenkins, Richard T. Tubman, O.N.Bryan
#8 - Dr. P.W.Hawkins, Frederick L. Dent, Townley
     Robey
#9 - Richard P. Wall, Jere Dudley, E.D.R.Bean

October 27, 1871, Vol. XXVIII, No. 25

Judson Wedding, deceased, property sold at Beantown,
not far from Baltimore and Potomac Railroad, 133
acres and dwelling.
N. Stonestreet warns trespassers on "LaGrange" or
"The Quiver" (the latter now occupied by Joseph
L. Murphy.)

Webster Sothoron, Esq. formerly of Charles County, now living in Montgomery, Alabama.

November 10, 1871, Vol. XXVIII, No. 27

ELECTION RESULTS

House of Delegates -
  Frederick Stone, Democrat - 1546
  Andrew G. Chapman, Democrat - 1588
  Dr. William R. Wilmer, Republican - 1400
  Edward W. Gardiner, Republican - 1301

State's Attorney -
  Eugene Digges, Democrat - 1577
  Daniel W. Hawkins, Democrat - 1067

Orphans' Court -
  Richard Barnes, Sr., Democrat - 1551
  Robert Digges, Sr., Democrat - 1573
  Dr. S.W.Dent, Democrat - 1357

County Commissioners -
  Dr. A.J.Smoot, Democrat - 1554
  Josias Hawkins, Democrat - 1532
  John H. Cox, Democrat - 1525
  Thomas R. Halley, Democrat - 1495
  Samuel Hanson, Democrat - 1530
* John R. Turner - 1375
* Egbert Carey - 1365
* Levi Hicks - 1376
* William H. Brawner - 1365
* Uzzial Wright - 1330

*This ticket, composed of Republicans and Democrats, was nominated by the Republican Convention.

Sheriff
  Luther A. Martin, Democrat - 1587
  William H. Welch, Republican - 1375

Surveyor
  James L. Brawner - 1902
  James A. Franklin - 421

George Passage has personal and real property sale.
E.P.Maddox found stray bull yearling.
Samuel G. Lancaster, B.J.Lancaster, B.H.Mattingley, Charles T. Carpenter and John L. Budd warn trespassers on their farms at Newport.

S.W.H.McPherson's residence in Pomonkey scene of
choral concert by ladies of the choir of St.
Paul's Church, Alexandria, supper and festival.
All to benefit St. John's Chapel, Pomonkey.
"...The ladies of St. John's desire to enclose
their church yard...and to make some much-needed
improvements to their church..."
Lawrence Posey has public sale of personal property.
Washington Norris shot and killed Walbert Bell (both
Negroes) at Harris' Lot. Norris is in jail.
The Rev. F. McAtee of St. Thomas' Manor has given
the Editor sweet potatoes "...grown upon the
Manor."
James H. Gough, John R. Turner and Thomas P. Turner
warn trespassers.

November 17, 1871, Vol. XXVIII, No. 28

Henry Delozier has a pair of stray mules.
Hannibal Milstead has stray bay mare mule.
George Taylor advertises for tenant for his farm
for 1872. He warns poachers and trespassers from
"Cherry Grove."
James A. Keech and Lucinda Gough warn trespassers.
Hugh Mitchell Marries Mary R., daughter of Daniel
Jenifer of Baltimore County at "Good Hope" resi-
dence of bride's father on Nov. 15th by the Rev.
James A. Mitchell, Rector of White Marsh Parish,
Talbot County.
Thomas Skinner, Doncaster, raised "...turnip of the
ruta baga variety..." 6½ pounds.

November 24, 1871, Vol. XXVIII, No. 29

Luther A. Martin, Esq. bonded as sheriff.
Sallie M. Swann will resume Oyster and Eating House
formerly operated by James Swann, deceased.
John M. Todd and John K. Todd, Newburg, sell 1000
superior cabbage.
R.A.Rennoe, T.A.Smith and Thomas P. Gray appointed
examiners to ascertain public convenience required
by closing road past Cross Roads to Blue Banks on
Potomac River and opening and making a public road
to Liverpool Point on Potomac River.

ROAD NOTICE

Notice is hereby given, That the undersigned and one
hundred others will make application to the County

Commissioners of Charles County, at the expira-
tion of thirty days, for a Public Road across
Zachia Swamp, about midway between the crossing at
Allen's Fresh and the crossing at Newtown, commenc-
ing at a point on the Public Road leading from Cen-
treville to Newport, near a private road of J.R.
Carlin, A.J.Boarman, across Zachia Swamp through
the lands of Dr. F.R.Wills, Samuel Cox, William
Nevitt and heirs, to the Public Road leading from
Newtown to Chapel Point and Port Tobacco.

[Signed] J.R.Carlin, Joseph S. Boarman, George M.
Lloyd, N.V.Miles, C.Claude Digges, Samuel Cox, Sr.,
John B. Lyon, John L. Budd, John T. Crismond, George
B. Shannon, Wm. L. Sheirbourn, R.T.Jameston, George
Spaulding, B.I.Lancaster, Geo. B. Lancaster, John
H. Kinnamon, A.J.Boarman, B.P.Donelly, J.G.Chapman,
C.A.Neale, and others.

George Forbes vs Samuel H. Berry and wife - Equity
    Court. Frederick Stone, trustee.

CATHOLIC MISSION FOR COLORED PEOPLE

We learn that Archbishop Spalding has donated sixty
acres of land in Charles county to the new Catholic
Mission about to be established in this county for
the benefit of the colored people. The property is
situated near Bryantown, and is said to be in good
condition and valuable. The mansion house upon it
(formerly used as an Academy) will for the present
accommodate the Mission, and will from time to time
be enlarged as the necessities of the case demand.
Four ecclesiastics, members of the St. Joseph's
Society for Foreign Missions, have recently arrived
from England and will take charge of the Mission.
They also contemplate establishing schools for the
children of colored parents, wherever practicable.

December 1, 1871, Vol. XXVIII, No. 31

Circuit Court cases

State vs John Turner - perjury - n.g.
State vs William Hill, colored, resisting constable
    L.A.Martin. Guilty, 10 days.
State vs Charles Bloice, colored, resisting con-
    stable L.A.Martin. Not'guilty.
State vs John C. Irwin, assault and battery.
    Guilty, $5 and costs.

75

State vs Charles Weamert, keeping disorderly
   house. Guilty, $5 and costs.
State vs Basil Clarke, cutting saddle flap. Not
   guilty.
State vs H.H.Bean, murder. Not guilty.
State vs Simon Chapman, colored, larceny. Guilty,
   3 months.

Board of County Commissioners met and elected
   officers:
   President - Dr. A.J.Smoot
   Clerk - John R. Robertson
   Bailiff - Asa Jenkins
   Keeper of Court House - J.D.Covell

Charles Bowls sells personal property at "Cedar
   Point Farm" in Cedar Point Neck.
Mrs. Mary Latimer's farm "Oak Grove" for sale near
   Pope's Creek on Baltimore and Potomac Railroad
   adjoining "Clifton."
Andrew G. Chapman, Esq. marries Helen Mary Chapman,
   daughter of Pearson Chapman at Christ Church, Port
   Tobacco on Nov. 29, 1871 by Rev. Dr. Lewin.
William P. Burks of Bedford County, Virginia marries
   Lizzie C. Gray, eldest daughter of Thomas P. Gray
   at the residence of the bride's father on Nov. 22
   by Rev. William J. Chiles.
Augustine W. Neale marries Jennie R. Matthews,
   daughter of the late Dr. Thomas Matthews of St.
   Mary's County at St. Aloysius Church in Leonard-
   town on Nov. 22 by Rev. Father DeWolf.
Mrs. Elender O'Bryan died near Gallant Green on
   Nov. 18th. She was 81 years old.

WOMEN AS PRINTERS

   A job printing office, conducted entirely by women,
is now in full operation in Washington, and is in
quite a flourishing condition. Four female composi-
tors are employed, and the work turned out by them
is pronounced excellent in every respect. There
are many things in the art typographical that must
utilize the peculiar talent women have for contrasts
of color and proportions of forms. To be a thorough-
ly accomplished job printer is to be an artist.

December 8, 1871, Vol. XXVIII, No. 32

Thomas Posey, deceased, Orphans' Court. Ellen C.
Posey and Thomas B. Delozier, administrators.

George Forbes vs Samuel Berry and wife. Equity
Court.
Richard A. Oliver marries Mary Bowls of Kent
County at Bohemia Church in Cecil County on
Nov. 21st by Rev. Father Vellager.
H. Maud Hanson died, 2 years, 4 months old. She
was the daughter of F. Alvan and Jennie R. Hanson.
"Little Maud, the priceless treasure of loving
hearts, bright as the sparkling dew drop of the
morning, blythe as the carolling songster, now
sleeps in the voiceless silence of the tomb..."

St. Columba lodge holds election

Worshipful Master - Henry G. Robertson
Senior Warden - Rev. Meyer Lewin, D.D.
Junior Warden - James L. Brawner
Secretary - John S. Button
Treasurer - J. Hubert Roberts
Tiler - William M. Morris

Case of State vs George W. Norris
    Those testifying C.C.Perry, Rufus Perry, R.G.
    Harris, Dr. A.J.Smoot, Lemuel Smoot, Joseph
    Norris, Andrew Boarman, Dr. B.Neale, Dr. F.M.
    Lancaster. Attorneys - Eugene Digges, Esq. -
    State; Hon. F. Stone and R.H.Edelen, Esq. and
    J.F.Matthews, Esq. - defense.

December 15, 1871, Vol. XXVIII, No. 33

Thomas Edwin Sandy marries Alice Virginia Milstead
    at the residence of the bride's father on Dec. 6th
    by Rev. William J. Chiles.
Mrs. Joanna C. Everett died at Middleburg, Loudon
    County, Virginia at the residence of her son in law,
    Rev. William S. Baird, on Dec. 3rd. She was 73
    years old and formerly resided at Newtown. "She
    had been a worthy member of the Methodist Church
    for more than 50 years..."
William B. Matthews advertises a buggy and harness
    for sale.
J.T.Mudd advertises to rent a house and blacksmith
    shop near Gallant Green.

A CARD

To Misses Lizzie Huntt, Hattie Wells, Mary Huntt
and Lydia Jenkins.

Young Ladies: You have to-day manifested your re-

spect to me by the presentation of a beautiful
hat, and let me assure you that I the more highly
esteem the present, because I believe it to be an
expression of your appreciation of my efforts to
advance you in your literary course, to render your
labors easy and to add as much as possible to your
happiness during that part of your scholastic life
in which we have been associated together. Be as-
sured that I shall ever hold you in fond remembrance, ever ready to make any sacrifice to secure
your welfare in the future.
  With affectionate regard, I remain, most truly,
your friend.
Dec. 16, 1871   F.PENNINGTON

December 22, 1871, Vol. XXVIII, No. 34

School Commissioners Appointed: Dr. Thomas A.
  Carrico, Judge Edmund Perry, John H. Mitchell,
  Esq.
W.E.W.Rowe writes to Editor deploring indifference
  of parents to their children education-wise.
Elizabeth Tompkins vs James R. Tompkins - farm to
  be sold "Part of Neale's Gift" 170 acres with
  dwelling. Also, "Part of Tompkins' Purchase"
  and generally known as "Tompkinsville." Lot
  has store-house, grocery-room attached and
  dwelling. R.H.Edelen, N.Stonestreet, V.Brent,
  Receivers.
R.G.Nevitt marries Mary G. Lee, daughter of the
  late Col. Dodridge C. Lee of Fairfax County,
  Virginia in Christ Church, Alexandria, Va. on
  Dec. 14th by Rev. Mr. McKim.
William H. Brawner died at his residence on Dec.
  16th. He was 61 years old.

December 29, 1871, Vol. XXVIII, No. 35

Julian Berry of Alexandria, formerly of Charles
  County marries Clara D. Gaines of Gainesville,
  Prince William County, Virginia in Washington,
  D.C. on Dec. 15th by Rev. Dr. Newman.
William H. Posey marries Philomenia Jane Baxter
  at the residence of Walter Milstead on Dec.
  26th by Rev. William J. Chiles.
James Linton died on Dec. 10th, age 68 years. He
  was formerly of Philadelphia.
George Taylor, Port Tobacco, will do stencil work
  and cut plates for marking hogsheads, sacks,
  farming implements, etc. "...A bottle of in-

delible ink and brush furnished with each
nameplate."
Francis Waters, deceased. Orphans' Court.
Albin Price, administrator.

January 5, 1872, Vol. XXVIII, No. 36

Hon. Barnes Compton temporarily called to the
chair in Maryland Senate and administered oath
of office. In the House of Delegates the Hon.
Frederick Stone was elected Speaker pro tem -
"...returned thanks for honor conferred upon
him..."

Dr. Thomas A. Carrico elected president of the
Board of School Commissioners and George M.
Lloyd, Esq. was elected Secretary-Treasurer.

William H. Blandiford of Baltimore City marries
Delia Wells, eldest daughter of the Editor of
the Times at Christ Church, Port Tobacco on
3 Jan. 1872 by Rev. Dr. Lewin.

January 12, 1872, Vol. XXVIII, No. 37

John H. Monroe and William N. Berkley vs Martha
Lunt, Henry W. Davis. Ratification order -
sale by John W. Mitchell, trustee. Samuel Lunt
sale fishing shore "Thorn's Gut" be ratified.
$1355 sale.

John B. Norris, Jr. - insolvent notice.

Thomas R. Newman marries Mrs. Mary B. Rose on
January 5th by Rev. Dr. Lewin.

Somerset D. Roby marries Georgie Richards of
Washington, D.C. on Jan. 9th at the residence
of the bride's father in Washington, D. C. by
Rev. Mr. Boyle.

John Grinder advertises that thirty wood cutters
are wanted at his farm at the mouth of the
Mattawoman Creek "...prime wood 75¢ per cord;
oak wood 85¢ per cord."

Mary A. Sanders deceased, Orphans' Court. D.
Ignatius Sanders, administrator.

Charles F. Hayden advertises blacksmithing, coach
repairing, wheelwrighting at Allen's Fresh.

January 19, 1872, Vol. XXVIII, No. 38

County Commissioners appoint constables:
    1st Election District - Hugh Clements,
    2nd Election District - Albin Price and Thomas
    B. Delozier,
    3rd Election District - Peter Wheeler and Thomas
    W. Wright;
    4th Election District - John W. Boarman,
    5th Election District - Lemuel Smoot and
    Francis McWilliams,

7th Election District - George R. Bryan,
8th Election District - Samuel Smoot.

James Richardson of Pomonkey district, escaped
from Port Tobacco jail - committed on charge of
abducting 13-year old girl.
Richard P. Wall, next friend Henry H. Bean, James
M. Bean. Estate of Thomas O. Bean, deceased -
sale be ratified, $4,810.98.
J.W.Warring marries Miss M.J.Miles on Jan. 9th
at St. Mary's Church, Alexandria by Rev. Father
Towles.
Mrs. Susan Chapman, relict of the late Hon. J.G.
Chapman died. Funeral held at Christ Church in
Port Tobacco at 12 noon on Jan. 20. "Interment
family burying place, St. John's"

January 26, 1872, Vol. XXVIII, No. 39

George H. Clagett marries Jane Brown at "Strawberry
Hill" residence of William H. Clagett, Esq. on
Jan. 4th by Rev. J. Towles.
Lemuel Wilmer, Assistant Assessor for Charles and
St. Mary's Counties gives notice to all planning
to sell liquor and leaf tobacco to obtain license.

February 2, 1872, Vol. XXVIII, No. 40

Mrs. Mary Latimer's former property "Oak Grove"
204 acres near Pope's Creek on Baltimore and
Potomac Railroad line, adjoining property
"Clifton" Rudolph Johnson, trustee.
"ALLEN'S FRESH LOOKING UP"
New blacksmith and wheelwright shop - Charles F.
Hayden;
Boot and Shoemaking Shop - Wesley Bowie;
J. Thomas Colton, Merchant.

Thomas S. Bridgett marries Jane S.A.Richards on
Jan. 30th at Rectory by Rev. Dr. Lewin.
Sylvester M. Mudd died Jan. 28th. He was 42 years
old "...in the Communion of the Catholic Church
and in the confidence of a certain faith." "...
A dutiful and affectionate son and brother..."

February 16, 1872, Vol. XXVIII, No. 42

Sarah Jane Button dies, wife of John S. Button, in

Port Tobacco Feb. 6, 1872. She was 26 years old
"...She died...a true believer in the Catholic
faith...A grief-stricken husband and an agonized
sister will find some comfort in remembering her
many virtues and prepare to meet her where she
awaits you with her angel babe..."

Thomas K. Ching, William A. Lyon, Samuel Swann,
trustees of School #3, 4th Election District,
need teacher.

H.M.Clements marries Mary S. Morris on Feb. 12th
by Rev. Dr. Lewin.

(The following is not Charles County-related, but
mighty interesting, nevertheless)

> "Married
> On Wed., 24th ultimo, on horseback,
> in front of the Tavern House of
> Wm. J. McLaughlin, in Pocahontas
> Co., Va. when the thermometer stood
> eight degrees below zero by the Rev.
> G.L.Brown, Daniel McCarty, Esq.,
> a pensioner for service in the War
> of 1812, aged seventy eight years,
> and Miss Ann Gabert, aged twenty-eight
> years, both of Pocahontas County."

Asa Jenkins died at his residence in Charles County
on Jan. 19th, age 82 years. He was a soldier in
the War of 1812.

William D. Massey died on Feb. 11th in Alexandria
after a brief illness of pneumonia. 56 years old.

Quenzel's store has valentines "prettier, funnier
and cheaper than ever."

Josias Hawkins, Trustee, vs Susan Chapman and others
appeal Circuit Court commenced by Vivian Brent and
R.H.Edelen for appellant, Alexander B. Hagner and
Frederick Stone, appellees.

February 23, 1872, Vol. XXVIII, No. 43

W.H.S.Taylor from "Poynton Manor" sends to Editor
"Extract - From the Spanish"

F.T.C.Dent died at Centreville in Charles County
on Feb. 14th, age 38 years.

John L. Herbert died at his home "Waverly" farm
Feb. 17th, age 64 years "...a kind, affectionate
husband and father..."

Ann Sinclair, deceased, Orphans' Court. Catharine
A. Oliver and Charles H. Oliver, administrators.

A.R.A.Murray advertises for rent "...a small farm near Bryantown...good dwelling upon it..."

Appointments by Governor

Warehouse #4 - Barnes Compton, Charles County, Tobacco Inspector. Inspector for St. Mary's Co. as well as Charles County. St. Mary's Beacon applauded Compton's appointment. He was named as no "gentleman outside our county more acceptable to it than the popular and genial Senator for Charles, who is pre-eminently qualified to discharge all the duties of the position, and is besides,

'...without alloy of fop or beau,
A polished gentleman from top to toe.'"

March 1, 1872, Vol. XXVIII, No. 44

Mrs. Adelaide R. Scott, formerly Mrs. A.R.Padgett, relict late J.T.Padgett of Port Tobacco died on Wed. last of pneumonia at her residence in Washington, D.C. She was 42 years old.

Susan P.A.Chapman died, widow of late John G. Chapman at "Glen Albin" 17 Jan. 1872. She was 71 years old.

John A. Burroughs, Esq. died at his residence in William and Marry Parish on Feb. 17th. He was 69 years old. "...has left behind him...a gentle christian wife and 10 children...[he] came to us more than 30 years ago from St. Mary's County where he was born..."

Henry A. Thompson's creditors noticed to file claims - V. Brent, auditor.

Mary T. Dent "...having determined to leave County..." advertises for sale and rent goods in store in Centreville, store fixtures, store house, barn, dwelling house and lot attached. Apply to Dr. E.V.Edelen or Dr. T.A.Carrico.

William Simmons will sell at Maddox's store, Pisgah, following parcels of land - house and lot where Canan now lives; house/land formerly belonging to Lucinda Thompson now owned by Ann A. Simmons, my wife; "...my life estate in farm adjoining Benjamin Simmons, formerly owned by Thomas Milstead."

March 8, 1872, Vol. XXVIII, No. 45

Sarah Ellen Cox died, daughter of William and Ellen
R. Cox on Feb. 16th. She was 6 years, 19 days
old.

Charles Fergusson, Jr. died at the residence of his
father in Baltimore on Monday last, 24 years old.

F.T.C.Dent died 14 Feb. at his late residence. He
was 33 years old. He left "...a young and interesting family...dear little ones...a wife..."

Amelia Josephine Burch died, wife of William M.
Burch of Bryantown on 28 Jan. She was 33 years
old. She left "...multitude of sorrowing friends,
...on so inclement a day, following the remains
to their final resting place in the consecrated
ground of St. Mary's Church..."

March 15, 1872, Vol. XXVIII, No. 46

William Maddox died on Feb. 28th of paralysis. He
was 67 years old.

John Carrington died "...suddenly of pneumonia..."
on the 15th. He was 67 years old.

March 22, 1872, Vol. XXVIII, No. 47

J.T.Mudd elected director of Southern Maryland Road.

Mrs. Charles J. Pye died last Tues, daughter [wife?]
of the late John Pye.

Richard M. Smoot, Esq. appointed keeper of the Upper
Cedar Point Lighthouse, salary $600 per annum.

Ella M. Marbury appointed registered clerk Dead
Letter Office in Washington, D.C., salary $900
per annum.

George W. Webb, Albert Renwick, William Saxton,
trading as G.W.Webb & Co. suit against William L.
Sheirbourn - sheriff sale one dwelling house and
lot in Newport.

March 29, 1872, Vol. XXVIII, No. 48

Dr. B.A.Jameson residence is where the Baltimore and
Potomac Railroad force is now working.

William R. Wilmer's name sent by President to Senate
to be Collector of Internal Revenue for the 5th
District of Maryland.

J.R.Murray lost a pair of leather saddle bags "...
containing very important papers..." also some
bundles of dry goods.

George J.H.Huntt and Julian E. Norris bought F.T.C
Dent's store at Centreville.
T.A.Smith, Cross Roads, asks creditors to settle.
Walter B. Wood marries Sarah E. Huntt at the resi-
dence of the bride's father March 27th by Rev.
J.T.Topp.
W.H.Bean died on March 11th at his residence near
Bryantown. He was the son of Mrs. Harriet Bean
and the late John H. Bean. He was 25 years old.
H.R.V.Cawood died in Washington, D.C. on March 18th.
He was 73 years old and formerly of Charles County.
Mrs. Martha A. Lacey "...beloved wife R.T.Lacey,
Esq..." she was 35 years old "...passed away...
fond and faithful wife and mother..."

April 5, 1872, Vol. XXVIII, No. 49

John A. Burroughs, deceased, Orphans' Court.
Eliza T. Burroughs and William McKennie Burroughs,
Administrators.
E. DeC. Mitchell's stallion will be let to mares at
Gerard Rison's, J.R.Murray's and Jonas E. Smith's
mill.
Henry Sothoron's trotting horse will make his 2nd
season.
William E. Bean died on March 11, 1872. He was 25
years old and "...he was an example for all, and
has left behind him a name unsullied and pure...
Oh, fond and devoted mother; oh, faithful and af-
fectionate sister and brother..."
Rev. Robert Smith, M.E.Church, South and Preacher
in Charge Charles Circuit will preach at Newtown
at 10 a.m. and at Robert Tucker's at 7½ p.m.
Joseph Price, O.N.Bryan, P.A.Sasscer appointed
Commissioners and Examiners. Would public be
benefitted by opening and making public a road
across Zachia Swamp one half way between crossing
at Allen's Fresh and that at Newtown, will ascertain probable cost - will meet at store of
Col. Samuel Cox.
T.C.Price advertises work and brood mare for sale.

County Commissioners Appoint County Collectors

1st Election District - John J. Brawner,
2nd Election District - Washington Page,
3rd Election District - A.T.Moore,
4th Election District - Townley Robey.

Mail Contracts

Washington, D.C. - Leonardtown - John C. Thompson,
    $2499;
Washington, D.C. - Fort Washington - John C. Howard,
    1,009,
Silver Hill to Pomonkey - Robert H. McCleave, 419,
Upper Marlborough to Nottingham - Robert H. McKee,
    340,
TB to Aquasco - J.C.Thompson, 249
Beantown to Port Tobacco - William M. Morris, 312,
Glymont to Port Tobacco - William M. Morris, 489,
Port Tobacco to Nanjemoy - Edward S. Welch, 390,
Port Tobacco to Harris' Lot with branch to Allen's
    Fresh and Newport - William M. Morris, 499,
Leonardtown to Ridge - Logan O. Smith, 480.

May 24, 1872, Vol. XXVIX, No. 4

John Donatius Middleton died in Jasper, Jasper
    County, Texas on March 11, 1872. He was 35 years
    old.
Samuel Sheriff died April 29, 1872 at his late resi-
    dence. He was 85 years old. "...We bid him fare-
    well, but the memory of his kindness and generous
    sympathy with the sick and suffering we can never
    forget. Few have equaled him in his attentions to
    the afflicted...He had walked about the yard,
    leaning on his son for support, on the day of his
    death..."
The Sunday Schools attached to Christ Church, Port
    Tobacco and St. James' Chapel, Newtown will be
    opened every Sunday at 5 p.m. and all childre,
    both white and colored, are cordially invited to
    attend.
Judge Francis H. Digges, deceased, large, old mansion
    near Allen's Fresh destroyed by fire. House re-
    cently owned by son, C.C.Digges. Sympathy to him
    and his two sisters who lived there.
T. Yates Robey, Sr. had tied his horse to a tree at
    Chapel Point when a severe storm passed over the
    county. Lightning struck that tree and instantly
    killed the horse.

                Editor's Note: An old gentleman
                in Pennsylvania walked forty miles
                to pay for his subscription to a
                paper. We know of some people in
                this county who would walk forty miles
                out of their way, over rough roads, to
                keep from paying.

Thomas Wright, deceased, Orphans' Court. Uzzial
    Wright, administrator.
Richard Jamieson has stray red bull and red cow.
Elkanah F. Franklin, deceased, audit report to be
    ratified.
F. Matthews Lancaster administrator Hezekiah
    Luckett, deceased. Notice to Creditors.
Alpheus Haislip secured scow or lighter at Rum Point
    on Mattawoman Creek.
George A. Skekell, proprietor of Glymont Pavilion,
    open to public.
Mrs. Sarah J. Mollyhorn, Harris' Lot, will sell
    "Mexico" 57 acres. It lies on public road lead-
    ing to (2 miles from) Lancaster's Wharf on
    Potomac River - good dwelling.

June 7, 1872, Vol. XXVIX, No. 6

Two murder trials reported on in this issue:

Case of Charles Newman who gave himself up for the
    murder of a colored boy, William Contee. Appear-
    in the trial were Frank Contee, 12 or 13 year old
    brother of William; John T. Colton, Esq., Justice
    of the Peace at Allen's Fresh; Dr. B.A.Jameson;
    Thomas A. Jones, Esq., George Dent, Esq., con-
    stable; Lemuel Smoot, Esq., constable.
    Newman came to this county from Virginia, some
    two or three years since, accompanied by his wife
    and a small child, took shelter with his family
    in a shed on the fishing shore of Mr. Pearson
    Chapman - most destitute condition - excited the
    sympathy and charity of the neighborhood. The
    house he lived in burned down - next moved to
    Pope's Creek, where homicide took place. He has
    been sentenced to the Penitentiary for five years.
    His wife is still in the county with two children,
    one an infant, and they are really in a pitiable
    condition.

Case of Winnie Jones, Alfred Dent and William Dent-
    All charged with murder of Alfred Jones, husband
    of Winnie, at his residence, near Middletown.
    Parties are all colored. Mary Matthews, first
    witness, lives at Mr. Richard McDaniel's; Dr.
    R.K.Compton examined; John Penny examined;
    Philip Thomas examined; Billy Jones examined;
    Amerson Early examined; Luther Clagett examined;
    Levi Hicks examined; T.C.Wilkerson examined;
    L. McC. Monroe examined; Walter McPherson ex-
    amined. State's Attorney moved that a judgment

of not guilty be entered in favor of Alfred and
William Dent - two prisoners were discharged. The
case of Winnie Jones submitted without argument.
Judge Ford stated that as there was a reasonable
doubt of the prisoner's guilt on his mind, it was
his duty to give her the benefit of that doubt,
and therefore adjudged her not guilty.

Edith Kate Dows died, youngest daughter of William
and Eleanor Dows, 9 months old at "Rosemary
Lawn" on May 25th.

Circuit Court

State vs John Francis Lacey (colored) assault and
battery, intent to kill Jane Linkins - guilty,
six months in jail, fine $25. Tried for similar
offense against Joseph Linkins - same sentence
and fine.
State vs David Johnson (colored) larceny of ox
yoke. Not guilty.
State vs Lemuel Williams, larceny four hogs from
William L. McDaniel - not guilty.
State vs Lemuel Williams and Henry Speake, larceny
eight hogs from W.D.Adams - not guilty.

Josias Hawkins, Esq. admitted to practice at bar of
Circuit Court, Charles County.
William A. Mudd, Esq., appointed Officer of Registration, 8th Election District, Charles County.
Charles Brown, colored, escaped from jail. Convicted of larceny of pair of pantaloons, sentenced
to six months. Was permitted by temporary jail
keeper to go for water at hydrant and kept going
"...thus reliev[ing] the county of any further
expense for boarding him."
Henry A. Thompson, deceased. Order of Ratification.

June 21, 1872, Vol. XXVIX, No. 8

A.H.Robertson graduated in second annual commencement
in the Department of Law at the University of
Maryland.
Robert D. Digges graduates from the Naval Academy.
He is the son of the late John D. Digges and
brother of our able State's Attorney, Eugene Digges.
George H. StClair purchased "Pye's Landing" on the
Potomac River near Glymont.
Morris C. Brotherton of Baltimore City marries Sarah
M. Mattingley at the residence of the bride's father
on May 18th by Rev. F. McAtee.

Ella Wilson dies, wife of Col. Thomas J. Wilson,
  in Baltimore Saturday last, 27 years old.
John I. and James A. Hurst vs William Dunnington,
  administrator for J.F.Dunnington, deceased.
Richard P. Walls vs H.H.Bean. Order Ratification.
John M. Whitty has moved to his new store at
  Lothair.
George N. Rowe, Duffield P.O., lost money ($98)
  somewhere in Port Tobacco.
Thomas A. Jones, insolvent docket.
Samuel Sheriff, deceased, Orphans' Court. Joshua
  B. Sheriff and Thomas R. Holley, administrators.
George Forbes, Sr. will sell farm near Patuxent
  City known as "Robertson Farm."

June 28, 1872, Vol. XXVIX, No. 9

The Ancient Records of Charles County

   The following from the old records of this county
was copied by a friend and handed to us for publication:

           August Court - Anno Domini, 1758
              Before the Worshipfull
Gustavus Brown,   John Winter,
Thomas Stone,   James Nevison,
Allen Davis,   Sam. Hanson,
William Eilbeck,   Daniel Jenifer,
Walter Hanson,   George Dent,
John Winter,   Richard Harrison,
Arthur Lee,
           Gentlemen Justices thereunto legally
authorized and assigned.
                   Phil. Rd. Fendall, Cl'k,
                   John Fendall, Sheriff
FREDERICK, Lord Baltimore, Proprietary.
HORATIO SHARP, Esq., Governor

                  ———

Wm. Hungerford Jr.,   ) Action on the Case:
)   Damages 4,812 lbs.
      versus   ) crop Tob. Costs 200
Charles Hungerford   ) lbs. Judg't non pros.
        John Hall, Att'y for plaintiff.
        George Johnson, Att'y for defendant.
              Cause of Action:

    Mr. Charles Hungerford   Dr.
1757 -- April   Tob.lbs Pounds s. d.
To John White's note of hand
 you won of me at gaming on
                       89

```
cards, 45 T, is in crop        423
To 40s. bill, Virginia curren-
cy, you won of me at ditto
on ditto, in Mary'd cur...                    2    10    0
To 10s. bill of ditto you won
of me at ditto on ditto...                         12    6
To 1 pence of gold you won of
me at ditto on ditto,  to the
value of..................                          13    6
To 1 trans'r note you won
of me at cards, Ced'r Pt.
Warehouse, quantity 371
Tob. is in crop...........     348
To 2 ditto at Port Tob. Ware-
house, you won of me at
cards, qt. 213 Tob. is in
crop Tob.................       201
To 1 crop note at Cedar Poin.
Warehouse, you won of me
at cards, with allow'e for
Cask.....................       859
To Rich'd Smith, Jr.'s bond,
payable to me for 2,981 crop
T. you won at ditto.......    2,981        _____
                              4,812          3   16   0
```

Errors Excepted.

Wm. Hungerford, Jun'r.

Maggie Hanson died May 5, 1872 of heart disease.
   She was 21 years old "...the beautiful faith of
   the Episcopal Church...sad petition to 'bury me
   by little Maud'...Bereaved mother...Kind sisters
   and brothers...She has 'crossed over the dark
   river'..."
Thomas C. Price, Joseph A. Gray, William H. Gray,
   Robert Prout, Thomas P. Gray petition County
   Commissioners to allow Thomas C. Price who bought
   small piece of land for building site of Joseph
   A. Gray - land cut off from farm of Price by
   present county road and allow Price at his expense,
   to lay off and open new road.
Hanson Clements has stray bay mare.
W. Mallinckrodt marries Nannie C. Harris, daughter
   of Henry R. Harris, Esq. on June 11th by Rev.
   J.M.Todd.

Death of an Old Citizen

   Francis R. Wills, M.D. died at his late residence,
near Port Tobacco, on Saturday morning last, at an
advanced age (70 years). (The name of his home was
"Preference.") Dr. Wills retired from the regular
practice of medicine nearly thirty years ago, and

devoted himself, we believe, almost exclusively
to agricultural pursuits, in which, by the exercise
of sound judgment, and of rare prudence and economy,
he was most successful, notwithstanding the heavy
losses, incident to the late war, which swept away
the fortunes of so many of our citizens. In the
death of Dr. Wills our community has lost a valuable
and useful citizen, and his family a devoted husband
and father. In speaking of him as a friend, we shall
be pardoned for mentioning that he was among the
first, when we came to this place to establish The
Times, over twenty-eight years ago, to give us encouragement, and promptly entered his name as a sub-
scriber upon our books, and has been a most punctual
paying one every year since. Thus, one by one, our
old friends are leaving the stage of busy life, and
we trust to find everlasting rest from their weary
labors.
F.A.Tolson, Post Master at the new post office at
    Riverside, 3 miles n.w. of Nanjemoy.
Simpson and Lloyd farm - small tobacco pen-house
    was struck by lightning and burned. Loss $80.
New lightning rods have, within the past week, been
    placed on the Court House and the two wings of
    the building. The old rod, which was upon the
    main building only, was in a condition to invite
    destruction, rather than to serve as a protection
    from the subtile element. Messrs. Bishop & Pugh
    furnished and put up the rods, which are said to
    be of excellent quality.

July 12, 1872, Vol. XXVIX, No. 11

Thomas I. Gardiner, J.M.Dudley, E.W.Haviland, Egbert
    Cary, T. Elzear Gardiner, Henry Gardiner, H.A.
    Burch, Albert Gardiner petition County Commissioners
    to open a public road, now private one, beginning
    on public road near Mrs. Eliza Gardiner's and
    passing through lands of Thomas I. Gardiner, T.
    Elzear Gardiner, E.W.Haviland, H. Canter, J.M.
    Dudley, and Egbert Cary to intersect county road
    at a point near Old Fields Church.
Miss Mary G. Garner, mantua maker can be found at
    the residence of her father William Garner on
    "Brentfield" (farm of J. Ware).
George H. StClair property - steamers between
    Washington, D.C. and Quantico now landing daily
    at Pye's Wharf instead of Glymont.
John A. Chapelear appointed by Governor to be Of-
    ficer of Registration for 9th Election Distrace
    of Charles County, vice Rufus Robey, declined.

Frank P. Hamilton's home "Oakland" caught on fire about 1 p.m. on Wednesday last, It was found impracticable to subdue it. It originated under the roof of the kitchen, which is connected with the main building by a long entry. A number of men working on the property and that adjoining joined forces to give assistance, but no efforts could save the building. In the attempt to cut away the entry, the timbers of which it was built were found so hard and heavy that the axe proved of no avail. This dwelling was erected by the late Charles A. Pye, and is said to have cost about $10,000. It was undoubtedly one of the most complete and valuable dwelling houses in the county. The furniture, window sash and some other parts of the house easily removed, we understand, were saved. The building is insured in the State of Maryland Mutual Fire Insurance Company of Baltimore to the amount of $5,000.

James T. Dyer marries Mary A. Adams at "Hawthorn" July 11 by Rev. Dr. Lewin.

Benjamin W. Blandford died at his residence Tuesday last after an illness of four days. He was 62 years old. (William Boswell registered a tribute of respect at the August 2 Vestry meeting of the Port Tobacco Parish.)

Mrs. M.E.Bowie died on July 3rd. She was 29 years old.

William B. Matthews advertises for rent, "Laidler's Ferry." Also sells 4 cows, 2 bulls, 2 heifer calves.

James F. Matthews, attorney at law, Port Tobacco.

August 2, 1872, Vol. XXVIX, No. 14

ANNUAL STATEMENT BY THE COMMISSIONERS OF
CHARLES COUNTY, MARYLAND
for the year ending June 30, 1872

Judges of the Orphans' Court

Richard Barnes, Robert Digges, Stouton W. Dent.

County Commissioners

A.J.Smoot, Thomas R. Halley, John H. Cox, Samuel Hanson, Josias Hawkins.

Judges of Election

George P. Jenkins, William Hamilton, Bennett Neale,
Thomas L. Speake, Charles E. Hannon, Richard B.
Posey, Henry S. Dent, Joseph Price, Washington A.
Posey, William Nevitt, sr., William L. Sheirbourn,
Thomas Posey, John H.D.Wingate, George T. Simpson,
Thomas B. Berry, William L. McDaniel, George F.
Bealle, Benjamin D. Tubman, William H. Cox, John A.
Wood, John W. McPherson, Jere W. Burch, James A.
Mudd, T.Elzear Gardiner, R.P.Wall, James T. Thomas.

Clerks of Election

John T. Davis, John I. Jenkins, James A. Franklin,
W.E.W.Rowe, Peter W. Robey, C.C.Digges, J.T.Dutton,
C.C.Perry, J.R.Sheriff, R.F.Blandford, J.W.Everett,
A.T.Monroe, F.L.Dent, Townley Robey, Rufus Robey,
J.H.Chapelear, William P. Flowers, Richard Price.

Guards at the Election

Lemuel Smoot, A. Simpson, use W.H.Gray, William E.
Dement, J.W.Dyson, J.Mollison, Charles J. Butler,
R.T.Halley, Joseph H. Mattingley, P.H.Turner,
William Fenwick, J.P.Murdoch, use J.H.Roberts,
Henry Thompson, Robert E. Rison, Samuel Smoot.

Grand and Petit Jurors - 1871 - November Term

George P. Jenkins, Townley Robey, William M. Jameson,
R.P.Wall, Francis L. Higdon, John W. Boarman, Joseph
H. Gardiner, B.L.Higdon, Francis Price, John B.
Carpenter, Joseph A. Gray, S.H.W.McPherson, use G.A.
Huntt, William B. Fergusson, Thomas A. Millar,
Joseph T. Ward, William Wolfe, Henry L. Mudd, sr.,
Washington A. Posey, William L. Sheirbourn, John R.
Turner, J.A.Mudd, use W.H.Moore, James M. Burch,
William P. Compton, Joseph E. Sanders, P.A.Sasscer,
T.Yates Roby, F.W.Weems, John E. Bailey, A.H.Robertson,
Samuel Hanson, Samuel Cox, Samuel Carrington, Charles
H. Wills, Benjamin Welch, Thomas J. Boarman, William
H. Berry, C.H.Dent, use G.A.Huntt, Charles F. Lancaster,
Benton Barnes, James A. Franklin, John T. Davis,
B.W.Hardy, use J.W.Warring, John F. Cobey, F.D.
Gardiner.

1872 - May Term

Samuel W. Adams, Francis Carpenter, James H. Neale,
John H. Freeman, C.C.Digges, William E. Dement, B.W.B.
McPherson, Edward L. Huntt, Benjamin W. Blandford,
John I. Jenkins, James A. Adams, A.W.Neale, William
B. Matthews, John W. Jenkins, William L. Harding,

Charles C. Bowling, Charles L. Gardiner, John S.
Gibbons, Marshall Chapman, William L. McDaniel,
Thomas Latimer, Charles H. Wood, G.C.Burch, E.N.
Stonestreet, use Col. Cox, Sylvester Mudd, Richard
W. Bryan, Thomas M. Welch, William H. Price, John G.
Chapman, Edwin A. Smith, Thomas Carrico, John
Crismond, John H. Kinnaman, William Turner, Edgar
Griswold, Benjamin F. Burch, William Cox, John W.
Fowler, Thomas B. Farrall, William F. Dement, Jere
T. Mudd, Yates Barber, E.F.Mason.

1871 - November Term - Talismen

Lemuel Wilmer, Francis Carpenter, John H. Hancock,
William M. Burch, Andrew J. Norris, Henry G.
Robertson, B.P.Donnelly, John H. Kinnaman, Joseph
S. Boarman, Richard Payne, John H. Jenkins, John S.
Gibbons, A.W.Fowke, R.A.Murray, Joseph Price, John
A. Price, William Nevitt, sr., Jere T. Mudd, Joseph
H. Padgett, William L. Cook, Henry A. Neale, Patrick
Murphy.

1872 - May Term - Talismen

John T. Davis, Richard Barnes, jr., George C. Davis,
James Owens, Michael Martin, B.F.Robbins, William
Cox, John H.D.Wingate.

Witnesses in State's Cases - 1871 - November Term

Francis Wedding, George J. Chapalear, P.A.Sasscer,
Thomas B. Delozier, Albin Price, Luther A. Martin,
John W. Cofer, Victor Matthews, M.McMahon, use
Latimer & Son, Charles Bowles, use Boswell & Co.,
George R. Bryan, Thomas Welch, William A. Boarman,
Mary E. Howard, Lemuel Smoot, Cox Nevitt, N.J.Miles,
John E. Wenck, A. Proctor, use E.V.Edelen, E.Tucker,
use J.H.Roberts, E.Proctor, use E.V.Edelen, Dr. A.J.
Smoot, Samuel Smoot, A.M.Burch, William Hicks, Dr.
R.F.Chapman, H.Robey, use J.H.Roberts, James E.
Stewart, J.M.Burch, C.C.Perry, Rufus Perry, Francis
McWilliams, Margaret Dale, James Jenifer, Richard
Lamar, J.Stewart, use J.F.Thomas, Mary A. Mason,
William H. Baxter, Joseph F. Thomas, Grandison
Stewart, R.V.Tucker, use J.H.Roberts, George A.
Huntt, John T. Davis, William Acton, James H. Dent,
John Wade, use William Burch, Rufus Robey, J.C.
Middleton, William M. Burch, G.C.Burch, B.P.Donnelly,
J.E.Ware, use Latimer & Son, F.Clements, M.McMahon,
C.M.Bond, A.Proctor, use E.V.Edelen, E.Proctor,
George D. Mudd, Lettie Golden, Thomas Martin, James
Ward, Alexander Smoot, Jere W. Burch, William J.
Burch, Marion Freeman, John C. Wenck, G.C.Burch,

J.A.Wenck, R.Y.Tucker, use J.H.Roberts, H.Robey,
E.Tucker, CC.Perry, Rufus Perry, Lemuel Smoot,
Hanson Bell, N. Burgess, use J.T.Dutton, H.A.Neale,
Bennett Neale, A.J.Boarman, F.M.Lancaster, William
E.Norris, J.W.Cofer, use A.Price, Albin Price, C.
Jordan, use J.H.Roberts, James Jenkins, John Brown,
use R. Payne, John C. Bush, John Nevitt, Levi McC.
Monroe, M.A.Mason, use G.A.Huntt, Oscar Penn,
J.Jenkins, use J.H.Roberts, George A. Huntt,
Humphrey Lenkfield, use J.I.Lacey.

1872 – February Term

G.C.Perry, Lemuel Smoot, Humphrey Lenkfield, use
J.I.Lacey, Hanson Bell, B.G.Harris, Henry A.Neale,
Bennett Neale, A.J.Boarman, Victor Matthews, use
J.H.Roberts and J.W.Fowler.

1872 – May Term

Samuel W. Adams, Francis Carpenter, James H. Neale,
John H. Freeman, C.C.Digges, William E. Dement,
B.W.B.McPherson, Edward L. Huntt, Benjamin W.
Blandford, John I. Jenkins, James A. Adams, A.W.
Neale, William B. Matthews, John W. Jenkins, William
L. Harding, Charles C. Bowling, Charles L. Gardiner,
John S. Gibbons, Marshall Chapman, William L. McDaniel,
Thomas Latimer, Charles H. Wood, G.C.Burch, E.N.
Stonestreet, use Col. Cox, Sylvester Mudd, Richard
W. Bryan, Thomas M. Welch, William H. Price, John G.
Chapman, Edwin A. Smith, Thomas Carrico, John Crismond,
John H. Kinnaman, William Turner, Edgar Griswold,
Benjamin F. Burch, William Cox, John W. Fowler,
Thomas R. Farrall, William F. Dement, Jere T. Mudd,
Yates Barber, E.F.Mason.

1871 – November Term-Talismen

Lemuel Wilmer, Francis Carpenter, John H. Hancock,
William M. Burch, Andrew J. Norris, Henry G. Robertson,
B.P.Donnelly, John H. Kinnaman, Joseph S. Boarman,
Richard Payne, John H. Jenkins, John S. Gibbons, A.W.
Fowke, R.A.Murray, Joseph Price, John A. Price,
William Nevitt, sr., Jere T. Mudd, Joseph H. Padgett,
William L. Cook, Henry A. Neale, Patrick Murphy.

1872 – May Term – Talismen

John T. Davis, Richard Barnes, jr., George C. Davis,
James Owens, Michael Martin, B.F.Robbins, William
Cox, John H.D.Wingate.

Witnesses in State's Cases-1871-November Term

Francis Wedding, George J. Chapalear, P.A.Sasscer,
Thomas B. Delozier, Albin Price, Luther A. Martin,
John W. Cofer, Victor Matthews, M.McMahon, use
Latimer & Son, Charles Bowles, use Boswell & Co.,
George R. Bryan, Thomas Welch, William A. Boarman,
Mary E. Howard, Lemuel Smoot, Cox Nevitt, N.J.Miles,
John C. Wenck, A. Proctor, use E.V.Edelen, E.Tucker,
use J.H.Roberts, E.Proctor, Dr. A.J.Smoot, Samuel
Smoot, A.M.Burch, William Hicks, Dr. R.F.Chapman,
H.Robey, use J.H.Roberts, James E. Stewart, J.M.
Burch, C.C.Perry, Rufus Perry, Francis McWilliams,
Margaret Dale, James Jenifer, Richard Lamar,
J.Stewart, use J.F.Thomas, Mary A. Mason, William
H. Baxter, Joseph F. Thomas, Grandison Stewart,
R.V.Tucker, use J.H.Roberts, George A. Huntt,
John T. Davis, William Acton, James H. Dent, John
Wade, use Wm. M. Burch, Rufus Robey, J.C.Middleton,
William M. Burch, G.C.Burch, R.P.Donnelly, J.E.
Ware, F.Clements, M.McMahon, C.M.Bond, A.Proctor,
E.Proctor, George D. Mudd, Lottie Golden, Thomas
Martin, James Ward, Alexander Smoot, Jere W. Burch,
William J. Burch, Marion Freeman, John C. Wenck,
G.C.Burch, J.A.Wenck, R.Y.Tucker, H.Robey, E.Tucker,
C.C.Perry, Rufus Perry, Lemuel Smoot, Hanson Bell,
N.Burgess, H.A.Neale, Bennett Neale, A.J.Boarman,
F.M.Lancaster, William L. Norris, J.W.Cofer, Albin
Price, C.Jordan, James Jenkins, John Brown, John
C.Bush, John Nevitt, Levi McC. Monroe, M.A.Mason,
Oscar Penn, J. Jenkins, George A. Huntt, Humphrey
Lenkfield.

1872 - February Term

C.C.Perry, Lemuel Smoot, Humphrey Lenkfield, Hanson
Bell, B.G.Harris, Henry A. Neale, Bennett Neale,
A.J.Boarman, Victor Matthews.

1872 - May Term

Thomas S. Dent, Thomas P. Gray, Sylvester Mudd,
Leonard Marbury, Victor Matthews, T.R.McDaniel,
Lucretis Hayden, C.Walker, use D.W.Hawkins, Thomas
W. Wright, Thomas Hanson, Alexander Washington,
Joseph Ross, George Brown, Elijah Davis, John W.
Clements, William Murphy, William F. Dement, Albin
Price, Thomas B. Delozier, Joseph Linkins, Ellen
Linkins, Matilda Murray, Ann Murray, Frank Contee,
F.L.Dent, Peter Wheeler, William Contee, Lemuel
Smoot, Samuel Murray, Philip Thomas, Vivian Brent,
W.W.Cobey, Luther Claggett, R.K.Compton, R. McDaniel,

R.B.Oliver, Dr. B.A.Jameson, W.A.Padgett, Lemuel
Smoot, Thomas H. Scott, H.R.Scott, Frank Tolson,
W.H.Farmer, James Shackelford, George A. Huntt,
William Dunnington, Grandison Willett, J.E.P.
Wedding, W.D.Adams, M.C.Scott, Mary Newman, Mary E.
Penney, Albert Milstead, F.P.Hamilton, M. Murray,
use M.M.Whitty, Ann Murray, S. Murray, P.Clements,
Reverdy A. Rennoe, C.Bowling, James Oliver, F.N.
Digges, C.C.Perry, Rufus Perry, Lemuel Smoot,
C.Yates, Humphrey Lenkfield, H.Bell, A.J.Boarman,
F.M.Lancaster, William Contee, F.Contee, William
C. Brent, Thomas D. Stone, Dr. B.A.Jameson, Lemuel
Smoot, Josephine Collins, Alice Harvey, William J.
Knott, J.T.Colton, J.P.S.Middleton, F.Mugleton,
C.Walker, Charles H. Sheirbourn, Lemuel Smoot,
Luther Claggett, Philip Thomas, Richard McDaniel,
John Penny, M.Matthews, Amerson Early, use L.McC.
Monroe, W.McPherson, W.B.McPherson, John Young,
T.C.Wilkerson, McCartney Monroe, Patrick Duffy,
James Moore, William Moore, Ned Williams, G.O.
Monroe, Eleanor Linkins, James Bateman, Joseph
Linkins, Jane Linkins, James Linkins, William H.
Welch, Henry Williams, Thomas Allen, William
Russell, W.L.McDaniel, P.A.Sasscer, Joseph Young,
Caleb Pickeral, William E. Dement, W.D.Adams,
J.E.R.Wedding William G. Willett, J.A.Moreland,
T.C.Wilkerson, W.L.Berry, Hezekiah Williams,
R.B.Oliver B.G.Harris, Dr. J.S.Conrad, use Dr.
R.Digges.

Bailiffs and Messengers

John D. Covell, Asa Jenkins, N.B.Crangle, John H.
Jenkins, Joseph H. Mattingley, J.Benjamin Mattingley,
Asa Jenkins, John D. Cove.1.

Election Rooms

John A. Price, T.A.Smith, Richard Payne, C.C.Perry,
Elizabeth Duffy, S.W.H.McPherson, G.C.Burch, use
B.F.Burch, E.D.R. Bean.

Crow Bill Certificates

T.A.Smith, Thomas Skinner, William B. Carpenter,
George N. Rowe, Reverdy A. Rennoe, John B. Carpenter,
Lemuel W. Maddox, Thomas M. Welch, C. Greenabaum,
Thomas S. Dent, Joseph T. Ward, C.C.Perry, J.M.
Latimer & Son, Albert Farrall, Joseph I. Lacey, Frank
McWilliams, W.W.Padgett, William Boswell & Co., John
R. Robertson, Richard T. Tubman, P.A.Sasscer, J.W.
Warring, Dr. T.A.Carrico, Townley Robey, Thomas R.

Farrall, Samuel Smoot. E.D.R.Bean, William H.
Moore, Jere T. Mudd.

Collectors for Assessments and Insolvencies

William H. Gray, John T. Dutton, John H. Hancock,
William M. Burch.

Coffins and Burying Paupers

William B. Carpenter, N.J.Miles, George Norris, use
Dr. R. Digges, Warren O. Willett, J.W.Warring, Dr.
E.Miles' heirs, Thomas Carrico, P.Douglass, use
E.D.R.Bean, Charles M. Bond.

Coroners' Inquests

R.W.Bryan, Coroner, J.Reverdy Carlin, Coroner, G.C.
Burch, Coroner, use B.F.Burch, Dr. A.J.Smoot, Post
Mortem, Dr. B.A.Jameson, Post Morten, Dr. R.K.
Compton, Post Mortem, Dr. G.D.Mudd, Post Mortem,
Thomas R. Halley, Winfield Halley, T.R.McDaniel,
D.R.McDaniel, Joseph T. Downs, C.C.Bowling,
E. Luther Clagett, John A. Wood, John H. Cox, John
C. Coomes, L.McC. Monroe, R. Benson Clagett, Thomas
D. Stone, John Ware, Richard Payne, W.W.Ware,
William Garner, James Taylor, R.H.Harbin, W.B.Wood,
George Dent, Francis Neale, Francis A. Carpenter,
John Dement, Mary Matthews, Witness, Philip Thomas,
Witness.

Registration

James A. Franklin, Charles C. Perry, William C.
Brent, John H. Freeman, use J.T.Ward, Marcellus
Thompson, use J.H.Cox, Rufus Robey, Townley Robey,
George W. Carpenter, Henry M. Hannon, John A. Price,
room rent, T.A.Smith, room rent, Elizabeth Duffy,
room rent, Thomas Latimer, room rent, G.C.Burch,
use B.F.Burch, room rent, E.D.R.Bean, room rent.

Material for Public Roads

Joseph Price, R.C.Norman, William T. Baker, Henry
A. Milstead, William Stewart, Mrs. Sarah Floyd, B.J.
Lancaster, Mrs. E.A.Middleton, James H. Gough, John
T. Crismond, Mrs. Eleanor Robertson, John Ware, John
M. Whitty, John L. Budd, G.B.Lancaster, Thomas D.
Stone, J.W.T.Simpson, Dr. S.W.Dent, E. Bowling,
Edgar Griswold, F.Rozier, J.H.Murray, F. Rozier's
heirs, John H. Cox, F.O. Medley, George F. Bealle,
Dominic Mudd, J.B.Sheriff, William B. Matthews,

Thomas S. Martin, Thomas S. Boarman, E.V.Edelen,
F.T.C.Dent, Dr. Hezekiah H. Bean, Josias H.Hawkins,
John Hamilton, William Berry, Dr. Thomas A. Carrico,
John F. Gardiner, Mrs. A. Bowling, Messrs. M. & D.
Waters, George E. Goldsmith, L.S.Robey, Mrs. B.
Smoot, George Gardiner, Joseph H. Huntt, William L.
Berry, Philip A. Sasscer, James Haviland, Captain
Reed, Mason L. McPherson, Merritt Haviland, E.D.
Boone, B.F.Bowling, John D. Bowling, Ambrose Adams,
Mrs. Fannie Show, James A. Mudd, John Webster,
Zachariah Swann, Jane Canter, George Morris, Henry
Canter, Robert Gifford, Samuel T. Swann, Dr.
William S. Keech, Chapman Lyon, Marion Freeman,
Mrs. E. Robinson, Thomas Bridgett, William Wheatly,
James M. Burch, Dominic Boarman, Rev. P.B.Lanahan,
Benjamin Gardiner, Truman Watson, H.W.Harned,
Thomas Carrico, Henry S. Dent, John B. Carpenter,
Pliny Bowie.

New Road to Liverpool Point

James L. Brawner, William P. Harvey, Henry J.
Kendrick, Price Gray, jr., George T.C.Gray, William
A. Smith, T.W.Price, use T.A.Smith, Timothy A. Smith,
Reverdy A. Rennoe, Thomas P. Gray, William P.
Flowers, R.C.Norman, Henry A. Milstead, Joseph Price,
_____ Barned, Childs & Harvey.

Material for Roads omitted in 1870

W.W.Padgett, F.A.Carpenter, Alexius Waters, Mason
L. McPherson.

Miscellaneous Items

County Commissioners for the following accounts:

George A. Huntt, Clerk to the Circuit Court	$1,105.80
Luther A. Martin, Sheriff	975.46
John R. Murray, late Sheriff	348.85
George N. Rowe, Crier of Circuit Court, use Samuel Cox	202.61
Joseph Stewart, Register of Wills	527.34
Eugene Digges, State's Attorney	1,355.00
Magistrates' and Constables' Fees	90.00
Roads and Bridges	6,000.00
Insane Paupers	
County Bonds and Interest	2,778.80
Contingent Expenses	500.00
Trustees of the Poor	2,250.00
Board of School Commissioners	3,133.18
Elijah Wells, for Printing	681.50

```
Vivian Brent, Attorney to County
  Commissioners                                      100.00
John R. Robertson, Clerk to County
  Commissioners                                      399.60
John W. Mitchell, fees for defending
  criminals                                           65.00
Richard H. Gardiner, fees for defending
  criminals                                           20.00
Daniel W. Hawkins, fees for defending
  criminals                                           38.33
Andrew G. Chapman, fees for defending
  criminals                                           40.00
Richard H. Edelen, fees for defending
  criminals                                           20.00
Vivian Brent, fees for defending criminals           15.00
John T. Dutton, for errors in tax                   119.00
Joseph I. Lacey, for errors in tax                    3.27
John D. Covall, Keeper of the Court House            20.00
John D. Covall, per account filed for clean-
  ing up Court House lot, etc.                        14.75
Edwin W. Duvall, Sheriff of Anne Arundel
  county for Jail fees                                13.45
John R. Murray, for clothing for prisoners           12.45
Dr. William Boarman, for medical services
  rendered prisoners                                   5.50
William H. Higges, per account filed for
  merchandise and burying paupers                     17.89
William Boswell & Co., per account filed for
  tax books, stationery, etc.                         34.02
George Speake, use Philip A. Sasscer, for
  hauling dead horse out of the road                   1.00
```

By order, J.R.Robertson, Clerk, County Com.
  Charles County, August 2, 1872

ROAD EXPENSES

```
1st Election District, Joseph Price, sup.    $1,370.46
2nd Election District, George Dent, sup.        896.74
3rd Election District, William Wolf, sup.     1,336.42
4th Election District, Joseph H. Padgett,     1,605.75
```

Joseph I. Lacey had large grey horse strayed or
  stolen "...from Port Tobacco Commons..."
John W. Jenkins advertises for rent "...farm on which
  I reside, with or without teams, and good comfort-
  able houses furnished."
Mrs. Sallie M. Lawson, Mrs. Jane Middleton, and Miss
  Emily Jameson, managers of "...pic-nic at 'Holly
  Springs' near Newport...benefit Newport church..."

Samuel Strong and wife deed of trust to W.H.S.
Taylor and Charles C. Callan, trustees Washington
Briscoe, sale of farm "Carrick" on Potomac River
in Pomonkey Neck - 150 acres, situated immediately above "Pomonkey Point Farm. Richard W.
Bryan , Trustee and John W. Mitchell, Attorney.
Henry Turner and wife Amelia Turner buried twin
sons, Samuel Henry died on July 22, age 10 weeks
and William Lewin died on July 27, age 10 weeks,
5 days.
Thomas A. Burgess, deceased, property sold, 250
acres immediately on Potomac River - dwelling
house - 1 mile Nanjemoy Stores. Formerly large
fishery.
Capt. James H. Neal's residence "Mount Air" now
school for young ladies has closed after the
first session. Miss Hortense Digges, teacher.
Rev. F. McAtee awarded premiums for excellent
examinations. From Charles County - Emily Welch,
Fannie Welch, Port Tobacco, Mary Millar,
Clotildis Franklin, Mary Emily Hamilton. Bertie
Fowler received a premium "...for learning how to
write and cypher very nicely..."
Joseph T. Herbert will sell livestock at "Tulip
Hill Farm" to satisfy creditors W.A.Padgett and
W.W.Padgett.
James R. Tompkins defendant - Elizabeth Tompkins
complainant. "Part of Neale's Gift" 170 acres.
Also "Part of Tompkins' Purchase" 30 acres and
known as "Tompkinsville" - store-house and
grocery room attached. Cobb Neck near Lancaster's
Wharf.
John Carrington, deceased, Orphans' Court. Mary E.
Carrington and John W. Carrington, executors.
John W. Guy, deceased, property to be sold "Dent's
Levels," "Independency" and others 384 acres -
upper side of Mattawoman adjoining land of B.D.
Tubman, Esq., dwelling house - sale at R.T.
Tubman's store near the premises.
J.D.Hanson sold "Part of Greenland" to P.A.Murphy.
On road from Port Tobacco to Newtown 200 acres,
$2500.00 cash.
Leonard Marbury of Glymont advertises for rent
"...small tenement...on river...any quantity of
land (not exceeding 100 acres.)..."
A.R.A.Murray - for rent - farm adjoining William
H. Berry and Mrs. Ann Murray. Presently occupied
by Mr. Padgett.
Elizabeth Skinner died August 1, 1872 at the resi-
dence of R.D.P.Radcliffe, Esq., 60 years old.
Mrs. Mary S. Clements died, wife Hugh M. Clements
on July 30 of congestive fever. 24 years old.

John N. Lomax died at Middleville on July 23rd
43 years old.
Maggie Mayo Sasscer died, infant daughter of
Philip and Ellen A. Sasscer, 10 months old, on
July 9, 1872 of brain fever. "Put away her crib
and playthings, Half-worn shoes and little dress,
For the relics of our darling Sadly on our spirits
press..."
Young man named Rollins living with his mother on
the farm of B.L.Higdon shot and killed his brother
who was pretending to be a stranger who broke open
the door. Dr. Robert Digges called upon the case.

August 16, 1872, Vol. XXVIX, No. 16

Agnes Darrow's land "Oak Grove" for sale - 250 acres
on Neale's Creek - 1½ miles from Lancaster's Wharf,
a steamboat landing - lies to right of the public
road from Port Tobacco to said wharf adjoining
lands of Mrs. G. Hamersley, C.H.Posey and Mrs.
Camilla Edelen - dwelling. Zadock Williams,
trustee; J.F.Matthews, attorney.
D.R.Spalding's residence at White Plains, livestock,
machinery, household furniture for sale. J.B.
Conklin, half owner; W.W.Willett, agent for C.M.
Joy; George N. Rowe, agent for Gibson and Imbrey,
part owners.
Valentine Zimmerman died at the "Briars" 16 years
old "...after a short and painful illness..."
Joseph I. Wills' residence will be scene of party
and supper given by the ladies of the congregation
of the Cobb Neck Church to raise funds to repair
church.
Martha F. Mason, Doncaster Post office has "Goose
Bay Farm" for rent - "...on Potomac opposite
Quantico."
John A. Burroughs, deceased, real estate to be
divided "Wycomoco Fields" by Commissioners -
Charles F. Shaw, John H.D.Wingate, John M. Page,
Henry R. Harris, Charles C. Perry.
A.R.A.Murray, agent for James Keath's heirs adver-
tise for rent "...farm adjoining lands of William
H.Berry and Mrs. Ann Murray...present occupant
Mr. Padgett."
Peter Wheeler sells "Oak Hill" - 330 acres adjoining
R.B.Posey - public road from Port Tobacco to
Budd's Ferry - 12 miles from Port Tobacco - 2½
miles to Budd's Ferry "...in full view of Potomac
River opposite railroad and depot at Quantico."

F. Price sells pair work mules or will trade for good draft horse.

Capt. Fantz caught illegally hauling seine in Wicomico River within 500 yards of the beach, also in any creeks or inlets. Captain gave word of honor not to escape but next morning he had gone.

John A. Burch injured in accident whereby unruly ox caught him between cart and tree - wheel hub fractured the thigh bone.

The following Registration Officers give notice of election:

William C. Brent, Election District #1, Port Tobacco,
James A. Franklin, Election District #2, Hill-Top,
George W. Carpenter, Election District #3, Nanjemoy,
John H. Freeman, Election District #4, Allen's Fresh,
Henry R. Scott, Election District #5, Harris' Lot,
Marcellus Thompson, Election District #6, Middletown,
Henry M. Hannon, Election District #7, Pomonkey,
James A. Mudd, Election District #8, Bryantown,
John H. Chappelear, Election District #9, Patuxent City.

Edwin A. Smith, secretary, St. Columba Lodge "reg. comm. will be held..."

Elizabeth Skinner, deceased, Orphans' Court. Thomas W. Wright, administrator.

William Higges, Charles Perry, P.A.L.Contee, F.M. Lancaster, Commissioners for the 5th Election District petition County Commissioners to change the road "...Peter Dill's wharf to his out gate, so as to run parallel with fence between said Dill's and Mrs. Hungerford's farm."

Francis R. Wills, deceased, Orphans' Court. Teresa O. Wills, executrix.

September 6, 1872, Vol. XXIX, No. 19

J. Walter Boarman's farm "Boarman's Rest," "Calvert's Hope," and "Hardship" for sale 422 acres - dwelling house.

Francis B. Green's residence will be scene of party by the ladies of St. Joseph's to raise money for a fence around the grave yard at Pomfret.

J.R.Robertson, Clerk to the County Commissioners asks for bids for 20 cords of good seasoned oak wood "for the Court house."

Margaret G. Stone, Comm of William B. Stone advertises for rent, for 1873, that part of "Habredeventure Farm" now occupied by J.H.Mattingly."

Terms, apply to F. Stone, Port Tobacco.
George M. Lloyd advertises for nine teachers for
    colored schools - $25.00 per month.

County Commissioners Appoint Judges of Election

1st Election District - George P. Jenkins, William
    Hamilton, Peregrine Davis
2nd Election District - Charles E. Hannon, Earnest
    Hanson, Benton Barnes
3rd Election District - Richard B. Posey, H.S.Dent,
    Joseph Price
4th Election District - W.A.Posey, William Nevitt,
    sr., William L. Sheirbourn
5th Election District - Thomas Posey, George F.
    Beale, Francis B. Green
6th Election District - Thomas B. Berry, George F.
    Beale, Francis B. Green
7th Election District - Benjamin D. Tubman, William
    H. Cox, John A. Wood
8th Election District - John W. McPherson, Jere W.
    Burch, James A. Mudd
9th Election District - James T. Thomas, R.P.Wall,
    T. Elzear Gardiner.

W.W.Cobey has livestock for sale.
J.G.Chapman advertises for sale livestock.
Francis W. Weems, near Newtown, advertises for sale
    150 acre farm adjoining John Hamilton.
Amos O. Horton and A.B.Horton, his wife, George W.
    Guy and M.A.Guy, his wife, vs W.E.W.Rowe, Joseph
    O. Guy. Sale of real estate of John W. Guy, de-
    ceased, be ratified. George Brent. George A.
    Huntt, clerk County Commissioners of Charles
    County. Amount $2750.

September 13, 1872, Vol. XXVIX, No. 20

Thomas L. Speake, deceased, Orphans' Court. James
    B. Franklin, executor.
William Thomas Wood died, eldest son of Thomas and
    Sarah Wood at the residence of his father on 4th
    of September "...aged about 6 years."
W.C.Brent - Officer of Registration for 1st Election
    District asks the residents to notify him of people
    who have left the district.
Leonard Marbury advertises public sale at Glymont.

Delinquent Taxpayers

Martha Cooksey - 10 acres; Joseph Parker's heirs

"Burch's Reserve" and "Part Monmouth" 176 acres
Reybold - Wharf property at Benedict.
James L. Brawner has a two-year old turkey gobbler
now making attempt to hatch a pumpkin. Gave up
on several watermelons.

Democratic Conservative Convention
Meets

Hon. Andrew G. Chapman - Chair. One member from
each county appointed Executive Committee -
John T. Davis will represent Charles County.
Charles County Members to convention - John T.
Davis, Vivian Brent, A.G.Chapman.

September 20, 1872, Vol. XXVIX, No. 21

R.H.Edelen has wheat seed for sale.
Charles Stewart, Charles R. Marks, Theodore Lyon,
trustees for school #1, 6th Election District,
advertises for teacher.

Tournament and Ball
at Marshall Hall

Capt. William F. Dement - Chief Marshal
J.W.Waring, Esq. & J.A.Brawner, Esq. - Aids
J.T.Halley, Esq. and J.M.Kendrick, Esq. - Heralds
Col. J.W.Jenkins, Judge R.T.Tubman, B.D.Tubman, Esq.,
Thomas S. Martin, Esq. and William H. Clagett, Esq. -
Judges
D.I.Sanders, Esq. - Orator of the Day
R.H.Gardiner, Esq. - Orator of the Evening
A.M.Bryan, Z.W.Halley, R. Turner Halley - Committee
of Arrangements

Sarah Rebecca Covell died, daughter of John D. and
Mary R. Covell of Port Tobacco on 26 July. She
was 7 months, 11 days. "The sweetest flowers are
culled first..."
Friend Wilson of the Marlboro Gazette calls
Editor Wells "modest" because he did not call at-
tention to new type. "...The editor (our friend
Wells) who is as modest and bashful as a boy with
a new coat, rather shyly donned this new dress,
and said nothing. We cannot permit the occasion
to pass without paying a compliment - richly
merited - to the worth of one of our most valued
and esteemed exchanges."

September 27, 1872, Vol. XXVIX, No. 22

J.G.Chapman advertises for a white woman to be his housekeeper.

October 4, 1872, Vol. XXVIX, No. 23

Richard T. Boarman, James A. Mudd and Emily Mudd, his wife, Mary Julia Bowling and Albert Boarman vs J. Walter Boarman and Mary Elizabeth Boarman, his wife, order Richard H. Edelen to ratify sale property to the amount of $3500.

Mary A. Slye, deceased, Orphans' Court. Richard P. Wall, administrator.

George Taylor, deceased, Orphans' Court. George Taylor, administrator.

Lawrence Posey dies in Baltimore on Sept. 16th. He was 48 years old. Late of this county.

Mrs. Lawrence Posey opens a boarding house in Baltimore. "...nothing will be left undone for their [boarders'] comfort."

R.H.Edelen, Esq., trustee, sold fine estate of 422 acres to William H. Moore of Bryantown, $3500.

October 11, 1872, Vol. XXVIX, No. 24

Maryland Editors' Association meeting. E. Wells is a member of the executive committee.

Edgar Griswold, near Pomfret Chapel, reports stolen dark roan horse, $20 reward.

Joseph H. Haviland warns trespassers on "Oakland."

R.Barnes, Jr. opens meat market "...in store adjoining 'Times' building."

Wm. Boswell and Co. sells selection of guns, rifles and pistols, also three English lever silver watches. "Reason for selling, the owner having no further use for them."

Quenzels have oysters - plate, gallon, bushel or barrel.

October 18, 1872, Vol. XXVIX, No. 25

George W. Howard, tailor, in store-house adjoining Mrs. M.A.Scott's millinery establishment in Port Tobacco.

October 25, 1872, Vol. XXVIX, No. 26

Robert Dudley Digges dismissed from Naval Academy

for "hazing" colored cadet, Conyers.
John F. Bradley warns trespassers from his farm on
    west side of Port Tobacco Creek, nearly opposite
    Chapel Point.
Mary A. Sanders, deceased, personal property to be
    sold at "Cedar Grove" "...also an old carriage."

Tournament at Marshall Hall

Knights - J.E.Martin of Hawthorne; John M. Halley,
    Potomac; R.M.Martin, Cat Ponds; Nathaniel Halley,
    Dolly Varden; Z.W.Halley, Forsaken; A.M.Bryan,
    Dead Duck; W.T.Clagett, Pomonkey; H.M.Thomas, Red,
    White and Blue; Sidney Miles, Night Before Last;
    and G.R.Bryan, Red Star. The following ladies
    were crowned: Kate Compton, Queen of Love and
    Beauty; Cecil Miles, 1st Maid of Honor; Eva
    Boswell, 2nd Maid of Honor; Ella Clagett, 3rd
    Maid of Honor.

Samuel Sheriff personal property sold. J.B.Sheriff
    and Thomas R. Halley, administrators.
Joseph Stewart, Register of Wills for Charles
    County gives notice that the free scholarship for
    Charles County to the Baltimore Female College is
    vacant.
Anderson Montgomery, colored, advertises that she
    wants information of the whereabouts of her chil-
    dren, Martha Ann, Susan, Jane and Nace Montgomery.
    She was owned by Alexander Haislip, near Port To-
    bacco for 22 years, now living in Richmond. Also,
    she is seeking information about Martha Ware, also
    owned by Haislip. Anderson was taken to New Orleans
    22 years ago and shortly thereafter purchased in
    Virginia.
E.C.Dutton, Allen's Fresh, has for sale a pair of
    mules and a lot of beef cattle.
W.A.Fowke and Ernest Hanson warn trespassers on
    "Gunston" and "Cold Streams."
Mary Henrietta Hancock dies, wife of T.T.Hancock,
    at her mother's residence (Mrs. Henrietta Roberts)
    on October 20th. She was 32 years old. "She
    leaves a sorrowing husband, three interesting little
    children, a devoted mother, kind brothers..."
Mrs. Eleanor Maddox dies at "Whitehall" on Sept. 12.
    She was 60 years old. "She was proud of her descent
    from illustrious pilgrims of Ark and Dove..."
Rev. P.F.Boyle will lecture in Port Tobacco - proceeds
    go to "completion of St. Thomas' Church..."

Golden Wedding

"The following, which we copy from the St. Joseph Valley Register, of the 24th ult., will doubtless be interesting to many relatives and friends of the aged couple mentioned still residing in Charles County:

The golden wedding of John H. and Sophia Robey, father and mother of Mrs. D.H.Harman and John A. Robey of this city, was celebrated at their home in Leesville, Carroll County, Ohio, on Thursday, Oct. 10, 1872. It occurred on the same day of the week upon which they were married just fifty years before. The children were all present, the first time that they had met together at the old home for eight years. They are six in number, three sons and three daughters, namely as follows: Mary E., wife of Jesse Mikesell; Malvine S., wife of Daniel W. Edgerly; John A.: James J; George W., and Elizabeth A., wife of David H. Harman. The husbands of the daughters were also present, and three children of John A. Robey, Eva T., James M. and Mary S., the only grand children of the aged pair. ...After dinner the father gave a brief account of his early life and raising of his family of six children, four of whom, the three daughters and one son, having married. After the conclusion of the address he presented each of the children at $10 gold piece. Including son-in-law and daughter-in-law there were ten in number, but death having severed the daughter-in-law (the wife of John A.), the aged sire said her children should receive her portion; but as there were three of them he would give each a five dollar greenback in lieu of the gold piece. The occasion was one of great pleasure and happiness to all concerned, and will long be remembered.

The aged couple came to Ohio in 1822 from Charles County, Maryland, and have lived at the above place ever since, being among the oldest settlers. They are nearly 73 years of age, but are hale and hearty and bid fair to live for years to come.

Capt. Leonard Marbury dies in Alexandria on Oct. 30th. He was 81 years old.

Margaret E. Bowie died at her residence in Nanjemoy on October 20th. She was the consort of Ethelbert Bowie, Sr., and was 51 years old.

George Brent warns trespassers on "Brentland."
Alexander Sanders, deceased, Orphans' Court. John
   H. Posey, administrator.

November 8, 1872, Vol. XXVIX, No. 28

John H. Cox warns trespassers on "Apple Grove" and
   "Walnut Grove."
F.P.Hamilton warns trespassers on "Oakland."
Joseph Parker, deceased, property "Part of Burch's
   Reserve" 56 acres and "Part of Monmouth" 120 acres
   on road from Centreville to Bryantown.

November 15, 1872, Vol. XXVIX, No. 29

Mrs. Catharine Posey dies in Washington, D.C. on Oct.
   20th. She was 56 years old and formerly from
   Charles County.
Mrs. Sarah Edelen dies at her residence near Bryan-
   town on November 8th. She was the relict of
   George Edelen "at an advanced age."
Uzzial Nalley, deceased, property "Part of Woodberry
   Harbor" sold 310 acres in Nanjemoy just below and
   adjoining Nanjemoy Stores. Thomas A. Millar and
   Samuel Hanson, executors.
Thomas M. Welch, overseer of Poors' House asks bids
   for 1000# pork. "Hogs to weigh from 125-200# each.
Bennet T. Clements, deceased, claims to be submitted
   to Sarah Ann Clements, executrix.

November 22, 1872, Vol. XXVIX, No. 30

Charles H. Milton, Port Tobacco, house and sign
   painter.
James Sykes, surviving partner of Sykes and Stackpole will have sale at Marshall Hall of personal
   property of partnership.
Harry B. Milton died at "Rich Bottom" on September
   15th, son of C.H. and J.D.Milton. He was one year,
   11 months, 26 days.
William Turner warns trespassers on "...my homeplace
   or the farm known as Dorsey's, belonging to John
   C. Morton, rented by me for present year..."
Quenzel's serve "breakfast, dinner and supper, during Court..."

December 6, 1872, Vol. XXVIX, No. 32

Death of Major William B. Stone

It becomes our sad duty to announce the death of Major William B. Stone, of this county. He died at his residence, near this place, on Sunday last, the 1st instant, of an affection of the brain, under which he had been suffering for several months past. Major Stone was the son of Judge Michael Stone, once Chief Justice of this Judicial District, and a nephew of Thomas Stone, Signer of the Declaration of Independence. Like his distinguished uncle and father, he was trained to the law; and practiced with reputation, and successfully, until 1844. In that year he was nominated as Chief Judge of this District by Governor Francis Thomas, and served until 1845. His political opponents being in the majority in the Senate, and having the Governor, his appointment was not confirmed, when he retired from the practice. Since that time he has been entirely engaged in agricultural pursuits, except on one occasion. In 1855 he and the late Senator Merrick were nominated by the Democratic party for the Legislature, and after a long and laborious canvass were elected in the last struggle made by the old Whig party in the county. With his colleague Major Stone served the county ably and faithfully in the Legislature, and after his term of service altogether retired from public life. In all the relations of life Major Stone furnished an example worthy of imitation. He was an examplary husband and father; a kind and affectionate relative; a social and hospitable gentleman; a kind and charitable neighbor, and, above all, he was a consistent Christian.

Thus are passing away, one by one, the men who were prominent in the professions, and as business and public men, when we first came to Charles county. Soon none will be left. A great change has been made in the social condition of our people since they grew up and lived—a change, we fear, which will not be favorable to the development of such a class of men in the future. Let us, then, treasure their memories, and imitate their virtues, that their characters may assist in moulding, as far as possible, those who will succeed them in the places and duties of life.

Captain James H. Neale died at "Mount Air" on November 12. He was 71 years old.
Dr. James B. Franklin died at his residence on November 8. He was 67 years old.
John Ware, Esq. died at "Brentfield" on Nov. 8. He was 55 years old.

110

John H. Robey, deceased, sale of personal property.
  John N. Robey and John A. Turner, administrators.
A mule, county property, found dead in Port Tobacco.
  "Whether it died of prevailing epizootic...re-
  cently suffering...found in narry alley, its
  throat being caught between sharp-pointed palings
  of a fence...strangulation."

St. Columba Lodge Election

Samuel Cox, Jr. - Worshipful Master
James L. Brawner - Senior Warden
George Taylor - Junior Warden
Edwin A. Smith - Secretary
John S. Button - Treasurer
William Wolf - Tiler

R. Young sells personal property
James D. Milstead, mortgagee will sell "Cornwallace's
  Neck" 550 acres adjacent to "Glymont" having valu-
  able wharf, recently put in good order - dwelling
  house recently built, owned by Charles H. Pye.
James H. Neale, deceased, Orphans' Court. Francis
  P. Hamilton, administrator.

December 13, 1872, Vol. XXVIX, No. 33

Tom Lovel, Hughesville, sells machinery.
Jane F. Sandy died at "Locust Hill" in Nanjemoy 20
  October, wife of Albert Sandy.
James H. Neale, deceased, personal property sale at
  "Mount Air." Francis P. Hamilton, administrator.
Edwin Adams' property on Potomac River for sale.
Joseph Parker property on road from Centreville to
  Bryantown for sale.

December 20, 1872, Vol. XXVIX, No. 34

W.D.Adams marries Sarah J. Robey on Tuesday last by
  Rev. J.H.Ryland.
J.P.Robertson has mules for sale.
Elizabeth Tompkins vs. James R. Tompkins - Equity
  docket.
John H. Robey personal property to be sold at his
  late residence.
F.A.Tolson, Riverside Post Office, has found 30' long
  lighter marked "Str National, Capt. Gregg."
J.T.Mudd, Gallant Green, advertises for competent
  clerk for "country mercantile business."

Francis Neale, Esq., dies in Baltimore. He was
   80 years old. He came to Baltimore in 1826.
W.A.Posey has a few barrels of winter apples for
   sale.

December 27, 1872, Vol. XXVIX, No. 35

John Edward Alvey marries Margaret A. Hamilton on
   Dec. 19th by Rev. Dr. Lewin at St. Paul's Chapel,
   Piney.
Henry Hawkins of Port Tobacco had horse and wagon
   stolen from Chapel Point.
Sarah Pennington, teacher at Port Tobacco school
   presided over Exhibition by the Scholars.
Railroad officials "passed over" the Baltimore and
   Potomac Railroad to its southern terminus. Col.
   Samuel Cox greeted them at Cox's Station through
   Eugene Digges, Esq. who delivered an address.
   Col. Cox invited the company "to the mansion" –
   they partook of more substantial comforts. They
   were entertained handsomely – sweet music by
   Prof. Gray's Band. After breakfast on Friday a.m.
   the visitors returned to the cars and departed
   for their homes.

VOTER REGISTRATION LIST SHOWING STRICKEN NAMES
issue of Nov. 1, 1872

District 1 - Port Tobacco
  Moses Cameron, Josiah Cooper, Lewis Edwards,
  Hanson Farmer, Nathan H. Farrall, Samuel
  Freeman, Alfred Green, William N. Jones,
  Patrick Smallwood, John Taylor
District 2 - Hill-Top
  James Brown, Ignatius Dyson, Alfred Easton,
  Washington Johnson, John T. Mattingley,
  Matthew Matthews, Samuel Manuel, Frank McPherson,
  Alonzo Shelton, William Joseph Thomas
District 3 - Nanjemoy
  Isaac Brown, Wesley Bowie, Joseph Dogan,
  Howard Daley, J.R.D.Gutheridge, Daniel Hensen,
  Thomas Henson, jr., Frederick Henson, Richard
  Johnson, Phil Jenifer, George S. Milstead,
  Franklin Pennington
District 4 - Allen's Fresh
  John T. Butler, James H. Good, Robert Jenkins,
  George Mills, Walter J. Randall, William R.
  Rollins, Orlander Thomas, John Thomas, jr.,
  John W. Turner, Charles H. Wood
District 5 - Middletown
  Aaron Butler, Thomas Dulany, Francis Gill,
  Rodgers Goodford, Francis A. Simms,
  James Thompson
District 6 - Harris' Lot
  Hanson Barber, L.D.Freeman, Jacob Johnson,
  George Luckett, Hanson Marshall
District 7 - Pomonkey
  Jourdan Brawner, William B. Dent, Francis Ford,
  Joseph Johnson, Thomas Marteall, Thomas Matthews,
  Wilson L. Moore
District 8 - Bryantown
  Adam Ford, Joseph Jenifer, John H. Jenifer, John H.
  Jones, Baptist Kimbo, Henry Proctor, George A.
  Proctor, Marion C. Reed, Charles Savoy, John H.
  Smoot, Charles J. Sidler, Richard W. Sidler, Thomas
  Elzear, Thomas Woodland
District 9 - Patuxent City
  Charles H. Butler, William H. Chapman, William
  Curtis, William H. Clayton, Richard E. Skinner,
  Richard Smallwood, Edward Skinner, Benjamin Spriggs,
  James E. Skinner, Richard Thomas, Fielder Wade

January 3, 1873, Vol. XXVIX, No. 36

Baltimore and Potomac Railroad commenced running a
regular daily train of cars for passengers on
Wednesday, January 1, 1873 from Cox's Station to
Bowie. Cox to La Plata to Beantown.
George Taylor sells mule for $125.
B.D.Tubman advertises for rent the farm lately owned
by Dr. Charles H. Pye and adjacent to "Glymont."
Lemuel Wilmer sells personal property.
Charles Robey, deceased, property for sale "at Cox's
Station" - formerly owned by four daughters of
the deceased Robey. S. Cox, Jr. attorney.
E.Dows has purchased the farm owned by heirs of the
late Thomas A. Burgess - 250 acres on Potomac
River, in Nanjemoy district - $2,000.
Thomas L. Speake, deceased, Orphans' Court.
William B. Carpenter, administrator.

January 10, 1873, Vol. XXVIX, No. 37

George M. Carpenter marries Mary E. Delozier on 31
December by Rev. R. Smith.
Hugh P. Posey marries Elizabeth E. Bowie on 2 Jan.
by Rev. R. Smith.
Noel R. Simmons marries Ida M. Delozier on Jan. 8th
by Rev. R. Smith.
Francis L. Smallwood marries Mrs. Aloysia L. Pickerell
on Dec. 24th at Christ Church, Accokeek by Rev.
J. Towles.
William J.R.Smallwood marries Catharine E. Coomes at
Pomphret Church on Jan. 2nd by Rev. Father McAtee.
Mr. Smoot, keeper of the light, Mrs. Smoot and assist-
ant keeper Mr. Hodgkins have been hemmed in by ice
for the past six weeks at Upper Cedar Point Light
House. Ice is piled up 16' high on every side but
the outer channel.

January 17, 1873, Vol. XXVIX, No. 38

William B. Matthews has livestock for sale.
John F. Swann has found two hogs and four shoats.
Samuel Strong and wife, deed of trust and sale $1,000.
Richard W. Bryan, trustee.
Smith Butler, negro, about 70 years old was struck by
locomotive on railroad and instantly killed - be-
tween Cox's Station and Middleville. Justice Carlin

held inquest. Butler got on freight train at
Brandywine, got off at La Plata. He intended to
continue on to visit a friend or relative near
Pope's Creek. Train left without him and he
started to walk - 6-7 miles to his destination.
On the way he purchased whiskey and became in-
toxicated.

January 24, 1873, Vol. XXVIX, No. 39

Edward J. Sanders marries Fannie Green at St. Jo-
seph's church on 21 January by Rev. F. McAtee.
Samuel Cox appointed Postmaster at Cox's Station
Post Office.
William B. Stone, deceased, Orphans' Court.
Margaret G. Stone, Executrix.

January 31, 1873, Vol. XXVIX, No. 40

Mrs. Celia Ann Albrittain died at the residence of
her husband, John W. Albrittain, Sr., on Jan. 14.
She was 59 years old. "An affectionate wife and
mother..."
Edward S. Welch and William Brown warn trespassers
on "Maryland Point Farm."
John W. Cox, James M. Harvey and Robert Sanders
took up a 10 oared boat, built in yawl fashion.
W.P.Flowers, justice of the peace.

February 7, 1873, Vol. XXVIX, No. 41

James T. Halley marries Mollie C. Wheeler, formerly
from Fairfax County, Va., at Pomonkey Methodist
Episcopal Church on 30 January by Rev. Mr. Townsend.
B.B.Burroughs marries Mary Judy of Madison County,
Illinois at residence of bride's father by Rev.
C. Nash of Centralia, Illinois.
Edward Radie, Jr., marries Josie Clara Farrall,
daughter of Stanislaus Farrall on January 8th at
St. John's Church, Baltimore by Rev. Father
McManus. The bride is formerly from this county.
Rev. Dr. Lewin placed a silver communion set on the
altar. It was the generous offering of a lady
parishioner. The service consists of a flagon,
paten and two chalices made of pure silver with
gilt on the inside.
Richard Garner, deceased, Orphans' Court. William
A. Garner, Administrator.

'Thomas Higdon found a brindle yearling.

February 14, 1873, Vol. XXVIX, No. 42

Mr. Morris was awarded the contract for conveying
mail to and from the railroad station. The mail
is brought by railroad and delivered at Murdock's
(or Salem) station. Service six times a week.
Beantown route discontinued. Duffield office
supplies this place as at present. The Post Office Department calls Port Tobacco Station
Murdocks; the Railroad calls it Salem.
Henry Brent died in Port Tobacco this a.m. He was
the youngest son of W.C. and Ida D. Brent.
Rudolph Carl Herman Thies, native of Oldenburg,
Germany died at Cox's Station on February 10th.
He was about 47 years old.
Professor A.C.Gray of The Brass Band and Musical
Association of Cox's Station will give a concert
at the Courthouse. John I. Jenkins is the Presi-
dent of the Committee.

February 21, 1873, Vol. XXVIX, No. 43

Mrs. Sympronia A. Corry, consort of Robert S. Corry,
died at her residence in Newport on 17 January.
She was 44 years, 5 months, 29 days. "She leaves
a husband and nine children to mourn their incon-
solable loss."
Baltimore and Potomac Railroad Co. is erecting at La
Plata station a warehouse and passenger room under
one roof. A platform 77' long and 8' wide will be
placed in front and one end of the building.

March 21, 1873, Vol. XXVIX, No. 47

James P. Smith died at the residence of Thomas D.
Simpson near Newburg on March 6th. He was 23 years,
2 months, 23 days old.
James Wills, colored, arrested for hog stealing.

March 28, 1873, Vol. XXVIX, No. 48

Editor Wells announces change of publishing day from
Friday to Thursday. The railroad now carries the
mail and each evening it is detained at Huntington.
Friday's papers would not be received until Monday
or Tuesday. Thurday's papers will reach everywhere

on Friday.

Charles A. Neale appointed 5th District Road Supervisor by County Commissioners. "When landlord Burch's dinner-bell sounded, the Commissioners proceeded forthwith to put things where they will do the most good."

Hannah Barnes died on 19 March. She was the wife of T. Benton Barnes, 26 years old. "Her gentle voice, which has been to him [her husband] as the sunlight of his existence, is now silent forever..."

Mary Alice Neale died on March 15th. She was the wife of E. Clarence Neale — 29 years old.

Lemuel Wilmer, deputy to Dr. W.R.Wilmer, Collector for 5th District, was directed to obtain search warrant and seize illicit distillery in Baltimore County by Seibold and Co. in 1868. After thorough search the still was found and seized.

Barnes Compton sells "Annapolis Woods" — 340 acres of wood and timber to Messrs Wecker and Houston. Number of hands at work felling trees for ship timber, railroad ties and cordwood. The tract is 4-5 miles west of Port Tobacco. Shipping from port on Potomac River.

Storehouse at La Plata Station will soon be built. "La Plata is one of the Stations on our railroad and will prove excellent place for business. Thomas R. Farrall, "...one of our energetic and thriving young merchants, will occupy station when finished, and we heartily wish him success. La Plata is about 3½ miles from Port Tobacco by county road and nearly two miles from Salem Station by railroad."

Thomas Latimer appointed postmaster at Newport vice John M. Latimer, deceased.

Edward S. Welch and William Brown warn trespassers on "Maryland Point."

John W. Fowler, Chapel Point, advertises for sale horses, cows and heifers.

Dr. John T. Digges in Port Tobacco offers services.

J.R.Robertson, Clerk to County Commissioners advertises "cash for four good mules to work on public roads..."

April 10, 1873, Vol. XXVIX, No. 50

Robert S. Corry to serve as Postmaster at Newport. Thomas Latimer, deceased.

Mrs. Owens' residence near Hill-Top will be scene of festival to benefit church "at that place."

Mr. Sanders, member of the brass band, will repeat
the amusing address delivered by him at Port
Tobacco.

Grand Jurors
Hugh Mitchell - Foreman

George J. Chappelear, C.L.Carpenter, C.H.Wood, A.M.
Dyer, J.B.Conklin, R. Barnes, Jr., Alexander Smoot,
W.L.McDaniel, Jere W. Burch, John E. Bailey, W.N.
Bean, S.N.Cox, Philip Harrison, William Nevitt, Jr.,
W.A.Lyon, W.F.Dement, G.C.Burch, W.W.Cobey, Edward
L. Huntt, T.S.Dent, Ernest Hanson, E.A.Smith.

Petit Jurors

J.A.Montgomery, J.T.Mudd, T.L.Hannon, G.H.Gardiner,
George S. Gardiner, C.L.Gardiner, E.N.Stonestreet,
W.M.Burch, F. Carpenter, C.C.Bowling, G.T.Brown,
H.L.Mudd, Yates Barber, John W. Jenkins, E. Griswold,
J.R.Carlin, H.H.Bowie, George Dent, J.F.Thompson,
T.R.Farrall, J.H.Gough, Townley Robey, P.A.Sasscer,
F.L.Dent, J.A.Adams.

William P. Compton advertises for sale three mules
and a yoke of oxen.
Letter to the editor. "...Confound the old antiquated
Court House! What if it does leak! Pull the old
thing down, and let us have in its place...a grand
temple...with its spire rising high up to the
clouds!..."
James D. Milstead vs Charles H. Pye, Equity Court.
W. Gibbons, A.B.Slye, J.R.Johnson trustees, want
teacher for P.S. #2, 9th Election District.
A.O.Horton and A.B.Horton, his wife and George W.
Guy vs W.E.W.Rowe, Joseph O. Guy, Equity Court.
C. Morton Stewart, Trustee, John Stewart, attorney,
sell property "Belmont" and "The Twin Sisters."
Land surrounded by lands of: Joseph Stewart, heretofore sold by B.D.Spalding to Sarah Chunn; land
owned by John Dement and children; land of W.C.
Willett, of Richard Willett, of George H. Gardiner's
heirs, of S.H.Robey, of W.T.Robey's heirs, land
occupied by late F. Montgomery, land of late H.A.
Moore, of H.D.Monroe's heirs, of W.M.Smallwood's
heirs, Christopher Wilkinson, Alison Hick's heirs,
land owned by Rev. George Berry and sisters, land
occupied by William Wolfe, land owned by heirs of
George S. Adams; including Mill Property, sometimes
known as Spalding's Mill, formerly the residence of
B.D.Spalding generally known as "Retreat," sometimes
called "Berry's Plains" - all known as "Cuttle

118

Manor" - 2,120 acres - frame dwelling house,
grist mill with 2 story frame near it, frame
store on line of Baltimore and Potomac Railroad,
(excepting the lot used as family burying-ground.)
Sale made at White Plains Station (Duffield Post
Office) which is on the premises.
John I. Jenkins, president and R.C.Fergusson, secretary of "The Brass Band and Musical Association of Cox's Station" will give two public con-
certs at Cox's Station.   Professor A.C.Gray will
direct.
W.H.S.Taylor writes to Editor Wells listing birds
resident all year, and migrating to be found in
Charles County:
Gray Eagle, bald Eagle, large horned Owl, screech
Owl, large hen Hawk, marsh Hawk, chicken Hawk,
sparrow Hawk, fishing Hawk, King Fisher, large
gray Crane, medium size Crane, Sea Gull, Woodcock,
Snipe, Sandpiper, Sora, or Rail; Indian Hen, Crow
Buzzard, crow Blackbird, red wing Blackbird, Star-
ling or Bobolink, Pheasant, Partridge, wild Pigeon,
tame Pigeon, Mocking Bird, French Mocking Bird,
Cat Bird, Baltimore Oriole, Lettuce Bird, Yellow
Bird, Humming Bird, Robin, Blue Bird, Wren, blue
Jay, Red Bird, Blue Bird, small, a light blue all
over, house Sparrow, hedge Sparrow, Snow Bird,
Lark, Swallow Dove Swallow, chimney Swallow, barn
Swallow, bank Swallow, House Martin, Bee Martin,
Chippoorwill,   bull Batt, leatherwing Bat, Cedar
Bird, Rain Crow, Woodpecker, Flicker, Sapsucker,
Tom-tit, Wood Bird, Kill-dear, Peewee Plover.
Aquatics - Swan Goose, brent or brant Goose, can-
vass back Duck, red neck Duck, shuffler Duck,
bald face Duck, Tumbler Duck, mallard Duck, dipper
or diver Duck, sprigtail Duck, summer Duck, blue
wing Duck, Walloon, Water Crow, Water Witch.   80
in all.

April 17, 1873, Vol. XXVIX, No. 51

Commissioners approve new public road across Zachia's
Swamp to Cox's Station.
Col. J.S.Ammon had two young apple trees pulled up by
the roots.
James R. Tompkins died Thursday a.m.   He was about
41 years old.
Mrs. Martha F. Mason died in Baltimore on April 15th.
She was 72 years old and formerly of Charles County.
Mrs. Augusta R. Hawkins died in Washington, D.C. on
April 11th.   She was the widow of the late Dr. John
L. Hawkins - 70 years old.

The name of the Post Office at Duffield changed
to White Plains and the site was removed two
miles east to the Baltimore and Potomac Railroad
station. George N. Rowe, Post Master, vice
Elizabeth Duffey superceded by change of site.
E.L.Huntt appointed Post Master at the new post
office at Mattawoman.
Edmund Perry of Port Tobacco had stolen old dark
bay mare.
Nace Smallwood advertises strayed sorrel filly.
Richard T. Tubman advertises for clerk.
Peter Dill, Cedar Point, wants good carpenter to
erect mill house.
Elizabeth A. Middleton, deceased, Orphans' Court.
Washington A. Posey, executor.

April 24, 1873, Vol. XXVIX, No. 52

James Owens was shot in Newport. Shot was intended
for man named Barber. Aggressor was Thomas Ward.

The Address
Mr. D. I. Sanders

...Really, my friends, the times of Port Tobacco--
the Port Tobacco Times (two dollars in advance,
cheap enough) is "alive and kicking.' It kicks
as hard, tho' not as erring, as those mules of our
county fathers--at poor old Oswald; they object
to 'the taking off.' I do not intend to tell
you all the good things about the Times, but I
will tell you something that is and will ever be
good for you--that is: Subscribe for it and see
the good things yourselves. Don't borrow it: If
it is worth borrowing, it is worth subscribing
for.--Help the generous, hard-worked editor and
printer in his untiring efforts to present a
paper, that every Charles Countian would be anx-
ious to see, read and subscribe for. Gentlemen,
subscribe for it, if you wish and expect success.
Ladies, subscribe--for it always records the
marriages, which you delight to read and generally
the first you look at, and I am sure its kind and
grateful publisher will insert, free of charge,
the marriages of all lady subscribers, and to
those already married, he will furnish newspapers
for bustles--not in the family. Subscribe, one
and all--let there be a full, strong stream flow-
ing to the Wells of Port Tobacco, 'till the Wells
there be full to overflowing..."

Joseph S. Turner marries Teresa R.A.Robey on
   April 15th by Rev. Dr. Lewin.
B.F.Burch sells hotel in Port Tobacco "...known as
   the Brawner House..."
Port Tobacco town commissioners elected - William
   Boswell, J.H.Jenkins, Joseph L. Lacey, J. Quenzel,
   and E. Wells.

May 8, 1873, Vol. XXX, No. 2

William Whitty of Chapel Point advertises the
   Chapel Point Mills.
Francis Posey of Prince George's County marries
   E.A.Jameson at "Westwood," the bride's mother's
   residence on April 29th by Rev. Father Murrer.
Notice in Marlborough paper "May Grand-pa Wells
   live long."
Hon. A.G.Chapman addresses alumni at St. John's
   College annual commencement.

Meeting at Harris' Lot, 5th District, to form
   Agricultural Club

Dr. F.M.Lancaster called to chair. Elected
   P.A.L.Contee, President; William McK. Burroughs,
   Secretary; By-laws committee - Henry R. Harris,
   C.C.Perry, and Charles H. Wood.

Nicholas Stonestreet and Mr. Albrittain lost sheep
   to dogs.
Marsh Robin omitted from bird list.
Elizabeth A. Middleton, deceased, personal property
   to be sold. W.A.Posey, executor.
John M. Latimer, deceased, Orphans' Court. Thomas
   T. Latimer and James B. Latimer, administrators.

May 22, 1873, Vol. XXX, No. 4

Lizzie Huntt died May 13. She was the second
   daughter of M. & M.T.J.Huntt. She was 12 years,
   9 months old.
Benjamin P. Donnelly - delinquent tax payer - house
   and lot at Allen's Fresh "Ward's Addition" and
   "Parnham's Amendment" - 170 acres.
Wife of Peter Smith, colored, burned severely try-
   ing to kindle fire with kerosene. Lives on farm
   in Cornwallis' Neck known as "Six Chimneys."
P.A.Sasscer erecting large store-house at Beantown Station on Baltimore and Potomac Railroad.
J. Quenzel lost a red buffalo cow.

121

Miss Alice A. Payne, Allen's Fresh, announces she
has new stock of spring and summer millinery.

May 29, 1873, Vol. XXX, No. 5

Thomas M. Welch, overseer Poors' House advertises
for 20 barrels of corn.
John J. Brawner, Collector asks all who owe for
taxes to please pay. 1st Collection District.
Philip Hawkins, colored, tried and convicted of
larceny. Sentenced to 4 years at the Colored
Boys House of Reformation and Instruction.
Timothy Dean, alleged lunatic and pauper. Jury
recommends that the County Commissioners provide
unfortunate youth board and room at public
expense.
James Wills, colored, sentenced to 5 months for
larceny of a hog, property of B.A.Gardiner.
Thomas Ward, guilty of assault.
Salem Station name changed by Baltimore and
Potomac Railroad to Port Tobacco Station.
J. Alexander Brawner appointed to a place in the
Custom House, Baltimore.
H. Clay Robey nearly severed his nose in a freak
accident. Skillfully dressed by neighbor,
A.R.A.Murray.
Bettie Short died, nearly 100 years old. She was
a former slave of Col. William Bruce, a soldier
in the Revolution who died many years ago.
C.H.Posey has a gate on his property which has been
swinging for 52-53 years - made of white oak
with iron hinges.
Egbert Carey, deceased, Orphans' Court.

June 5, 1873, Vol. XXX, No. 6

Benedict J. Edelen, deceased, property to be sold
"Part of Assington" 280 acres on east side of
Zachia Swamp, opposite Cox's Station on the
Baltimore and Potomac Railroad - dwelling house.
R.H.Edelen, trustee.
Washington Page, Collector of Taxes for 2nd Col-
lection District asks delinquent taxpayers to pay.
James Sykes, Surveying Partner will sell leasehold
interest of "Marshall Hall" under lease from
John M. Little.
Thomas I. Speake, candidate for Register of Wills.
Peter Wheeler, Esq., died at his residence on May
27th, former sheriff for about 60 years.
Rev. Meyer Lewin, D.D., rector of Port Tobacco

Parish was re-elected as a Member of the Standing Committee by the Episcopal Convention in Baltimore.
The buildings of the Townsend Street Station in Baltimore on the Baltimore and Potomac Railroad will be taken down and removed to the Port Tobacco Station in erecting a warehouse there.
James H. Montgomery's two sons were injured in a horse jumping accident. One son died the next day and the other is dangerously ill.
Mr. Farrall has moved into "the fine store at La Plata and from evidences appears to be doing a prosperous business..."

June 19, 1873, Vol. XXX, No. 8

J. Philip Stuart sells farm on Potomac River 1½ miles from Pope's Creek. Baltimore and Potomac Railroad passes through the eastern portion and a county road through the center. 450 acres. 4,000 cords of wood - dwelling. Apply to the residence of R.H.Stuart near the White Plains Station.
J.F.Matthews of Lothair advertises a 420 acre farm convenient to steamboat wharves, railroad, church, schoolhouse, post office.
Richard W. Bryan, agent for J.A.Brawner advertises for sale at the residence of J.A.Brawner in Pomonkey Neck personal property.
Peter Wheeler, deceased, Orphans' Court. James D. Milstead, administrator.
John T. Mattingly advertises stray black mare "...last seen going up Mount Hill..."
Ladies of the Oakland congregation of the Methodist Episcopal Church. South, will hold festival in the grove "...purpose...to plaster said church..."
A.B.Slye, Hughesville - rent farm near Benedict.
Jere Herbert marries Maggie Springsteen of Baltimore in Baltimore on the 10th of June by Rev. J.J.Webster.
Maria Josephine Roberts died in Port Tobacco on Sunday night. She was the second daughter of J.Hubert and Lilla L. Roberts. She was 6 months old.

July 3, 1873, Vol. XXX, No. 10

Alexander Jones (colored) petitions Governor for pardon - he was convicted in Charles County court for burglary, sentenced to penitentiary for 14 years.

W.W.Cobey, Nanjemoy Post Office, sells cotswold
buck lambs and jersey red pigs.
Margaret G. Stone advertises for sale that part of
farm "Haber de Venture" "...that is now occupied
by Mr. Joseph Duffey..." - small dwelling -
300 acres. Apply F. Stone, Port Tobacco.
John M. Latimer, deceased, personal property sold.
T.T.Latimer and J.B.Latimer, administrators.
Mary M. Pye died in Washington, D.C. on June 20th.
She was the relict of the late Charles A. Pye
and was 66 years old.
Mr. Button "...our persevering assistant..."
writes Editor Wells.
Philip Harrison's tobacco house in Cobb Neck -
8000# tobacco, was struck by lightning and en-
tirely destroyed.
Peter Wheeler, deceased, personal property to be
sold. James D. Milstead, administrator.
R.H.Gardiner advertises for stolen dark bay horse,
buggy, bridle and rug - reward.
Thomas A. Burgess, deceased, property petition
John B. Burgess in case of Washington Deatly vs
Jane Lewis for sale of real estate of William H.
Lewis. John B. Lawson, trustee. B.G.Stonestreet
Commissioner in Equity.
Joseph F. Thomas "of Mount Pleasant, in County of
Charles..." is declared bankrupt.

July 10, 1873, Vol. XXX, No. 11

Port Tobacco Times returning to publishing day of
Friday because of mail delivery.
W. McK. Burroughs addresses Farmers' Club at
Harris' Lot.
Daisy Mallinckbrodt died on 27 June at the residence
of her grandparents in Charles County. She was
the only child of William and Nannie C. Mallinck-
brodt.
C. Claude Digges advertises for sale fine, large
mule.
Benjamin F. Oliver marries Mary V. Tucker, former
wife of Thomas W. Tucker, at residence of bride's
father on June 30 by Rev. Robert Smith.
Thomas R. Gardiner, Esq., of St. Mary's County,
formerly of Charles County marries Lucy A. Higdon,
youngest daughter of the late John F.S.Higdon at
St. Mary's Church, Bryantown on June 25th by Rev.
Peter Linaghan.
Sallie J. Luckett died at Hughesville on July 4th.
She was the youngest daughter of James H. and
Mary E. Luckett. She was 5 years, 9 months.

"Sallie was as sweet a bud as ever blossomed to
be nipped by the early frost of death."
B.M.Edelen's valuable young horse was killed by
lightning - near Bryantown.
Duffield Post Office restored.
Mrs. Cecilia Miles' team of horses became frighten-
ed and ran off. Occurred at Brawner House where
play-goers had gone after the play "The Rivals"
at the Courthouse.

August 1, 1873, Vol. XXX, No. 14

H.H.Owen, "Rose Hill" near Port Tobacco advertises
a mare "taken from an enclosure..."
B.L.Higdon, near Port Tobacco, offers pair oxen
for sale.

William and Mary Parish Festival Officers

Mrs. John T. Colton, president; Mrs. McK. Burroughs,
vice president; Miss Esther Burroughs, secretary;
Miss Bettie Mortan, treasurer of the Ladies'
Society [Names of president and vice president show
in paper as men's names. Surely, Editor Wells errs!]
[In later issue, Editor Wells recognizes error and
apologizes.] Festival to be held at residence of
Charles A.F.Shaw, Esq.

J. Richard Cox, teacher at School #2, 4th Election
District annual examination and exhibition.
Mortgagee's sale of property "Margaret Ogleton"
lying between Pomonkey Creek and farm of William
H. Clagett, running with main road from Pomonkey
Creek to Semmes Hill. Sarah Massey, assignee
mortgage. Mortgage from Sandy A. Butler to James
Massey - dwelling house.
William Queen announces he found fishing scow,
32' long, 11' wide in Potomac River near Mathias'
Point.
Jere T. Mudd of Gallant Green and J. Thomas Colton,
Allen's Fresh, are local agents for Maryland Life
Insurance Co. Also, Dr. Robert Digges of Port
Tobacco.
B.I.Edelen - insolvent petition - R.H.Edelen, trustee.
Mary Edmonia Pye, deceased, property sold "Longevity"
245 acres - 4 miles from Port Tobacco - convenient
to steamboat and Baltimore and Potomac Railroad -
dwelling house, brick stable.
Cox's Station Hotel - guests the last few days have
numbered 52 - mostly from Baltimore and Washington.
John H. Jenkins received an appointment for the

125

[The August 1, 1873 issue of the <u>Port Tobacco</u>
<u>Times</u> contained three articles which may prove
interesting to the reader. They are copied in
their entirety.]

Last week, in noticing the proceedings of the
Ladies' Society of William & Mary Parish, we were
in error. We should have said <u>Mrs</u>. John T. Colton
had been selected President and <u>Mrs</u>. McK. Burroughs
Vice President of the Society, and not that their
liege lords had been assigned to the duties of these
respective positions. Ladies have their rights, and
in recognition of their rights in this particular
we are pleased to make the correction in this in-
stance. We would further state that the ladies will
have everything very nice and very abundant at their
festival and we insist that their right to look for a
large attendance and liberal patronage on the coming
festive occasion is entitled to the most favorable
encouragement.

One of our Town Commissioners is sojourning for a
term at the "Canal Hotel," [jail] Sheriff Luke Martin,
proprietor. Domestic incompatibility on the one hand,
and a too strong, <u>spirit</u>-compatibility on the other,
brought about the change of the Town Commissioner's
habitation. He had just re-opened bar and flung his
flag to the breeze on Monday last, and, on Wednesday,
under escort, goes to the "Canal Hotel." When he
reached the hospitable hotel and after being duly
registered, he asked that he might be allowed to occupy the parlor of the house, but Mr. Bateman, room
clerk of the establishment, could not "see it," and
assigned him to an apartment with pretty lattice
work of iron about the door and windows, and "the
mother of Siscra looked out at a window, and cried
through the lattice." He asked to have a keg of his
lager brought to him for his use at the hotel, but
Mr. Bateman, thinking that would be a reflection on
the <u>bars</u> of the house, couldn't tolerate the propo-
sition. Things were very much fermented without it.

According to previously arranged programme the excursion of the poor children of Washington, to Glymont, came off last week. An eye-witness to the
festivities of the occasion informs us that there
were about a thousand of these waifs of the street
on hand when the ice cream and <u>t'other</u> <u>fixins</u> were
dealt out. A more ragged, motley crowd of the city

gamin, he says, it is difficult to imagine. White and black promiscuously mingled together in one common herd, from the little girl in faded, soiled calico, to the full grown youth in ragged, striped trousers and the little chaps in short frocks. Everything, we learn, passed off quietly, and the crowd returned to Washington, well pleased with the trip. These excursions are conducted, we believe, under the auspices of the "Chronicle Newspaper Publishing Company," and will be several times repeated during the season.

Port Tobacco

We publish elsewhere in our paper this week an article taken from the Marlboro' <u>Gazette</u> headed "Salem" and written by the Editor pro tem. of that journal. The occasion of the article in question was a recent visit of the writer to our ancient town. As we mentioned last week, several errors appear in the article touching interesting matters connected with the early history of our village. Before proceeding however to lay before our readers such facts as we have been able to collect in that connection, we would remark that the present rail-road station, spoken of as "Salem," takes its name from a small collection of houses located on the road leading from Port Tobacco to the railroad.-- Salèm proper being at least half a mile distant from the station of that name. The station too is now more generally known as Port Tobacco Station, being the most convenient depot for this place and adjacent country.

We have been unable to discover any data by which we can conclude that the original county seat was at Pope's Creek. Until the appearance of the article in question, we never heard that the county seat had ever, at any time, been elsewhere than where it is at present. Pope's Creek doubtless was original-ly an Indian settlement, and oysters in great abundance are supposed to have been found in the Potomac near that point. The immense amount of oyster shells to be seen banked up and imbedded at Pope's Creek are believed to have been deposited there by the abori-gines through a long course of years. We have no hesi-tation in saying there is error in the supposition that the county seat of this county was ever at any time located at Pope's Creek.

In reference to the name of our town we have ga-thered some interesting information from a very old map, which is now in the possession of a gentleman of this county. This map or chart was published in London, and is dated in the year 1606, and was no-ticed by us editorially some few years back. The notice we then made was generally republished in the papers of the State, and the map spoken of, as it doubtless is, as being a valuable relic of an early period in our history. It is a copy of a map ori-ginally made by Capt. John Smith, previous to his settlement in Virginia and some years before the first settlers of Maryland set foot on the shores of St. Mary's. Captain Smith appears to have ascended the Potomac, penetrating all the different inlets of the river and making explorations of the adjoining lands. Among other points visited by him was the Indian village of Potopaco at the head of a creek or inlet of that name and located precisely where the village of Port Tobacco now stands. On the map referred to the topography of the country seems to have been noted with faithful accuracy, and the Indian word Potopaco is interpreted to mean "the town between two hills." Soon after the coming of white settlers from Europe, Potopaco, being situated at the head of navigable water, offered an eligible site for the white man's settlement as being advantageously located for the purposes of trade and traffic with the Indians. Accordingly, some enterprising Scotchmen improved the opportunities offered, and to that fact we are indebted for the existence of the present town of Port Tobacco. Port Tobacco is but an Anglicized corruption of the Indian word Potopaco, doubtless suggested by a striking similarity of sound in the pronunciation of the words, as well by the fact that in colonial or provincial times a considerable commerce in tobacco was carried on with the mother country by means of ships trading directly from this point to Europe.

Years after the settlement of the white man here, however, the legal name of the place was Charlestown, and we remember to have read, some years since, a speech or published letter of the late Judge LeGrand, in which he announced that in the Revolutionary period the first military company in all the Colonies that ever marched beyond its own colonial limits to the defence of a sister Colony was organized by Capt. William Smallwood at Port Tobacco, in Charles County. They marched to Long Island and fought with marked bravery under their leader in the bloody fights there for the defence of New York. General Smallwood died and was buried in this his native county, but, strange to say, the exact spot of his interment is unknown. No stone or other memorial is to be found marking his place of burial.--Although Charlestown appears at one time to have been the legal name of this town, it does not seem to have grown in general use, and the village, from its earliest settlement, has been almost continuously known as Port Tobacco, the county seat of Charles county.

The following appeared in <u>The Times</u>, Aug. 1, 1873

SALEM

On Tuesday evening of last week we were sudden-
ly made aware that there was such a place in
Southern Maryland and that those who seek the
ancient village of Port Tobacco by rail must get
off at Salem. The artistic flourish with which
the Conductor made the announcement left no room
for doubt in our mind in regard to this suburb of
the metropolis of Charles County. A thought oc-
curs to us here, which, for the benefit of the un-
suspecting, we will set down: Salem, like many
other places, must be seen to be appreciated--the
eyesight however must be good or one loses half
the benefit.

The occasion of our trip to Port Tobacco was
partly to meet old and valued friends--many
whose friendship was fostered under far less pleasing circumstances than accompanied our recent meet-
ing--for when we first met 'twas during the stormy
days of the last war, to which our sister county
sent so many of her brave sons. The first face
whose kindly smile greeted us was that of our old
friend ,Captain Dement. We found him the same
whole-souled,generous fellow, and were happy to see
that he wears his years as gracefully as he did gal-
lantly and deservedly his military laurels. Surrounded by those we love as brothers in the "lost
cause," we lived over again in a few hours our soldier days. We missed some faces that we shall never
see again--the forms of those are sleeping where
they died--they made "their country's flag their
shroud"--a heart's requiescat we drop o'er their
silent and narrow homes.

The primary cause of our visit, however, was to
witness the Dramatic Association reader Sheridan's
bright and interesting comedy of the "Rivals," and
we were amply repaid for our restless expectation.--
We have never yet seen it put on the stage by ama-
teurs so well--the costuming were in every respect
faultless and the acting very fine. Of course our
limited power of criticism renders it impossible to
do justice to both actors and acting--but where all
did so well it would be superfluous to draw compari-
son. Our weakness for the ladies renders it out of
the question to be an impartial judge. One of the
main features of the occasion was the music. Prof.

130

Gray with his band were in attendance. Some
squibs that appeared in the "Huntingtonian" may
have left the impression that the "Charles County
Band" was a myth. Such however, is not the case.
The Band is an accomplished fact, and the selections
as well as their execution were exceedingly fine.
A word or two in regard to the town itself may not
be amiss. The oldest inhabitant knows nothing of
its infancy--and historians differ in regard to the
exact location of the Indian settlement, "Port To-
bago," from which the present town derives its name.
At the water terminus of the B. & P. R. R., Pope's
Creek, may be seen a huge and almost inexhaustible
mound of oyster shells. No one knows how they got
there--but from time to time relics of the dustly
settlers are found at such a depth among the shells
that many believe this spot to have been the original site of what is now known as Port Tobacco. The
quaint style of some of the out-buildings carry one
far "down the corridors of time." That venerable
old pile, the "Indian King," tells its story of a day
that is dead, and the visitor will hardly imagine
that the little stream that trickles past the town
was once the bed of a river, or at least a large
creek. We were told that ships were loaded here
for Liverpool and other foreign ports. A dilapi-
dated and weather-beaten warehouse marks the spot
where once all was bustle and energy. No vestiges
of anything like wharves are to be seen, and one's
imagination has to clothe the scene with garments of
the past to invest it with anything like business.
The reflection is not devoid of its lesson; the
actors in these scenes are gone; and their memory
almost extinct.

> "And the stately ships move on
> To their haven under the hill--
> But oh! for a touch of a vanished hand,
> And a sound from a voice that is still."

But the writer of this is far more interested in
the present population of Port Tobacco and its
neighborhood, than with those gone before. A more
generous and hospitable people we never met, and
their kindness to us will long be remembered and
gratefully appreciated. We visited the Editorial
Sanctum of the "Times," and found it like the paper
itself, a marvel of neatness. From its genial Editor and Staff we received a kind welcome. To the
"Times-man" on this as on other occasions we are indebted for many kind attentions. We met a young Bal-
timorean in the village, whose business seemed to

have been to superintend the putting into successful operation a threshing machine--the pattern of
late and improved design. We were intimate in our
school days with one that came from the Emerald
Isle--that as a thresher was a decided success.

We were glad to learn that the amount realized by
the entertainment amounted to about six hundred
dollars, which goes to rebuild St. Thomas' Church,
which was burned some years ago. We shall remember
with pleasure the bright, sweet faces we met during our stay, and would like very much to put down
here our impressions, but will only console our-
selves with the idea that "there are feelings that
words cannot measure." With many thanks to our
Charles County friends for one of the pleasantest
visits, we bid them good-bye.

Office of Registration for Port Tobacco, vice
W.C.Brent, resigned. Mr. Jenkins declines to
accept.
Dr. E.V.Edelen had two very valuable mules struck
by lightning and killed - storm was particularly
severe along the Zachiah Swamp.

August 8, 1873, Vol. XXX, No. 15

Democratic and Conservative Convention meets in Port Tobacco for election

Thomas R. Halley, Esq., President; John T. Davis
and Samuel Cox, Jr., Secretaries. Body to se-
lect three delegates; Tellers-J.W.Mitchell and
James F. Matthews. Delegates elected- John W.
Mitchell, Esq., Col. Samuel Cox and Eugene
Digges, Esq. Alternates-Col. J.W.Jenkins, John
W.Mitchell, Esq., Dr. T.A.Carrico.

Hon. Andrew G. Chapman addressed the St. John's
College graduates in Annapolis.
Mary Aphilia Wenk died, wife of Henry, at
"Normanda" on July 22. She was 21 years, 6
months. "...she lived in the Communion of
Christ's Holy Catholic Church..."
Catharine E. Carpenter died at her home, beloved
wife of Marbury Carpenter, devoted daughter of
J. Arthur and Elizabeth J. Golden. She was
23 years old.
John R. Murray is a candidate for Sheriffalty.

Tournament at Glymont

John T. Davis, Chief Marshal; D.I.Sanders will deliver address to Knights; Eugene Digges will
give the coronation address in the Pavilion at
night. 25¢ admission to grounds; Dinner-75¢
and will be served at 4 p.m. in large dining
room in Pavilion; supper-50¢ and 50¢ admission
for "a gentleman and ladies to the Ball in the
Pavilion, at night."

Elizabeth C. Smallwood, deceased, Orphans' Court-
James M. Moore and Philip A. Sasscer, admin-
istrators.
Augustin W. Neal "farmers' candidate for the
House of Delegates."
Thomas K. Ching's visitor named Levy from Bal-
timore was thrown from a horse and had his right
arm broken.

[The following letter appeared in the August 8, 1873 issue of the Port Tobacco Times in connection with the two articles which appeared in the August 1, 1873 edition.]

Charles County, Md.
August 4th, 1873.

Editor of the Port Tobacco Times:

Dear Sir: In your last issue is an editorial relative to the ancient village of Port Tobacco, the capital of Charles county, and such it always has been from the first settlement and organization of the county, and Pope's Creek, on the river, was not its site, as supposed by another writer.--It was an Indian village, called, as you correctly state, "Potapaca," which signifies "a town between high hills," and was located precisely where it now is, at the head of the present Port Tobacco Creek, then navigable to and from the town by vessels of any size used in the trade of the country. When the county was organized it was named "Charles Town," or "Charleses Town," which continued to be its legal designation until a comparatively recent period, and long within my recollection, when it was changed to its ancient anglicized Indian name by a special act of the Legislature.

The following, from the oldest record book, which is or ought to be, and certainly was a few years ago, in perfect preservation in the Clerk's office, being the original and strongly bound in parchment, may not be uninteresting. I give it in the quaint old spelling of the time:

"Records for Charles Countie, within the Province of Mariland, It being erected into A Countie by the Hon'ble Josias Ffendall, Esq., Gov'r of the sayd Province, May Ao., 1638."

This was during the last year of the Protectorate of the celebrated Oliver Cromwell, one of the greatest men in English history, who died September 3d, 1658. The first suit brought in the county is thus recorded:

"1658, May 25.--Arthur Turner demanded Warrant against John Ashbrooke in an action of debt to the valew of 1,300 lbs. Tob'o. Warrant to the Sheriffe of Charles Countye to arest, &c. Retur'e next Countie Court, to be holden at Humphrey Alwick's, the 4th of June next."

Where the locality of "Humphrey Alwick" was, we are in the dark.

"At A Court Held in Wensday, in Charleses Coun-
tie, the 26th of October, Ao., 1658.
                "PRESENTES:
"Josias Ffendall, Esq., Gov., Mr. John Hatch,
Mr. James Linsey, Mr. James Waker, (quare Walker?)
Mr. Henrie Addamas."
                "NOT PRESENT:
"Gov'r Captain William Stone, Secr't Mr. Baker
Brooke.
"John Courts, Plantive.   )   The Plantives
Hanniball and Elizabeth   ) Aresting the de-
 Spicer, Defendants.   ) fendants in an
action of Defamation, the sayd Plantive desireth
that the oaths of John Piper and Daniell Johnson
mought bee taken in open Court, which was granted.
   "John Piper, aged 30 years, or thereabouts, sworne
and examined in open Court sayeth that hee hard
Haniball and Elizabeth Spicer say that goodman
Courts was a slanderous man, and hath slandered the
whole cuntrie; and further, this deponant sayeth,
that hee hard the sayed Spicer and his wife say
that they hard goodman Courts say that William
Empson was a theefe from his cradell, and further
sayeth not.
   "Daniell Johnson, 23 years, or thereabouts testi-
fieth word for word as John Piper had done, and
then follows the judgement of the Court.
   "It is therefore ordered that the sayd Haniball
Spicer and Elizabeth Spicer shoold have six lashes
apeece, which the Sheriffe is to cause them to re-
ceave, but the sayd Elizabath alleging that * * *
   "Vera ex originie Copia ita Testor.
                "George Thompson, CT'k."
   Referring again to Port Tobacco, there was an
Episcopal Church there previous to the year 1684,
(Tempo. Charles II.) The original Church was built
on the western side of the creek, of which there is
now no trace of its foundations discoverable. We
know that it was occupied by the Rev. Mr. Moore, in
1692, (Tempo. William and Mary,) and that from him
to the present Rector there has been in the Parish
a regular succession of fourteen ministers, covering
a period of 177 years. The two last, the Rev. John
Weems, installed in 1787, died in 1821, and the Rev.
Lemuel Wilmer, elected in 1822 and died in 1869, occupied the pulpits of the old and present Church
for the unusually long period of 82 years, a very
high compliment, I think, to the devotion and stead-
iness of the parishoners.
   About 130 years ago, or "thereabouts," Port Tobacco was very near being utterly extinguished by
the removal of the county seat, or capital, to

Chapel Point, and nothing but the then powerful
influence of the Scotch merchants of the former
place prevented it. The site of the new town was
surveyed and laid out by a competent Engineer, and
I well remember, some fifty years ago, when the old
Clerk's office near the centre of the public square
was pulled down, seeing a very handsomely executed
plat of the same, colored and framed, which was
named "New Edinburg." The public square for the
Court House, &c, with streets running to it and to
the river were well laid down, together with ample
ground for wharves, for the accommodation of trade
and commerce, on water then deep enough for any
vessel that could go to Alexandria. This shows
that the movement was seriously entertained in in-
fluential quarters, prompted, no doubt, by the rapid
filling up of the creek and the fast growing destruction of the navigation at Port Tobacco. In my
younger days I have heard many of our best men regret that the plan of removal did not succeed.

                                                    T.

Mrs. Sallie B. Pennington, Newtown, had examination
and exhibition of pupils at school. Capt.
Pennington addressed pupils and visitors. At
close of speech, effort was made to increase
the teacher's salary. It took 20-30 minutes,
but $50 was raised.
Richard Cox conducted examination and exhibition
at Newport. Thomas D. Stone made brief address.
Kate McPherson, daughter of Samuel W. McPherson,
Esq., Pomonkey district, gave a statement of her
account of the tragic fire aboard the Wawaset.
She went aboard with Miss Marbury at Glymont.
Minnie Turner Padgett died - only child of J.V. &
Roberta Padgett on July 29. She was 9 months
and 5 days old.
William H. Moore, candidate for House of Delegates.
John H. Bishop, mortgagor of personal property to be
sold - D.F.Burch, mortgagee.
Miss E.S.Dent, teacher at School #3, 4th Election
District. held examination and exhibition. Children
were addressed by Dr. S.W.Dent.

August 22, 1873, Vol. XXX, No. 17

Joseph I. Lacey of Port Tobacco appointed by Gover-
nor as Officer of Registration.
Miss Elizabeth Duffey re-instated Postmistress of
the Duffield Post Office.
Dr. F. Matthews Lancaster announces candidacy for
House of Delegates.
A. Richards warns trespassers off land of late
Francis Montgomery.

Officers of Registration

Joseph I. Lacey, 1st Election District, Port Tobacco
James A. Franklin, 2nd E.D. - Hill-Top
George W. Carpenter, 3rd E.D. - Nanjemoy
John H. Freeman, 4th E.D. - Allen's Fresh
Henry R. Scott, 5th E.D., Harris' Lot
Marcellus Thompson, 6th E.D. - Middletown
Henry M. Hannon, 7th E.D. - Pomonkey
James A. Mudd, 8th E.D. - Bryantown
John H. Chappelear, 9th E.D. - Patuxent City

August 29, 1873, Vol. XXX, No. 18

W.E.W.Rowe appointed Justice of the Peace by Governor,
vice R. Oscar Wade declined.

Number of passengers at Port Tobacco Station be-
    tween 26 July and 19 August - 248. Average 12
    passengers per day.
Mortgagee's sale - Mortgage from Robert Oliver and
    Sarah A. Oliver, wife, to Francis Tennison, Ben-
    jamin P. Donnelly, Zachariah Lloyd to sell lot of
    land near Lothair or Middleville between forks in
    road leading to Allen's Fresh, very near Baltimore
    and Potomac Railroad. John W. Mitchell, attorney
    assignee.
Mrs. Juliana White died in Baltimore on August 21st.
    She was born in Charles County June 19, 1803.
Alexander Penn died in Baltimore on August 24th. He
    was 58 years old, formerly from Charles County.
Ann McCarty Blacklock died in Alexandria, Virginia
    on August 17th. She was 23 years old and the
    daughter of the late Dennis B. Blacklock.
Henry Matthews died at the home of his mother, Mrs.
    Amanda Matthews on August 20th. He was 22 years
    old.
Bill Brookes, colored, committed to jail by Constable
    Smoot for attempting to rape a white girl in
    Harris' Lot district.
George N. Rowe announces that the White Plains Sta-
    tion on the Baltimore and Potomac Railroad can
    accommodate persons with meals anytime. Also has
    accommodations for horses.

September 5, 1873, Vol. XXX, No. 19

M.A.Scott asks payment for debts.
J.H.Gough, Secretary, announces a meeting of the
    Farmers' Club of Newport.
T.W.Wright of Doncaster Post Office has an ad-
    vertisement for horse strayed or stolen from
    Glymont.

Tournament at Glymont

Judges - Col. Samuel Cox, Edgar Brawner, John H.
    Warring. Marshals - John T. Davis, Dr. J.T.Digges
    and Sydney A. Miles.
    W.H.Miles - Knight of Cornwallis
    E.H.Brawner - Knight of Potomac
    Marshall Thomas - Knight of Glymont
    J.H.Mattingly - Knight of La Plata
    Marcellus Cox - Knight of Mattawoman
    Hughes Wills - Knight of Saint Thomas
    Albin Wills - Knight of Hard Times

D.I.Sanders gave address.

Queen of Love - Linda Rhodes
1st Maid of Honor - Maggie Miles
2nd Maid of Honor - Cecie Miles
3rd Maid of Honor - Cora Dement
Alexander Robertson was unexpectedly called upon
to make the coronation address and "...acquitted
himself handsomely."

F. Stone and J.H.Mitchell announce a co-partnership
   for the practice of law.
Mrs. Amanda King died on Sunday in Charles County.
   She was the relict of the late James A. King, formerly of Port Tobacco.

September 12, 1873, Vol. XXX, No. 20

Jim Adams, colored, shot and killed himself while
   hunting on the Newtown farm of Mrs. Luke Hawkins.
James A. Mudd and B.M.Edelen, Bryantown, recently
   erected a steam saw and grist mill.
John W. Mitchell, Francis W. Weems and A.J.Smoot,
   State Central Committee of the Democrats and
   Conservatives of Charles County announce a meeting to elect delegates.
Walter Swann's farm "Prospect" will be the setting
   for the Grant Colored Tournament and Ball.
George M. Lloyd, secretary to the School Board
   gives notice to the Trustees of such schools as
   may need repairs or stoves to report same and
   give estimates.
John Hamilton advertises for rent two dwelling
   houses, blacksmith and wheelwright shops, on
   same lot in Port Tobacco.
Joseph H. Mattingly has found stray red bull
   yearling.
Mary Matilda Rowe died on September 6th at age
   one year, six months, twenty six days. She was
   the youngest child of Charles H. & Lizzie S. Rowe.
O.N.Bryan of "Locust Grove" sends to the Editor a
   pair of "...genuine Colorado potato beetles
   (bugs)." It took ten years to reach Charles County.

September 19, 1873, Vol. XXX, No. 21

Eugene Digges writes a letter to the public stating
   that he has nothing to do with the "political
   course of the Port Tobacco Times." Strictly
   Captain Wells' views and opinions (true Democrat).

139

Col. J.S.Ammon writes to the Editor to say he
  will grade and gravel Mount Hill Road for $1200.
  Will use "ravine through Mr. Boswell's land" and
  will culvert road where it passes over the run
  at the foot of road.
Thomas S. Turner marries Rose Good on Sept. 5th at
  Bethel Church in St. Mary's County by Rev.
  Robert Smith.
F.J.Maddox marries Rebecca D. Burroughs on September 11th at St. Peter's Church in Baltimore by
  Rev. Dr. Grammer.
Ardella Wood died on September 6th. She was the
  daughter of C.H. & Jane Wood. "...Remember,
  mother, God has called her, Do not murmur, do
  not weep, Your little one is only resting In a
  calm and peaceful sleep."
Mr. Lawrence, proprietor of "Hard Bargain" estate,
  thanked by ladies of William and Mary Parish
  "...for the use of his commodious mansion and
  beautiful grounds." [Article by assistant editor showed different picture of "Hard Bargain"--
  overgrown, etc.]
Pricey Ann Downing, deceased, property to be divided -- suit of George W. Downing vs Benjamin
  Wade. Commissioners - Jeremiah T. Mudd, Sylvester
  Mudd, Gonzaga C. Burch, George H. Gardiner and
  James A. Mudd.

September 26, 1873, Vol. XXX, No. 22

Democratic and Conservative County Convention

Dr. Peter W. Hawkins - President; Dr. T.C.Price and
W.A.Posey, Esq. - Vice Presidents; John T. Davis
and Thomas R. Farrall, Secretaries
Following announced as candidates:

Hon. Barnes Compton, Officer of Registration;
A.G.Chapman, Esq. & Richard P. Wall, Esq., House of
  Delegates;
George A. Huntt, Esq., Clerk of Circuit Court;
Joseph Stewart, Esq., Register of Wills;
Nominations for County Commissioners -
Thomas R. Halley, Josias Hawkins, Joseph T. Ward,
Philip A. Sasscer, Dr. A.J.Smoot, William E. Dement,
Francis Dunnington, Thomas M. Posey, Charles H.
Wills, John H. Cox and Joseph Price.
Hawkins, Smoot, Posey withdrawn.
Sasscer, Ward, Dunnington, Dement and Price elected.
John R. Murray, Esq., Sheriff;

140

William L. Cooke, Esq., name withdrawn;
James L. Brawner, Surveyor

Mrs. Jane Murphy died on Sept. 12th in Bryantown.
   She was the wife of Francis A. Murphy, 41 years
   old.
Rev. Joseph Mettam of Pikesville will "hold a protracted meeting" at Good Hope Baptist Church in
   Piccawaxen.
Twenty five cords of oak needed for the courthouse.
W.W.Cobey of Cross Roads Post Office advertises for
   sale 2-3 year old colts, one brood mare, one
   cheap work horse, one old mule, a lot of Jersey
   red pigs.

<u>October 10, 1873, Vol. XXX, No. 24</u>

[Voter registration lists for Election District
Numbers 4, 5, and 6 appear in this issue. Because the names are the same as those appearing
in the last listing, included here will be the
changes to the list only -- List of Names Newly
Registered and List of Names Stricken Off.]

Election District #4 - John H. Freeman, Officer
   of Registration
List of Names Newly Registered:
Blair John Baptist, Robert C. Ching, Richard Contee,
Hanson Farmer, Benjamin Hawkins, William Benjamin
Miles, James F. Matthews, Thomas A. Queenan, Lewis
Smothers, Robert H. Turner, William Whitty, jr.

List of Names Stricken Off:
John W. Boarman, Richard H. Bond, Eugene Digges,
Edward C. Dutton, John Dorsey, Henry Good, James L.
Hill, John H. Kinnaman, John M. Latimer, James H.
Neale, Sylvester Pye, George Rustin, John Ware.

Election District #5 - Henry R. Scott, Officer of
   Registration
List of Names Newly Registered:
John W. Cash, E.C.Dutton, John P. Nevitt, Alexander
Penn, James Thomas.

List of Names Stricken off:
George W. Berry, Richard Contee, John T. Digges,
V.T.Hayden, Charles Hayden, Wirt Harrison, Josias
Jenkins, George H. Short, J.R.Tompkins.

Election District #6 - Marcellus Thompson, Officer
   of Registration

List of Names Newly Registered:
Spencer McPherson, H.C.Page

List of Names Stricken off:
William L. Atcherson, jr., Bennet T. Clements,
Richard B. Clagett, Josiah Duckett, Charles
Mulholland, Francis G. Murray, Thomas D. Perry,
Franklin A. Robey, Henry Speake, Fielder D. Willett.

Judges of Election appointed by County Commissioners

1st Election District - George P. Jenkins, William
   Hamilton, B.L.Higdon
2nd Election District - Charles E. Hannon, Ernest
   Hanson, Benton Barnes
3rd Election District - Richard B. Posey, Henry S.
   Dent, Alexander Haislip
4th Election District - W.A.Posey, William Nevitt,
   Sr., William L. Sheirbourn
5th Election District - Thomas Posey, J.H.D.Wingate,
   Thomas Semmes

December 20, 1873, Vol. XXX, No. 34

W.D.Adams married Sarah J. Robey on Tuesday last by
   Rev. J.H.Ryland.
J.P.Robertson advertises mules for sale.
Elizabeth Tompkins vs James R. Tompkins - Equity
   docket.
John H. Robey, deceased, property to be sold at his
   late residence.
F.A.Tolson, Riverside Post Office, has found a 30'
   long lighter marked "Str National, Capt. Gregg".
J.T.Mudd, Gallant Green, advertises for competent
   clerk for "country mercantile business".
Francis Neale, Esq. died in Baltimore, 80 years old.
   Came to Baltimore in 1826.
W.A.Posey has a few barrels of winter apples for sale.

December 27, 1873, Vol. XXX, No. 35

John Edward Alvey married Margaret A. Hamilton on
   December 19th by the Rev. Dr. Lewin at St. Paul's
   Chapel, Piney.
Henry Hawkins of Port Tobacco, had a horse and wagon
   stolen from Chapel Point.

Sarah Pennington, teacher at Port Tobacco school,
   presided over Exhibition by the Scholars.
Railroad officials "passed over" the Baltimore and
   Potomac Railroad to its southern terminus.
   Col. Samuel Cox greeted them at Cox's station
   through Eugene Digges, Esq. who delivered an address. Colonel Cox invited the company "to the
   mansion" -- partook of more substantial comforts.
   Entertained handsomely - sweet music by Professor
   Gray's Band. After breakfast Friday a.m. the
   visitors returned to the cars and departed for
   their homes.

ANNUAL STATEMENT
BY THE
COMMISSIONERS OF CHARLES COUNTY, MD.

Amount of Assessable Property and Rate of Tax-1873

Orphans' Court.	$ 644.00
County Commissioners.	412.60
Judges and Clerks of Election	396
Grand and Petit Jurors.	1,488.50
Witnesses, State's cases.	267.50
Bailiffs and Messengers	385.50
Crow-bill Certificates.	174.00
Registrars.	
Assessments and Insolvencies.	476.02
Rent of Election Rooms.	25.00
Coffins for Paupers	77.00
Coroners' Inquests.	67.71
Material for Roads.	264.57
Miscellaneous Items	23,900.21
Collectors' Commissions for collecting State and County Taxes.	2,177.98
Amount overrated.	245.26

	$ 31,453.10
Treasurer of Maryland for State Taxes.	5,215.20
	$36,668.30

Amount levied on Baltimore and Potomac
   Railroad Co.* 4,200.00
*The above tax of $4,200 on Railroad, being in liti-
  gation, is not included in the amount of County
  Expenses.

Judges of the Orphans' Court

Robert Digges, Stouton W. Dent, Richard Barnes,
George P. Jenkins, J.H.Roberts, John S. Chapman,
William Boswell & Co.

County Commissioners

A.J.Smoot, Thomas R. Halley, John H. Cox, Samuel
Hanson, Josias Hawkins.

Judges of Election

George P. Jenkins, Charles E. Hannon, Richard B.
Posey, Washington A. Posey, Thomas Posey, Thomas B.
Berry, Benjamin D. Tubman, John W. McPherson,
T.Elzear Gardiner, Ernest Hanson, Benton Barnes,

John H.D.Wingate, Thomas Semmes, Henry S. Dent,
Richard Price, Jere W. Burch, P.A.Sasscer, William
Nevitt, W.L.Sheirbourn, James T. Thomas, R.P.Wall,
George F. Bealle, F.B.Green, William Hamilton,
Peregrine Davis, W.H.Cox, John A. Wood.

Omitted in 1871

George P. Jenkins, William Hamilton, Bennet Neale,
Thomas L. Speake, Charles E. Hannon, Ernest Hanson,
R.B.Posey, H.S.Dent, Joseph Price, Washington A.
Posey, William Nevitt, sr., W.L.Sheirbourn, Thomas
Posey, John H.D.Wingate, George T. Simpson, Thomas
B. Berry, William L. McDaniel, George F. Bealle,
Benjamin D. Tubman, W.H.Cox, John A. Wood, J.W.Mc-
Pherson, Jere W. Burch, James A. Mudd, T. Elzear
Gardiner, R.P.Wall, James T. Thomas.

Clerks of Election

John T. Davis, John I. Jenkins, James A. Franklin,
F.A.Hanson, J.H.M.Dutton, Philip Harrison, James F.
Carpenter, William P. Fowler, F.L.Dent, James E.
Higdon, C.C.Digges, Peter W. Robey, Rufus Robey,
John H. Chappelear, William L. McDaniel, Benjamin
F. Blandford, D.D.Everett, Theodore Dent.

Omitted in 1871

John T. Davis, John I. Jenkins, James A. Franklin,
W.E.W.Rowe, William P. Flowers, Richard Price,
Peter W. Robey, C.C.Digges, John T. Dutton, Charles
C. Perry, J.B.Sheriff, Benjamin F. Blandford, J.W.
Everett, A.T.Moore, F.L.Dent, Townley Robey, Rufus
Robey, John H. Chappelear.

Grand Jurors - 1872 - November Term

William Boswell, Clinton H. Dent, John Hamilton,
John Hancock, J. Hubert Roberts, J.B.Gardiner,
John T. Davis, Francis P. Hamilton, Joseph Price,
James M. Burch, Samuel H. Cox, Richard Price,
Samuel Hanson, Thomas A. Jones, William L. Cook,
John F. Cobey, Benjamin M. Edelen, Thomas M. Posey,
Alfred Q. Lloyd, John R. Murray, Samuel Hawkins,
J.C.Wenk.

1873 - May Term

Hugh Mitchell, George J. Chappelear, Charles L.
Carpenter, Charles H. Wood, R. Barnes, jr., W.W.
Padgett, Alexander Smoot, William L. McDaniel,

John E. Bailey, William N. Bean, Samuel N. Cox,
Philip Harrison, William Nevitt, jr., William A.
Lyon, William F. Dement, G.C.Burch, William W. Cobey,
Edward L. Huntt, Ernest Hanson, use W.W.Padgett,
A.M.Dyer.

Petit Jurors
1872 - November Term

Peregrine Davis, George F. Bealle, T. Yates Roby,
William Wolfe, Charles C. Perry, Charles E. Hannon,
Walter B. Wood, Francis B. Green, James H.M.Dutton,
T. Elzear Gardiner, Edmund Perry, John T. Dutton,
John T. Higdon, Thomas B. Delozier, William H. Cox,
John L. Budd, Joseph A. Gray, William H. Gray,
Francis Price, Thomas K. Ching, William P. Flowers,
B.L.Higdon.

Talismen

Samuel N. Cox, John T. Digges, Benjamin F. Robbins,
William Cox, Lemuel Wilmer, use J.H.Roberts.

1873 - May Term

F.L.Dent, James H. Montgomery, Jere T. Mudd, George
H. Gardiner, George S. Gardiner, Edward N. Stonestreet,
William M. Burch, Charles C. Bowling, Yates Barber,
John W. Jenkins, Edgar Griswold, J.R.Carlin, Henry H.
Bowie, George Dent, John F. Thompson, Thomas R.
Farrall, James H. Gough, Townley Robey, Philip A.
Sasscer, James A. Adams, Thomas L. Hannon, William L.
Cook, omitted in 1871, John I. Jenkins, omitted in
May Term, 1872.

Talismen

John R. Murray, James L. Brawner, John T. Davis,
Thomas O. Hodges, E.L.Clagett, William Cox, T.Yates
Robey.

Witnesses to the Grand Inquest - 1872 -
November Term

George S. Simpson, Thomas B. Delozier, Albin Price,
Thomas W. Wright, George A. Sheckels, Charles P.
Reese, James Garner, William Burke, Henry Lacey,
William Butler, John S. Richmond, Frank Wedge, Henry
Datcher, Peter Wheeler, Lemuel Smoot, Vivian Brent,
John Dement, William McDaniel, A.M.Brook, R.H.Harbin,
Robert Oliver, James H. Gough, Joseph H. Mattingley,

Thomas Skinner, James R. Cracrofts, James H.
Luckett, George Monroe, Theophilus Smoot, Thomas
M. Wolfe, Thomas H. Murray, Henry R. Scott,
George A. Huntt, Mary C. Scott, Richard H. Edelen,
Clem Rozier, Miley Taylor, Allen B. Milstead, Peter
Trotter, Edward Murray, William Hill, sr., Charles
H. Posey, N.J.Miles, Albert Milstead, John G.
Bealle, Joseph T. Herbert, Jane Key, use William
Cox, Thomas E. Grinder, Harriet Grinder, R.C.
Woodburn, Benjamin D. Tubman, J.H.Montgomery,
George F. Baker, Thomas F. Nicholson, J.C.Hayden,
James Mason, John T. Davis, Charles E. Wade, Anna
Allen, William Dunnington, Taylor Hayden, William
Baxter, George A. Huntt, William Trotter, Meyer
Greenbaum

1873 - May Term

Albin Price, Lemuel Smoot, Theophilus Smoot,
William Baxter, Thomas W. Wright, John F. Barber,
use J.M.Latimer & Son, Samuel Smoot, Dennis Smith,
George T. Simpson, F.L.Dent, Thomas J. Latimer,
Benjamin D. Tubman, James Owens, John W. Fowler,
Thomas J. Boswell, George Sewall, James E. Higdon,
William Hill, use William Hamilton, Thomas B.
Delozier

WITNESSES IN STATE'S CASES
1872 - November Term

Charles E. Reese, E.B.Hickman, John Penny, Mary E.
Penny, Sarah Penny, George Crage, Thomas W. Wright,
Eliza Tolson, Joseph Murray, James T. Bateman,
Thomas Newman, Michael Martin, William Butler,
William Burke, James Garner, Henry Lacey, Samuel
McPherson, R.K.Compton, David D. Horton, James H.
Luckett, Jas. B. Cracroft

1872 - July Term

George H. Sheckels, Charles Reese, R.B.Hickman,
James Whaley, Albert Tackey, George Swann

1873 - February Term

Thomas W. Wright, John H. Dement, Joseph Stone,
Robert H. Harbin, Thomas A. Jones, John W. Neale,
B.A.Jameson, Robert J. Lloyd, J.C.Howard

1873 - May Term

Benjamin D. Tubman, John T. Davis, Benjamin P.

Donnelly, Albert Milstead, Robert H. Harbin,
John H. Dement, George A. Huntt, Luther A. Martin,
W. Baxter, E.L.Clagett, Nicholas Contee, James
Owens, Francis Clements, John E. Ware, J.S.Simpson,
C.P.Bailey, H.Luckett, J.B.Cracroft, George P.
Jenkins, James L. Brawner, R.Payne, R.T.Clements,
William Hill

BAILIFFS AND MESSENGERS TO CIRCUIT, ORPHANS' AND COMMISSIONERS' COURTS

Joseph H. Mattingley, J.B.Mattingley, John H.
Jenkins, John D. Covell, H. Turner Rowe

CROW-BILL CERTIFICATES

Thomas S. Dent, John B. Carpenter, William Simmons,
George N. Rowe, William Cox, Timothy A. Smith,
M. Greenbaum, C. Greenbaum, William B. Carpenter,
John J. Brawner, Thomas Skinner, William Boswell
& Co., John T. Colton, George T. Simpson, Joseph
T. Ward, Albert Farrall, Charles C. Perry, E.C.
Dutton, Washington A. Posey, J.M.Latimer & Son,
C.C.Digges, E.P.Maddox, John R. Robertson, John
H. Hancock, William H. Moore, Philip A. Sasscer,
J.W.Warring, Huntt & Norris, B.W.Moore, William
R. Acton, C.C.Murphy, Mason L. McPherson, Jere T.
Mudd, Thomas R. Farrall, R.D.P.Radcliff

COLLECTORS FOR ASSESSMENTS AND INSOLVENCIES

John J. Brawner, Washington Page, Alfred T. Monroe,
Townley Robey, William H. Gray

REGISTRATION

James A. Franklin, William C. Brent, J.H.Freeman,
Marcellus Thompson, Henry R. Scott, Henry M. Hannon,
John H. Chappelear, James A. Mudd, George W.
Carpenter, C.C.Perry, Thomas T. Latimer, Elizabeth
Duffy, C. Greenbaum

RENT OF ELECTION ROOMS

C. Greenbaum, Charles F. Hayden, Elizabeth Duffy,
Charles C. Perry, Thomas H. Murray

COFFINS FOR PAUPERS

William F. Brawner, James L. Brawner, Alex. Dent,
R.S.Corry, Samuel Cox, William Hamilton, Joseph R.

148

Huntt, John W. Warring, Thomas Carrico, E.D.R.
Bean, J.B.Sheriff, William H. Higgs

POST-MORTEM AND JURORS' INQUESTS
Physicians

B.A.Jameson, John H. Reeder, A.M.Brooke,
F.M.Lancaster

Coroners

John T. Colton, Reverdy A. Carlin, James H.M.
Dutton, John F. Bailey

Jurors

P.Harrison, R.H.Clagett, H.Fowler, J.C.Hayden,
L.T.Hayden, M.Hayden, J.Fowler, L.Hayden, J.C.
Russels, F.Mattingley, C.Miles, B.Hayden, T.D.
Hayden, C.C.Perry, A.Hayden, B.G.Hayden, H.R.
Scott, T.M.Briscoe, J.R.Perry, W.Sheirbourn,
Wm. Hamilton, Edwin Dutton, Charles Key, William
Yates, Thomas Wood, J.B.Norris, L.P.Freeman, J.B.
Maddox,R.J.Bailey, Samuel Smith, N.W.Simpson,
W.F.Simpson, A.J.Walker, F.Freeman, J.T.F.Wingate,
James E. Norris

Witnesses

Henry Newman, Josephine Newman

MATERIAL FOR ROADS AND BRIDGES

Walter Mitchell, John H. Posey, Mrs. Ann Harvey,
Henry H. Posey, John Hamilton, William T.
Hindle, Walter R. Franklin, John Grinder, Peter
Wheeler, Alexander Rison, Gerard Rison, Walter
A. Haislip's heirs, Thornton Bell, R.A.Rennoe,
Richard Price, John B. Carpenter, E.F.Mason & Bro.,
Charles H. Wills, Reubin Butler, George Taylor,
R.W.Hanson's heirs, William P. Compton, Edward
J. Sanders, Mason & Green, Henry S. Dent, William
H. Price, John B.F.Burgess, Richard B. Posey,
Cyrus Wheeler, Thomas Posey of Roger, George R.
Posey, Joseph Gray, Thomas C. Allen, William S.
Perry, Mrs. Sarah Floyd, Richard Burgess,
William Boswell, John G. Chapman, Mrs. Sally M.
Sanders, Robert Lawson, Nicholas J. Miles,
Mrs. Margaret Hawkins, Henry R. Harris, Thomas
D. Simpson, Mrs. Glovia Hamersley, Mrs. Lucy
Coffer, J.R.Cassin, Samuel T. Berry, J.L.Hicks,
Edward Sanders' heirs, Hugh Mitchell, John H.

149

Mitchell, J.W.Thomas, Edgar Brawner, George P.
Jenkins, Leonard Marbury, Thomas Jenkins, Mrs.
J.E.Brawner for Highland, Samuel Cox, E. Briscoe,
Mrs. T. Harris, E. Griswold, Patrick Duffy, B.D.
Tubman, Thomas S. Martin, John Delozier's heirs,
Capt. Stackpole, Mrs. John Monroe, Philip A.
Sasscer, W.H.Clagett, James S. Moore, George S.
Moore, Henry Mudd, _____ Keech, Alfred Battles,
Catharine Stewart, C.M.Berry, W.A.Tucker, Thomas
Jenkins' heirs, N.B.Hannon, E.Myers, E.Miles'
heirs, Mary Page, John W. Carrington, Samuel Mudd,
E.D.Boone, George H. Barber, E.D.R. Bean,
Mrs. Jameson, William L. Berry, Philip A. Sasscer,
James T. Farrall, Robert Canter, John Bowling,
George J. Chappelear, Ambrose Adams, Thomas J.
Boarman, Thomas Carrico, George Dent, H.H.Bean,
Josias H. Hawkins, Mason L. McPherson, William
Boarman, Robert Dent, Joseph T. Ward, Samuel Cox,
Andrew G. Chapman, Francis Freeman, Joseph Price,
Philip A. Sasscer

MISCELLANEOUS ITEMS
Estimates to the County Commissioners for Clerk of
the Circuit Court, Register of Wills, Crier of the
Circuit Court, Sheriff, and States' Attorney

Elijah Wells, per account filed
Vivian Brent, Attorney to County Commissioners
John R. Robertson, Clerk to County Commissioners
John W. Mitchell, defense fees
Daniel W. Hawkins, defense fees
Dr. Robert Digges, Medical attendance at jail
William Boswell & Co. tax books and stationery
Charles H. Posey
John D. Covell, Keeper of the Court House

Judge Brent is ill with pleuro-pneumonia. Attended by "Dr. Robert Digges of our village," Dr. Thomas C. Price, consulting physician and on Monday Dr. Allan P. Smith, his family physician when in Baltimore was with him.

John A. Hindle's son left an ear of corn in Editor's office which had 20 rows of 52 grains each--upwards of 1,000 grains!

Thomas A. Burch was married to Ella E. Dement, all of this county at St. Paul's Chapel, Piney, on January 6 by the Rev. Dr. Lewin.

Thomas A. Millar and F. R. Speake, Trustees of School #1 write a protest to Mr. Lloyd, Superintendent.

W.H.Moore gives notice that he plans to leave the county and will remain in Bryantown long enough to settle accounts.

James A. Canan, well digger and pump maker has reduced his prices "to suit the hard times and I will take in exchange for work any kind of stock or grain."

B.D.Tubman advertises that the store house of R.T.Tubman, in Pomonkey, will be rented for another year--has kitchen "with a pump in the yard," barn with granary and stable and two lots, one of which has an orchard.

John W. Carrington, deceased, personal property to be sold. F.C.Carrington and A.J.Norris, administrators.

John M. Latimer, deceased, personal property to be sold at his late residence "Charlesboro'," near Newport. T.T.Latimer and J.B.Latimer, administrators.

Charles H. Wood, deceased. Marion A. Wood and John T. Dutton, administrators.

William Hill deceased. Samuel D. Hill, administrator.

George W. Thompson vs Peter W. Robey - Sheriff's sale of "Green Spot" - 8 acres, addition to same of 10 acres and improvements.

County Commissioners Appoint Constables

1 Election District - no appointments
2 Election District - N.E.Barnes and Richard Posey
3 Election District - A. Judson Groves and Thomas W. Wright

4 Election District - No appointments
5 Election District - Martin Hayden and B. Maddox
6 Election District - No appointments
7 Election District - No appointments
8 Election District - Samuel Smoot and John H. Chappelear
9 Election District - John Lamar

Joseph Murray marries Alberta E. Owen at the rectory on Monday, January 12 by Rev. Dr. Lewin.
Thomas Wilson Tucker died at his residence near Newtown. He left a widow and children. "Notwithstanding the inclemency of the weather his funeral was largely attended. At the grave it was whispered, 'the last of Wilson Tucker--how sad!'"
Richard Farrall, Hughesville, advertises for "Raymond Chapman, colored, who is indentured to me as apprentice, having left my service without my consent..."
Henry Sothoron advertises Havelock, by imported Havelock will stand at stud.
Mrs. Hamilton of Philadelphia advertises "A lady, known to many of the residents of Port Tobacco and vicinity, now residing in Philadelphia, having a superior Teacher for her children, will receive in her family a limited number of young girls, where the comforts of home will be combined with thorough instruction in English, French, German and Music."

[On May 8, 1873, the mast head of this newspaper changed. It now reads "Port Tobacco Times" and the line under it reads "Published at Port Tobacco, Charles County, Maryland every Thursday morning by Elijah Wells, Editor and Proprietor, at Two Dollars Per Annum in Advance" Succeeding pages still carry "Port Tobacco Times and Charles County Advertiser."]

Josias Hawkins advertises attorney at law in Boswell Building, Port Tobacco.

January 23, 1874, Vol. XXX, No. 39

Barnes Compton elected Legislative Treasurer of the State of Maryland for the next two years.
Dr. John T. Digges marries Cassie Mitchell in Baltimore on Thursday, January 15 by the Rev. Mr. Foley.
Mrs. Elizabeth A. Clark died, age 66 years.
J.F.Bradley's residence the scene of a "Pay Ball." "Tickets $1 admitting single gentlemen and ladies; married gentlemen half price."

Dr. Lancaster has introduced several bills in the House of Delegates.

J.T.Mudd, Gallant Green, advertises for hands to cut ties for the Southern Maryland Rail Road. Also, he has for rent blacksmith and wheelwright shop with bellows, anvil, vise and other tools attached.

William W. Ware, deceased - Elizabeth C. Ware and A.G.Chapman administrators.

C.F.Hayden, Allen's Fresh advertises wheelwright and blacksmith work.

Dr. John T. Digges has located himself in Port Tobacco.

John H. Jenkins is an undertaker in Port Tobacco.

R.S.Corry is an undertaker in Newport.

Charles H. Milton, house and sign painter, also hangs wallpaper, in Port Tobacco.

January 30, 1874, Vol. XXX, No. 40

Dr. A.J.Smoot appointed Commissioner to replace Mr. Ware, deceased.

William H. Wade appointed Constable, 1st Election District; William Hicks appointed Constable, 6th Election District; Thomas L. Hannon appointed Constable, 7th Election District.

James Mason's barber shop in Port Tobacco entered and trunk, containing money, was stolen.

Post Office in Marshall Hall discontinued.

R.H.Edelen suit as administrator for W.N.Bean vs William L. Robey "Part of Two Brothers," "Widow's Pleasure," and "Widow's Place" 240 acres to be sold.

February 6, 1874, Vol. XXX, No. 41

George Carpenter caught four men stealing his firewood stacked along banks of Potomac River awaiting shipmant to Alexandria and Washington. Marched them to meathouse and locked them up. Captain of ship who had remained on board made sail for Quantico. Brought back two men. Carpenter, his son and Mr. Mudd who lives with them took white man as decoy and boarded ship. Hand to hand fight took place. Carpenter and his crew prevailed. Captain escaped in small boat. The two men were released and sent home. Other three men in jail and ship moored off Chapel Point waiting for the Captain to come and claim her.

Bernard Tennison marries Ella C. La Motte of Hampstead, Carroll County, at St. John's Catholic

Church, Westminster, on the 27th inst. by Rev.
Father Gloyd.

Richard A. Acton marries Frances O. Canter in
Washington, D.C. on the 29th inst. by Rev.
Charles D. Andrews.

R. Payne, J. Thomas Colton, J.H.Reeder, trustees
of the Primary School #2, 4th Election District
near Allen's Fresh advertise for a teacher.

February 13, 1874, Vol. XXX, No. 42

J.A.Price, Esq. appointed by Governor to be tobacco inspector to serve until March 1 in place of
Barnes Compton, Esq. who resigned.

John W. Mitchell was admitted and qualified as attorney of the Court of Appeals.

William W. Cobey married Bettie, daughter of J.D.
Carpinter at the residence of the bride's
father on 8th inst. by Rev. R. Prout.

Homer B. Hammack married Miss Emmet Deakens in
Nanjemoy on 3rd inst. by Rev. R. Smith.

John T. Bowie married Susannah W. Posey in Nanjemoy on 4th inst. by Rev. R. Smith.

Louis Gwynn married Lucetta Hayden at the residence of Notley Bateman, Esq. in William and
Mary Parish, on 20th inst. by Rev. J.M.Todd.

Nicholas Miles, Esq. married Mamie Thompson of
Baltimore at St. Ignatius Church, Baltimore, on
the 27th ult. by Rev. Father Denny.

J.H.Roberts announces partnership with Thomas T.
Owen - name of company J.H.Roberts & Co.

N.E.Berry, trustee for Thomas Mason advertises
for sale farm and fishery "Upper Goose Bay" on
Potomac River adjoining Budd's Ferry, 700 acres,
frame dwelling, tobacco and grain barn, stable,
carriage house, corn house, meat house, two laborers' houses and other farm buildings. Across
river is "Quantico" rail road station and steamboat landing from which a steam ferry to Maryland
is contemplated.

Walter H. Stone administrator for Jesse J. Stone,
deceased.

Charles H. Scroggins administrator for William F.
Scroggins, deceased.

February 20, 1874, Vol. XXX, No. 43

Washington Burch, colored bailiff of County Commissioners was in court - was told that court appointed its own bailiffs. He said he was directed
by the County Commissioners to attend.

Col. J.S.Ammon operates sawmill near Cox's Station
and James A. Mudd's sawmill near Bryantown "doing at profitable business. Success to enter-
prise!"
Mrs. Mary R. Covell, wife of John D. died in Port
Tobacco on Saturday p.m. last of typhoid pneumonia, 42 years old.
"Farmers' and Planters' Mutual Aid
Association if the State of Maryland"

George H. Hardiner, Dr. S.A.Mudd, T.B.Robey, Dr.
W.J.Boarman, J.T.Mudd, B.F.Bowling, Dr. P.W.
Hawkins, T.P.Turner, William Queen, B.M.Edelen
elected.
F.P.Hamilton administrator for J.H.Neale, dec.
Mary E. Carrington, administrator for John
Carrington, deceased, personal property for
sale.

February 27, 1874, Vol. XXX, No. 44

Charles County Appointments

Justices of the Peace - 1st E.D. - William Boswell;
2nd E.D. - Henry H. Bowie and Allen B. Milstead;
3rd E.D. - William P. Flowers and Thomas E. Bowie;
4th E.D. - John T. Colton, Edward L. Smoot;
5th E.D. - Charles H. Posey; 6th E.D. - Thomas C.
Wilkinson and Joseph Stewart; 7th E.D. - Richard W.
Bryan; 8th E.D. - Thomas Carrico, G.C.Burch and
Henry Turner, Sr.; 9th E.D. - Edward D.R.Bean.
Officers of Registration - 1st E.D. - Joseph I.
Lacey; 2nd E.D. - Robert Ryson; 3rd E.D. - George
W. Carpenter; 4th E.D. - John H. Freeman; 5th E.D. -
Henry R. Scott; 6th E.D. - John Hancock; 7th E.D. -
Henry M. Hannon; 8th E.D. - James A. Mudd; 9th E.D. -
William Turner.
John H. Mitchell, Esq. declines to accept re-appoint-
ment as school commissioner.
George W. Makell married Sarah E. Leland at the resi-
dence of the bride's father the 12th inst. by Rev.
William J. Chiles.
Edith Wilmer died, youngest and beloved daughter of
William and Mary F. Boswell. She was 17 years, 2
months and 7 days old. "...The same father's
hand which led her to her first Communion, sustained
her bodily weakness at her last. As hand in hand
she went to the altar two years ago..."
Leonard Smallwood Robey died on 7 January after
several months illness. He was 74 years old, the

second child of Major Townley and Annie Robey and
grandson of William Marbury Smallwood. "...On
the morning of the day of his death he told his
household that he would die that day...it was not
until about 9 o'clock in the evening that his
family became really alarmed. From that time he
sank rapidly, and breathed his last without a
struggle or a groan, in a few minutes thereafter."
G.M.Lloyd,appointed by the Governor to the State
Board of Education.
Alfred P. Willett died at his residence Monday last
of pneumonia. "...He was a thriving citizen,
industrious almost to a fault..."
John M. Latimer, deceased, and Susan Latimer, wife -
real estate to be valued and divided. George M.
Lloyd, John L. Budd, J. Thomas Colton, John B.
Lyon and S. Cox, Commissioners.

March 6, 1874, Vol. XXX, No. 45

Dr. Samuel Mudd is chief officer of the Bryantown
Grange.
Sheriff William L. Cooke took the three prisoners
from the ship to Baltimore for trial.
Mrs. Mary Jane Randell died at Clifton on 10
February. She was 29 years old.
John William Cash died at Tompkinsville. He was
24 years old. "Willie, thou has left us,
We regret thy broken life,
Link by link 'twas severed -
Death has won the fearful strife..."
Charles E. Hannon, Clerk to the County Commissioners,
advertises for 10 cords of wood for the Court House.
County Commissioners Appoint Road Supervisors

1st E.D. - Joseph E. Sanders; 2nd E.D. - William E.
Burtles; 3rd E.D. - James L. Hicks; 4th E.D. - John
S. Gibbons. Fifth Corps - Christopher Blair, colored.
Sandy A. Butler mortgage to James Massey, property
"Margaret Ogleton" between Pomonkey Creek and farm
of William H. Clagett, running with main road to
Semmes Hill. Sale at Court House door. Sarah
Massey, assignee of mortgage.
James F. Matthews, attorney at Port Tobacco.

March 13, 1874, Vol. XXX, No. 46

Dr. A.D.Cobey, dentist, has been absent from county
during winter, has returned to practice in Port
Tobacco.

Mary R. Covell died on February 14. She was 41
years, 17 days old. She was the wife of John D.
Covell and leaves three children. "She was an
affectionate wife and mother, and devoted to the
care of her family..."

March 27, 1874, Vol. XXX, No. 48

Crescentia Grange Formed

Master - Hugh Mitchell; Overseer - John G. Chapman;
Lecturer - John H. Mitchell; Steward - William B.
Fergusson; Asst. Steward - William P. Compton;
Treasurer - Samuel Cox, Jr.; Secretary - William
Boswell; Gate Keeper - Isaiah Roby; Chaplain -
John W. Albrittain, Sr.; Ceres - Mrs. Mary R.
Mitchell; Pomona - Mrs. Cecilia W. Mitchell; Flora-
Miss Lizzie Hawkins; Lady Asst. Steward - Miss
Emily Hawkins.
Oliver N. Bryan's name prominently named as appoint-
ment to Commission of Fisheries of the State.
J. Cocking and Mrs. Sarah Floyd have agreed to pro-
vide suitable pond for cultivation of trout.
Andrew Jackson Smoot administrator for James R.
Tompkins, deceased.

Delinquent Tax Payers
Samuel Baggot's heirs - "Baggot's Boot," 60 acres.
Reybold - wharf and lot attached

Thomas K. Ching, William A. Lyon and Samuel T.
Swann, trustees for Colored School #1, 4th E.D.,
schoolhouse located near Newport Episcopal Church
needs teacher "...Either white or colored who can
furnish (second grade) certificate."

April 10, 1874, Vol. XXX, No. 50

F. Richard Burgess married Lizzie, youngest daughter
of John Cocking, Esq. on 31 ultimo by Rev.
Robert Prout.
John E. Edwards married Mary E. Stewart at St.
Thomas' Church on 8th inst. by Rev. F. McAtee.
Hon. A.G.Chapman appointed by Governor to be In-
spector General. "...Duties mainly to inspect
generous wines and fine dinners of which the
Governor and his Staff may be invited to partake
on public occasions. Long may General Chapman
add weight and grace to the militia of the State!"
John Mason, colored man of intemperate habits, found
dead on path not far from house where he lived on
Judge Jenkins' farm.

Andrew G. Chapman, A.M. gave commencement address
at St. John's College. "reflects great credit
upon our esteemed fellow-citizen."
Dr. George D. Mudd, State Senator from Charles
County furnished Editor a copy of report of Commission to adjust boundary between Maryland and
Virginia.
Charles H. Wills, Esq. presented Editor with bouquet
formed by daughter, Lottie. "...We accept it as
a good-will (Wills') offering."
J. Thomas Colton of Allen's Fresh has blooded
filly for sale.

April 17, 1874, Vol. XXX, No. 51

Grand Jurors

Samuel N. Cox, William Wolfe, George S. Gardiner,
George W. Berry, Joseph B. Gardiner, Thomas K.
Ching, Thomas S. Dent, Francis McWilliams, Yates
Barber, George W. Carpenter, William N. Bean,
George Digges, Thomas P. Gray, Charles C. Hardy,
John E. Bailey, Jere W. Burch, William A. Boarman,
James A. Mudd, John Hamilton, E.D.R.Bean, James H.
Montgomery, Thomas M. Posey, S.W.H.McPherson.

Petit Jurors

Joseph Price, Benjamin F. Bowling, John H. Hancock,
Ambrose Adams, John W. Halley, Samuel W. Adams,
Edgar Brawner, Albin Price, Marcellus Burch,
Reagan Deakins, Edward L. Huntt, G.C.Burch, John F.
Thompson, Francis Price, Townley Robey, Joseph T.
Ward, William L. Harding, D.I.Sanders, Mason L.
McPherson, James H.M.Dutton, Thomas C. Wilkerson,
Joseph S. Boarman, James A. Cochran, John W.
Boarman, Benoni W. Hardy.
James and Cutler Mason, two colored citizens, nearly
drowned in Port Tobacco Creek. Jim is the Port
Tobacco barber. "...We are glad we are not called
upon to say -- tho it may appear selfish in us --
that 'our loss is his gain.'"
William Kendrick died Sunday last, 12th inst. 69 years.
Margaret Willett and Richard Willett, administrators
for Alfred P. Willett, deceased.
A.W.Marlow tells of narrow escapt on road at hands of
"young bloods with fast teams and fine buggies..."
Washington Page, Collected for 2nd E.D., says pay taxes.
F. Stone advertises yoke of oxen for sale.

April 24, 1874, Vol. XXX, No. 52

Dr. Henry R. Scott, while handling tobacco in his barn, fell 8-10', struck his head against a timber, and was "killed almost instantly." He resided in lower section of the county, for a long time "an esteemed and valuable inhabitant of Port Tobacco." Born in St. Mary's County, he spent his early manhood in Prince Frederick. He was about 59 years old "a man of gentle and pleasing manners - kind-hearted-industrious, and withal a good manager upon the farm."

Rev. William J. Chiles died at his residence the 18th inst. He was 64 years old. A native of Caroline County, Virginia, he resided in Charles County for the last 37 years and for the same length of time, was pastor of the Baptist Church. "He was a most useful citizen, an ornament to society and died as he had lived--without an enemy."

F.D.Gardiner and William Queen dispute letter of A.W.Marlow concerning a buggy accident near Beantown.

James H. Neale, deceased, property "Mount Air" being sold at public sale at Court House. 588 acres on Potomac River ½ mile from Baltimore and Potomac Rail Road - dwelling house and all necessary out-houses, such as barns, stables and some tenant houses.

John B. Maddox has fine young jack "Blue Dick" to be let to mares "at my stables, near Cox's Station..."

Washington Page, Collector, 2nd E.D. requests taxes to be paid.

May 1, 1874, Vol. XXXI, No. 1

E. Wells notes that 30 years have passed since the Port Tobacco Times began. "Whether it has been faithful and beneficial to any degree to the interests of our community is for others to say, but we do say that it has been untiring in its efforts to that purpose with a zeal that has never flagged. Thirty years ago! We were young then, we are old now..." "With thanks to our friends, and with zeal unabated, we shall continue our efforts to make the Times worthy of their patronage."

Governor Appoints County Assessors

1 E.D. - John T. Davis, George A. Huntt, William H. Gray;

159

2 E.D. - Richard P. Wall, Josias Hawkins, John T.
Crismond.

County Commissioners appoint Collectors
of County and State Taxes

1 E.D. - William B. Carpenter;
2 E.D. - Francis McWilliams:
3 E.D. - John A. Marlow;
4 E.D. - George J. Chappelear. William H. Welch,
"fellow townsman" declined to let his name go before Board, citing his present ill health.
Samuel Smith and G.T.Simpson dissolve partnership.
New name is G.T.Simpson.
Mrs. Alice A. Payne opened new stock of spring and
summer millinery at Allen's Fresh.
J.T.Thomas - delinquent taxpayer.

June 26, 1874, Vol. XXXI, No. 9

Oliver N. Bryan obtained patent for fish hatching
box. "We know our friend from Pomonkey was
science on bugs, birds, etc., but we did not know
before that he was an inventive genious.--But
then he is a bachelor and has no other way to occupy his time!"

Agricola Grange formed in Pomonkey

Townley Robey organized and the following officers
were elected:
Master - Thomas R. Halley;
Overseer - R.W.Bryan;
Lecturer - W.E.W.Rowe;
Chaplain - B.W.B.McPherson;
Steward - H.M.Thomas;
A. Steward - R.A.Chapman;
Treasurer - B.D.Tubman;
Secretary - A.W.Thomas;
Gate Keeper - E.H.Brawner;
Ceres - Mrs. J.S.Warren;
Pomona - Mrs. R.K.Compton;
Flora - Mrs. B.D.Tubman;
Lady A. Steward - Miss M.A.Cox
Thomas Gross, proprietor of Marshall Hall, invites
PEOPLE OF THE COUNTY to a pic-nic July 4th. "...
There will be no boats at the wharf on that day,
and no fighting or disturbance likely to occur."
Samuel Contee, John T. Colbert, George W. Dyson,
Committee, announce first anniversary celebration
of Young Men's Moral and Mental Improvement Associ-
ation of Charles County at Wingate's Grove near
Shiloh M.E.Church. Rev. C.W.Walker, annual orator.

Thomas A. Millar warns owners of trespassing
stock.
John F. Semmes, deceased, property sold at Court
House door "Tompkin's Purchase," 270 acres, adjoining property known as Tompkinsville, fronts
on Cuckhold Creek - commodious dwelling - 7 rooms-
4 good tenant houses - out-houses - steam or sail
vessels at its own shore. J.C.Hayden and wife
complainants vs John B. Harrison and wife and
others, defendants.
William Boswell administrator, James Swann deceased.
William S. Chiles administrator, William J. Chiles,
deceased.
Mary J.C.Welch and Thomas T. Owen administrators,
William H. Welch, deceased.
B.Z.Tennison administrator, B.P.Donnelly, deceased.
William S. Chiles administrator, Henly Barnes,
deceased.
J.T.Thomas' property "Molly's Delight" and "Simp-
son's Delight" sold for taxes.
Thomas E. Bowie administrator, Samuel C. Dent,
deceased.
B.Z.Tennison advertises for rent store house - lot
and orchard adjoining - good barn, stable and
carriage house owned by late B.P.Donnelly at
Allen's Fresh.

July 3, 1874, Vol. XXXI, No. 11

Governor Appoints Officers of Registration
3 E.D. - T.A.Smith, vice George W. Carpenter, re-
signed;
5 E.D. - Washington Page, vice H.R.Scott, deceased.
J.R.Wilmer graduated from St. John's College in
Annapolis.
Mitchell, youngest son of Richard F. and Violetta B.
Nelson died on 18 June, 7 years old.
S.F.Gardiner, William L. Harding, William N. Hamilton,
Samuel T. Berry, George S. Gardiner, Thomas B.
Berry, Dominick Mudd, J.W.F.Bealle, citizens of
the 6th E.D. apply for public road: commencing at
public road on Mattawoman Swamp, near residence of
S.F.Gardiner; east thru Gardiner's farm to gate
between Dominick Mudd and Gardiner; north to Mudd's
Mill - 1 mile; east thru estate of Daniel Monroe's
heirs and portion of Thomas B. Berry's farm inter-
secting Washington and Port Tobacco road; distance
of 2 miles. "Road now used as public road and is
the only road to Mudd's Mill, Beantown Station and
other public roads from this section."

161

July 10, 1874, Vol. XXXI, No. 11
(No. 11 is same number shown on
issue for July 3)

"Goose Bay" farm belonging to Mason estate has been
sold to man from North for $9000 cash.

A locust tree near Mr. Bateman's house on land of
William Boswell, Esq. was struck by lightning.
John G. Chapman's barn at "Glen Albin" also
struck by lightning.

Joseph R. Wilmer will deliver the Salutatory oration
at St. John's College commencement.

Olive Grange organized at "Hard Bargain" in Picawaxen

Master — Dr. A.J.Smoot
Overseer — Francis Maddox
Lecturer — William McKenny Burroughs
Chaplain — C.A.F.Shaw
Steward — B.G.Harris
A. Steward — P.A.L.Contee
Treasurer — I.J.Lancaster
Secretary — J.M.Page
Gate Keeper — Washington Page
Ceres — Mrs. Nannie W. Smoot
Pomona — Mrs. Nannie G. Hungerford
Flora — Miss Lizzie Hungerford
Lady A. Steward — Mrs. I.J.Lancaster

Fourth of July Celebration by Colored Citizens of Charles County, Maryland

Young Men's Moral and Mental Improvement Association
of Charles County, Maryland held its first annual
at Wingate's Grove. Rev. C.W.Walker was not present.
Moses A. Hopkins, late graduate from Lincoln University, Chester County, Pennsylvania agreed to speak.
President is J.W.Dyson. The Shiloh Chorus under the
direction of Alonzo Sims sang. J.B.Key led in prayer.
The debate "Do inventions have tendency to improve
conditions of laboring class?" was decided in the
negative. M.A.Hopkins, J.B.Norris, Jr. and William
J. Norris, Jr., Judges. N.W.Dyson, Recording Secretary.

B.L.Higdon asks owner of black spotted sow to take
their property from his farm.

July 17, 1874, Vol. XXXI, No. 12

Columbus Robey married Louisa Robey on 24 June at the
residence of Thomas McDaniel, the bride's brother-
in law. Rev. W.H.Seat married the couple.

162

Charles E. Fowler married Rachel A. Beall in Bal-
timore on the 5th inst. by Rev. G.W.Hobbs.
Hezekiah Franklin died at his residence near Hill-
Top on the 11th inst. He was 84 years old and a
soldier of the War of 1812.
F.L.Boarman advertises a pair of young sorrel
horses and a yoke of young oxen for sale.
C.C.Bowling has a public sale of personal property
"...intending to leave the county..."
Percival Padgett, son of late J.T.Padgett of Port
Tobacco passed examination in Greek in the Sopho-
more class, cum honore, at Trinity College in
Hartford, Connecticut.
Mrs. M. Jameson's dwelling house and kitchen consumed by fire -- near Beantown. "...no insurance...we trust that aid will be extended promptly so as to enable the unfortunate sufferers to
meet the needs of the coming winter."
James F. Matthews, trustee, sold farm in Cobb Neck
to F. Stone, Esq. for $1,000.00.

July 31, 1874, Vol. XXXI, No. 14

James F. Owens, boot and shoemaker, Port Tobacco.
W.H.Stone and Sons want to rent farm.
Miss R.V.Mudd's school #3, 6th E.D. will have exhibition.
Charlotte Reed vs Richard Wade case in Circuit Court.
Charlotte Reed filed petition for revocation or
annulment of indenture of apprenticeship of her
son to Capt. Wade.
John M. Whitty bought of late William W. Ware
"Lothair" 11 acres, 3 roods bounded on the west
by the Baltimore and Potomac Rail Road and on
the east by the county road to Port Tobacco -
large and well-arranged storehouse - small dwelling house, blacksmith shop "...and a pump of excellent water in the yard..." R.H.Edelen, trustee.
John W. Mitchell, trustee, sells property "...at
La Plata Station..." farm 175 acres - 1 mile above
La Plata - ¼ mile to rail road - small dwelling -
farm of late Mark L. Semmes.
George N. Rowe of White Plains died. 65 years old.
Crier of Orphans' Court and Circuit Court for 25
years "...always been a consistent and earnest
member of the Methodist Church."

Officers of Juvenile Base Ball Club

President - J.W.Shackelford
Vice President - J.E.Stewart
Secretary - J.R.Lacey

163

Treasurer - John Matthews
Capt. 1st Nine - H.H.Boswell
Capt. 2nd Nine - John Stewart

J.Richard Cox, teacher school #2, 4th E.D. an-
nounces examination.
Thomas C. Wilkerson, Justice of the Peace, had
John A. Marlow before him asking owner of a cow
to remove it from his property.
Thomas M. Welch, Overseer of Poor, has resigned.
William F. Hammack administrator, Eleanor Barnes,
deceased.
Richard H. Edelen and John W. Mitchell trustees,
B.P.Donnelly, deceased, sell property "Thomas's
Plague," etc. 200 acres - dwelling, tobacco
barn, out-houses, small tenement - lying on Gil-
bert Swamp above village of Newport.

September 18, 1874, Vol. XXXI, No. 21

James Somervell, Esq. died - resided in Charles
County for several years. He was Inspector of
#4 Tobacco Warehouse.
J.W.Mitchell and R.H.Edelen, trustees, will sell
several farms and small tracts of land belonging
to the late Peter Wheeler. The property consists
of a small farm of 35 acres, upon which he resided - new and comfortable 2 story dwelling -
store house - stable and out-houses - suitable
for a country business; 118 acre farm adjoins
the above; farm in Chicamuxen of 250 acres, comfortable dwelling, necessary outbuildings; 45
acres near last mentioned; 1 or 2 acres on
Smallwood Church Road - small house used as store
and dwelling; 100 acre farm on Ward's Run - log
house and corn house.
Benton Burgess' dwelling house entirely consumed
by fire.

Registration Notices

Joseph I. Lacey, Officer of Registration, E.D.#1
Robert E. Rison,   "   "   "   , E.D.#2
Timothy A. Smith,   "   "   "   , E.D.#3
Samuel G. Lancaster,   "   "   "   , E.D.#4
Washington Page,   "   "   "   , E.D.#5
John H. Hancock,   "   "   "   , E.D.#6
Henry M. Hannon,   "   "   "   , E.D.#7
James A. Mudd,   "   "   "   , E.D.#8
William Turner,   "   "   "   , E.D.#9

W.W.Cobey advertises a lot of fine breeding ewes.

P.A.Sasscer, A.W.Marlow, John T. Langley advertise for a teacher at school #6, E.D.#6.
Mary A. Scott advertises a sale of personal
property.
T.A.Smith, F.Dunnington and J.H.Henderson advertise for teacher at school #3, 3 E.D.
Alice McNantz lost a bundle containing a gold cross,
silver medal, etc. on road near Centreville. Re-
ward at Huntt and Norris, Centreville.
Mrs. Amanda E.D.Brawner died, wife of James L.
Brawner, Esq. on Tuesday at her residence. "...
Mrs. Brawner had nearly reached the limit assigned
by the Palmist for human life, being in the 61st
year of her age..." She left nine children.
William Nevitt, Jr., deceased was honored by mem-
bers of Zachiah Grange, Patrons of Husbandry -
J. Thomas Colton, A.W.Neale, George Dent, Jr.,
Committee and Peter W. Robey, Secretary.
Allison Hicks, deceased, property to be sold
"Friendship" and "Two Sisters" 300 acres in Bean-
town neighborhood - dwelling, kitchen, barn
and other out-houses.
Dr. William R. Wilmer announces Republican Candi-
date for Congress.
Samuel Baggot heirs' property to be sold for taxes.
Samuel C. Moran, deceased, property sold at
Patuxent City - 237 acres.
Mary M. Moran, deceased, property assessed as her
dower sold, 184 acres - dwelling house, several
barns, necessary out-buildings - 2½ miles from
Patuxent City between Woodville and Patuxent City.
Belt, Williams and Co. vs John F. Parker, Equity
Court.
H.H.Bowie administrator, Hezekiah Franklin deceased.
B.I.Edelen, insolvent.
Z.R.Morgan, guardian, etc. vs E.F.L.Robertson.

September 25, 1874, Vol. XXXI, No. 22

Joseph Hunter, canny Scotchman from Glasgow, has
taken over the bakery in Port Tobacco and "...
proposes to make all of our good wives happy by
furnishing them with a superior quality of bread..."
Francis N. Digges addressed Zachiah Grange.

Peter Wheeler's Property Sold

Albin Price bought store property-32 acres-$1,000
Albin Price bought small adjoining tract-$351.50.
James D. Milstead bought farm at Chicamuxen near
church-$955.
James D. Milstead bought small (1½acres) adjoining
tract-$145.

Charles Hart, colored, bought 45acres-$250.
Capt. R.V.Welch bought 100 acres on Ward's Run-
$475.
Total $3,176.50
James R. Perry married Miss R.D.Scott in Washington,
D.C. on Sept. 21 by Rev. Father McCarthy.

Judges of Election

1 E.D. - Nicholas Stonestreet, C.J., George P.
Jenkins, Peregrine Davis;
2 E.D. - James A. Franklin, C.J., Daniel J.
Bragonier, James D. Milstead;
3 E.D. - George M. Barnes, C.J., Alexander Haislip,
James Harvey;
4 E.D. - Samuel Hawkins, C.J., Joseph N. Harrison,
Samuel T. Swann;
5 E.D. - Yates Barber, C.J., John B. McWilliams,
John M. Page;
6 E.D. - J.B.Sheriff, C.J., Henry E. Mudd, George
F. Beall;
7 E.D. - L.M.Sutherland, C.J., William DeC.
Mitchell, Theodore Dent;
8 E.D. - E.D.Boone, C.J., Thomas I. Boarman,
Philemon A. Sasscer;
9 E.D. - Thomas E. Gardiner, C.J., E.D.R.Bean,
Henry Gardiner.
Mary C. Clements died August 26th, wife of Thomas
A. Clements, 35 years old. Member Holy Catholic
Church.
A.G.Chapman, administrator, Gerard W. Hungerford,
complainant vs George Dent, Sr., defendant -
"Prospect Hill" to be sold at Court House door -
450 acres on Potomac River at Pope's Creek, ter-
minus of Baltimore and Potomac Rail Road, opposite
Matthias Point, Virginia "...comfortable, capa-
cious brick mansion in good condition and neces-
sary out-buildings..." S.Cox, Jr., trustee.
Bernard Z. Tennison, administrator, Benjamin P.
Donnelly to sell "Westwood Manor" - 100 acres -
lies on both sides of road from Newport to Centreville, adjoins lands of Thomas Carrico, Thomas
Higdon, Lucretia Lancaster and Joseph Wathen...
has upon it a small dwelling."
J.W.Waring and S.A.Miles, administrators, Edward
Miles, deceased.

October 2, 1874, Vol. XXXI, No. 23

"...road from Dent's Mill to Tolson's Wharf via
Poplar Spring School House and Tayloe's Mill..."

Daniel Webster Hawkins, a public official, came
   to the office of the Times and stopped his paper,
   thinking that no criticism of him is proper by
   the Editor.
W.L.Robey's property sold for the third or fourth
   time, this time to the Hon. F. Stone for $300.
   "...We would advise the purchaser to swap it off
   for a bull pup and then drown the pup. He would
   thus get rid of both land and pup..."
Samuel Cox, Jr. received no bids for "Prospect
   Hill." He later sold it to Dr. William R. Wilmer
   for $4800.

Tournament and Ball at Cox Station

Affair under the auspices of the "Social Club" of
   this neighborhood.
   Chief Marshal - Samuel Cox, Jr.;
   Aids,- R.C.Fergusson, F.P.Hamilton;
   Heralds - J.T.Crismond, A.W.Neale, B.G.Harris,
   William Queen, W.P.Jameston;
   Judges - F.W.Weems, Thomas Simms, Hugh Mitchell,
   Capt. W.F.Dement, William P. Compton;
   Committee of Arrangements - A.W.Neale, Hughes
   Wills, John T. Davis, C.A.Neale, C.C.Digges;
   Treasurer - James Bateman.

Festival and Tournament held at "Hard Bargain" for Benefit of William & Mary Parish

B.G.Harris crowned Mrs. Nellie Crane Queen of Love
   and Beauty;
Washington Page, Jr. crowned Miss Wattles of Alexandria 1st Maid of Honor;
William Gough crowned Cornelia Burroughs 2nd Maid
   of Honor; and
William Posey crowned Miss E.E.Burroughs 3rd Maid
   of Honor. Profit from festival $385.00.

Mrs. Cecilia Miles died "...passed to the Better
   Land...from her earliest youth, when a white dove
   flew into the room where she was preparing for
   church and alighted near her, to the hour of her
   holy death, her character was remarkable for its
   purity, sincerity and perfect unselfishness..."
E.D.Turner advertises that a lady living four miles
   from Port Tobacco having engaged the services of
   a governess for her daughters, would receive
   three or four young Pupils as boarders.
John Cocking advertises one sheep stolen from his
   home "Retreat."

John H. Cox, H.W.Robey and F.B.Green, trustees
at Bensville school, 6th E.D. advertise for a
teacher.

Vivian Brent writes to Editor complaining about
article in Independent which falsified facts
about his altercation with Mr. Hawkins. "Mr.
Button, whose name appears at head of Independent,
informs me that the article in question was
written by the Hon. F. Stone, who is the proprietor of the paper...in his character as a public
journalist it is his duty to ascertain the truth
and to publish that alone..."

J.W.Waring and S.A.Miles administrators for Edward
Miles, deceased, sell personal property at deceased late residence in Pomonkey district.

Ann Edelen, Laura Edelen and Maria Edelen vs Benjamin P. Donnelly. Sale $2600.

October 16, 1874, Vol. XXXI, No. 25

A grand tournament and fox race will be held at "Bunker Hill" owned by W.B.Wood near Allen's Fresh.

John Thomas, Allen's Fresh, writes comical letter
to friend, Elijah Wells.

Republican Meeting in Port Tobacco

John W. Mitchell, Esq. called meeting to order.
John Hamilton, Esq. elected President; Thomas M.
Posey, John H. Cox, Joseph B. Gardiner and John T.
Crismond - Vice Presidents; Thomas R. Farrall and
E. Wells - Secretaries. Dr. Eli J. Henkle, can-
didate for Congress spoke.

R.H.Edelen, trustee, sells at Court House door
property of George W. Robey "Dolley's Purchase,"
"Griffin's Seat," "Ferrall" and "Ferrall's Addition - 233 acres. Property located one mile from
White Plains station on Baltimore and Potomac Rail
Road - dwelling house, two tenement houses, barn,
stable, corn house and out-buildings.

John H. Mitchell warns trespassers on "Hanson Hill."

John W. Mitchell, trustee Equity Court case will sell
at public sale "Oak Grove" on Cobb Neck on Neal's
Creek near Lancaster's Wharf - 250 acres - dwelling house and out-buildings.

R.H.Edelen, trustee George Bailey, deceased will sell
"Pennsylvania" 254 acres on Cuckhold's Creek - two
dwelling houses, two barns, out-buildings and store
house where good business could be done.

Francis A. Posey sells "White Hall" - 393 acres adjoins St. Thomas' Estate on Potomac River - formerly owned by Mrs. E.A.Middleton.

Brother William M. Morris' death will be mourned
at Masonic meeting.
Cox's Station "a thriving town, with its hotel,
stores, dwelling houses, machine shops, and its
newly finished 'Grangers' Hall' for public purposes" held tournament. Samuel Cox, Jr. - Chief
Marshal. John H. Mitchell addressed gathering
in place of D.I.Sanders.

Knights	Names
Allen's Fresh	E. Posey
Lost Cause	L. Burch
Modoc	R. Martin
St. George	Reed Wills
St. John	J. Maddox
Charlotte Hall	A. Carrico
Patuxent	J. Wall
Arlington	C. Neale
Bryantown	G. Carrico
Oakvale	H. Carrico
Normandy	W. Mitchell
Sir Percival	W. Page
Brittania	T. Cocking
Beverly	V. H. Neale
Manor	C. Howard
Oakley	J. H. Hawkins, Jr.
Grange	James Bean
Port Tobacco	R. D. Digges

Queen of Love and Beauty - Miss Nannie Hawkins
1st Maid of Honor - Miss J. Boarman
2nd Maid of Honor - Miss Annie Stone
3rd Maid of Honor - Miss Linie Wills

Virginia Mudd and Sylvester Mudd, administrators of
J.T.Mudd, deceased, will rent store house, dwell-
ing house, barn, blacksmith shop at Gallant Green.
F.P.Hamilton, William Dows and William B. Fergusson
warn trespassers on "Oakland," "Rosemary Lawn,"
and "Cedar Hill."
P.H.Murphy warns trespassers on "Greenland."
Frederick William Linton married Sarah A. Gray at
Nanjemoy Episcopal Church on Wednesday, Oct. 7
by Rev. Robert Prout
        "Its right, since 'tis ordained,
            That man should wed,
            The law's obeyed,
            May happiness be had."

William M. Morris, Esq. died at his residence
near Port Tobacco Monday a.m. last 19th inst.
after a protracted and painful illness. He was
43 years, 3 months, 3 days old. "He died in the
communion of the Episcopal Church .."

November 6, 1874, Vol. XXXI, No. 28

Thomas D. Simpson died at his residence in the
County Tuesday last. He was 67 years old.
Master Thomas W. Norris died at Centreville 2nd
inst. of congestive fever. He was the son of
A.J. & Elizabeth C. Norris. He was 13 years,
2 months, 1 day old.
Peter Wood died in GeorgeTown Tuesday a.m. last of
apoplexy. He was 64 years old.
Joseph I Lacey advertises new fall and winter
goods in store in Port Tobacco "...our friend
across the street."
B.L.Higdon warns trespassers on "Locust Hill."
William B. Matthews and William Boswell warn trespassers on "Plenty" and "Chandler's Hope."
F.B.Green's residence was to have been the scene of
a party to benefit Pomfret Church - postponed
indefinitely.
Dr. Lewin has been absent for several weeks attending the General Episcopal Convention in New York
as a delegate.
E. Briscoe's property "Part of Clark's Inheritance"
270 acres sold for taxes.
Theodore Gross advertises that he has just opened
a store house at "Oak Grove," formerly occupied
by R.T.Tubman.
Thomas I. Milstead found off Craney Island, a gunning skiff, 15' long, painted a lead color.
F.W.Weems and J.B.Norris warn trespassers on "Fair-
view" and "Mount Republic."

November 13, 1874, Vol. XXXI, No. 29

Robert Cutler Fergusson married Katie S. Fergusson
at Christ Church, Port Tobacco Tuesday Nov. 10
by Rev. Dr. Lewin.
E. Hyland Brawner married Maggie J., daughter of
the late Dr. Edward & Cecilia A. Miles at St.
Charles Church the 4th inst. by Rev. Father McAtee.
Charles Howell of "Federal Hill" near Hughesville
has melodeon for sale.
J.G.Chapman and Margaret Stone warn trespassers.
M.C.Morris and Henry G. Robertson, trustees for
William Morris, deceased.
Thomas Croft warns trespassers on "Spring Gardens."

Rev. F. McAtee and Rev. Mr. Wiget conduct a re-
ligious retreat or mission at St. Thomas - as-
sisted by Rev. Messrs Murer and Guibitosi. Rev.
Mr. Wiget was pastor here about 20 years ago.
William M. Morris funeral Masonic order. Part of
it was conducted in Lodge room and then moved to
Piney where service and burial took place.
Present: Henry G. Robertson - Master; James L.
Brawner - Senior Warden; J. Hubert Roberts -
Junior Warden; John G. Chapman - Treasurer; John
S. Button - Secretary; George Taylor - Senior
Deacon; W.A.Fowke - Junior Deacon; A.D.Coby and
John J. Brawner - Stewards; Rev. Dr. Lewin -
Acting Chaplain; Samuel Cox, Jr., - Acting Mar-
shal; William Wolfe - Tiler. Members: Edgar
Griswold, William E. Dement, F. Stone, Josias
Hawkins, W.E.W.Rowe, Lemuel Smoot, W.H.S.
Taylor, Vivian Brent.

November 20, 1874, Vol. XXXI, No. 30

Zachariah T. Hayden, near Harris' Lot Post Office,
certifies he took a stray red cow. James H.M.
Dutton, Justice of the Peace.
F. Hughes Wills married Mary Digges, daughter of
the late John H. Digges, on Tuesday last 17th
at the residence of the bride's brother.
W.E.W.Rowe warns trespassers.
Thomas M. Ratcliff warns trespassers on "Wellington."

Circuit Court Cases

Michael Heard - riotous and disorderly conduct -
one month in Jail, fine $10.00.
Robert Brown, colored, convicted of rape on Martha
Kelly, colored - Penitentiary 10 years.
Henry Williams, colored, convicted of stealing a
calf - Penitentiary 2 years, 6 months.
Alexander Simms indicted for assault with intent to
kill Daniel Mullen - guilty, fined $15.00.
Wedding vs Robey; State vs James Burfy - larceny -
guilty, sentenced to Penitentiary 2 years, 6 mos.;
J. L. Richmond; O.N.Bryan vs Halley.
James Burfy and two other colored prisoners escaped
from Port Tobacco jail during the night.
Wesley Simmons' house on Glymont road burned. Also,
William Cox's fine residence at Salem was nearly
destroyed by fire.

December 4, 1874, Vol. XXXI, No. 32

Mrs. Lucy Gough's home near Trinity Church will be

scene of Fair and Festival to benefit church.
Hugh Mitchell, near Port Tobacco, has two stray
heifers.
Thomas L. Gardiner married Fannie T. Mudd at St.
Patrick's Church, Washington, D.C. November 19
by Rev. Father Lenigham.

St. Columba Lodge Chooses Officers

Worshipful Master - George Taylor
Senior Warden - Dr. A.D.Cobey
Junior Warden - J.H.Roberts
Secretary - H.G.Robertson
Treasurer - J.G.Chapman
Tiler - William Wolfe

December 25, 1874, Vol. XXXI, No. 35

M.A.L.Delozier and A.T.Delozier complainants and
Sarah M. Delozier and M.A.B.Delozier defendants
"Part of St. Matthews" formerly owned by John
Delozier - 123 acres on public road from Port
Tobacco to Pomfret Church and adjoins lands of
T.Y.Robey.
Turner Rowe resigned position of Crier of Orphans'
Court. John D. Covell appointed to fill vacancy.
Mr. Covell has been Bailiff for many years.
James H. Montgomery's farm "Simpson's Delight" -
100 acres sold by F. Stone, trustee,to Thomas
Carrico for $250.
Nannie G. Hungerford warns trespassers on
"Waverly" and "Sunny Side."
Zachariah V. Posey certifies he has taken up a yawl-
built boat - now in Neale's Creek.

REGISTRATION LISTS
  First District

Lists of persons newly registered and stricken off
by the Register of the First Election District of
Charles County. Published according to the Act of
Assembly of 1874.

Newly Registered

W. Owen Cooke, James A. Linkens, Gregory Mattingley,
P.A.Murphy, P.C.Murphy, Franklin Pennington, William
Tubman.

Stricken Off (Removed)

George W. Gray, John D. Hanson, George W. Howard,
James H. Lacey, John S. Long, Adam Smith, G.H.
Turner, Lemuel Wilmer, William R. Wilmer.

                    (Dead)

A.P.Willett, William H. Welch.

  Second District

Newly Registered

Thomas J. Arnold, John W. Boarman, William L.
Brawner, J.Wesley Carpenter, Jerome Dixon, Frederick
Frederick, James W. Franklin, Arthur Golden, Richard
W. Hart, Francis Price, Adam Smith

Stricken Off (Removed)

Alexander Bowie, John S. Baxter, Thomas Beall,
John W. Boarman, John Barnes, Basil Brooks, John
Henry Beall, Wesley Beall, Barnes Compton, John H.
Chunn of Edward, John Digges, Francis Dyson, John
Dotsen, Elijah Davis, Delvey Hawkins, Thomas Jones,
William Nicholas Jones, William A. Lutrell, George
Lutrell, Ferdinand T. Maddox, Thomas Maddox, James
Maddox, Isaac Maddox, David McElroy, Josias
Milstead, Allen B. Milstead, Victor Matthews, F.M.
Nelson, James Newman, Henry Norris, Francis Owen,
John A. Price, James L. Powers, Gerard Rison, James
Rison, A.H.Robertson, Jr., James H. Ransom, John H.
Randall, Joseph I. Smith, Richard G. Simmons, Clem
Smith, Timothy Smith, William B. Thompson, Sydney
Thompson, Henry Willis, James L. Willis, James R.W.
Willis, J. Noble Willis, George W. Willis.

(Dead)

Richard Butler, Francis Beall, Hezekiah Franklin, William H. Kendrick, William B. Maddox, Jesse J. Stone, Phillip Spriggs, George T. Simmons.

(Transferred)

Alexius Butler, Gregory Mattingly.

Third District

Newly Registered

Moses Coats, Asa B. Fargo, John S. Long, William H. Murdoch, George Morris, Llewellyn Scott, William A. Smith.

Stricken Off (Dead)

Hendley Barnes, William J. Chiles, Samuel C. Dent, James Howard, John Murdoch, Thomas R. Posey, James Sanders.

Fourth District

Newly Registered

Thomas A. Burch, J. William Farrall, C. Lorenzo Gardiner, Jr., Samuel J. Lancaster, Sanford Whalon.

Stricken Off (Removed)

Thomas Carter, Thomas Young.

(Dead)

Benjamin P. Donnelly, William Queenan, William W. Ware.

(Transferred)

Richard H. Cook, Francis Price.

Fifth District

Newly Registered

Frank Boadly, Robert G. Bell, Thomas C. Dyson, William D. Posey, Joseph I. Wills, Jr., Francis C. Wills.

Stricken Off (Removed)

G.T.Brown, F.B.Cooksey, Samuel W. Dyson, Richard
T. Fowler, A.B.Posey, Robert H. Plowden, John
Shorter, William Worton.

(Dead)

John William Cash, George Murray, H.R.Scott,
James Philip Smith, Charles H. Wood.

Sixth District

Newly Registered

Charles C. Jones, Charles F. Lucas, John E. Mudd,
James T. Padgett.

Stricken Off (Removed)

L. Brook Berry, Patrick Brown, George W. Berry,
E.L.Clagett, Sandy Digges, Lewis Edwards, Thomas
T. Hancock, Joseph Jenkins, P.A.Murphy, P.C.Murphy,
Charles R. Marks, James A. Murray, Thomas D. Perry,
Samuel C. Robey, C.E.Robey, Patrick Slattary,
Thomas E. Sandy.

(Dead)

Levin Carr, William Carrington, William Hill, John
H. Mason, Henry Robey, George N. Rowe, Ben Swann,
Henry Thomas, Thomas H. Willett.

Seventh District

Newly Registered

W. Jackson Alexander, Marion Banks, Charles A. Swann.

Stricken Off (Removed)

Charles H. Jones.

Eighth District

Newly Registered

George Chapman, Jr., T. Raymond Chapman, John
Robert Edelen, Richard Forbes, Henry J. Hawkins,
William Wilson Moore, Winfield Smoot, John Hanson
Skinner, J. Samuel Turner, Marcellus Washington.

Stricken Off

Joseph Henry Boswell, James T. Canter, Michael
Chew, Robert Craig, Samuel Cole, James R. Dyson,
Josias Duckett, Dominick Edelen, Phil. V. Edelen,
Adam Ford, T.Y.Hawkins, Patrick Harney, John T. Joy,
Samuel Johnson, James R. Lawson, George A. Miller,
John Horace Marshall, Edwin M. Murray, Joseph
Queen, L.S.Robey, Arthur D. Smoot, George Smith,
Joseph Sembly, J. Hy. Turner, P. Wilmer, L. Allison
Wilmer.

(Transferred)

Richard Harrison, Peter Jones, Robert Henry Proctor,
James E. Skinner.

Ninth District

Newly Registered

Upton Green, Henry Hawkins, Richardson Harrison,
Benjamin Larkins, Edward Skinner, James E. Skinner.

Stricken Off

John H. Craig, James B. Craycroft, John Dorsey,
Richard Forbes, Alfred Sewell

ANNUAL STATEMENT
BY THE COMMISSIONERS OF CHARLES COUNTY
June 30, 1874

(Following are the persons named in the statement
of the expenses of Charles County. The amount of
money they received for various services has been
omitted, believing that names are more important
than a dollar here and two dollars there)

Judges of the Orphans' Court

Robert Digges, S.W.Dent, Richard Barnes.

County Commissioners

Albert Milstead, P.A.L.Contee, A.W.Marlowe, Z.Swann,
A.J.Smoot, Thomas R. Hally, John H. Cox, Josias
Hawkins, Samuel Hanson.

Judges of Election

George P. Jenkins, Charles E. Hannon, Richard B.
Posey, Washington A. Posey, Thomas Posey, Thomas
B. Berry, Benjamin D. Tubman, John W. McPherson,
William Turner, William Hamilton, B.L.Higdon,
Ernest Hanson, Benton Barnes, Henry S. Dent,
Alexander Haislip, William Nevitt, Sr., William
L. Sheirburn, John H.D.Wingate, Thomas Simms,
George F. Bealle, F.B.Green, William H. Cox, John
A. Wood, Jere W. Burch, George H. Gardiner, Thomas
E. Gardiner, James F. Thomas.

Clerks of Election

John T. Davis, John I. Jenkins, James A. Franklin,
F.A.Hanson, William P. Flowers, J.W.Wheeler, Peter
W. Robey, C.C.Digges, Phillip Harrison, use E.Dutton,
Charles C. Perry, B.F.Blanford, William L.McDaniel,
Theodore Dent, P.D.Everett, F.L.Dent, J.E.Higdon,
Henry A. Burch, John H. Chappelear.

Grand and Pettit Jurors - 1873 - November Term

O.N.Bryan, Joseph A. Gray, George F. Bealle,
Francis P. Hamilton, William Hamilton, William L.
Berry, Josias H. Hawkins, Charles F. Lancaster,
James L. Brawner, James E. Wingate, Edmond Perry,
Thomas B. Berry, Thomas F. Darnell, William B.
Matthews, John T. Davis, William H. Berry, E.F.Mason,
James A. Franklin, Alexander H. Robertson, A.W.
Marlowe, Thomas B. Delozier, Robert J. Lloyd,

Richard Farrall, John W. McPherson, Thomas R.
Halley, Henry S. Dent, James B. Latimer, William H.
Moore, John B. Lyon, James A. Keech, R.P.Wall,
William P. Flowers, Richard Price, Francis B. Green,
J.H.Freeman, Thomas Posey, Charles C. Perry,
William M. Jameson, Walter B. Wood, Albert Milstead,
Joseph L. Watson, John S. Higdon, John T. Crismond,
Warren O. Willett.

Talesmen

John W. Newberry, Thomas S. Martin, George N. Lyon.

1874 - May Term

Joseph Price, Benjamin F. Bowling, John H. Hancock,
Ambrose Adams, John W. Halley, Edgar Brawner, Albin
Price, Marcellus Burch, Regan Deakins, Edwin L.
Huntt, G.C.Burch, John F. Thompson, Francis Price,
Joseph T. Ward, William L. Harding, D.I.Sanders,
Mason L. McPherson, James H.M.Dutton, Thomas C.
Wilkerson, Joseph S. Boarman, B.W.Hardy, Townly
Robey.

Witnesses in State Cases - 1873 - November Term

Patrick Quinn, Charles A. Neale, John A. Burch,
Julian E. Norris, Thomas R. Halley, Washington
Burch, Alexander Haislip, John W. McPherson,
Edwin Cox, John A. Burch, William P. Flowers,
John H. Freeman, L.A.Martin, George A. Huntt,
B.F.Burch, H.H.Bowie, George T. Simpson, N.T.Cox,
Henry A. Turner, James A. Mudd, Peter Trotter,
Edward M. Murray, Joseph T. Herbert, John R.
Murray, John H. Chappelear, Mary R. Sheirburn,
Thomas B. Delozier, William F. Hammack, Thomas W.
Wright, Thomas H. Murray, Samuel G. Lancaster,
F.L.Dent, Lizzie Datcher, Samuel Smoot, William
L. McDaniel, Robert J. King, Silas D. Lewis, A.H.
Westphal, Ignatius Moore, John Bowling, Alexander
Cooper, Richard Thomas, Adrian Posey, Bearnard
Matthews, Samuel Cox, Sr., Joseph H. Mattingley, Jr.,
R.Dudly Digges, use W.L.Cooke, Richard Lamar,
James W. Chappelear, John W. Lamar, use Benjamin
G. Stonestreet, J.J.B.Barnes, William E. Dement,
John H. Washington, A.B.Milstead, Richard H.
Burch, Stephen Burch, John L. Budd, Richard B.
Posey, J.B.Sherriff, Albert Wade.

1874 - May Term

J.A.Groves, Charles Jones, Samuel Smoot,

178

John Humphries, W.O.Cooke, J.H.Roberts, William
L. Cooke, Scott Hicks, Charles A. Neale, George
Worrick, Thomas W. Wright, Thomas T. Owen, Robert
E.Rison, John H. Chappelear, J.C.Hayden, William
F. Hicks, John Edelen, A.E.Canter, O.N.Bryan,
Lemuel Smoot, Richard Burke, Noble E. Barnes,
W.T.Simmons, F.M.Lancaster, F.L.Dent, Robert
Simmis, George N. Simmis, G.C.Burch, James Bateman,
James H.M.Dutton, Francis Coats, J.Henry Turner,
Charles H. Neale, Charles Carey, M.M.Carey, John
Thomas Herbert, John T. Crismond, George Chapman,
J.W.Copher, Andrew Jackson, B.G.Harris, Louisa
Young, John H. Hancock, Mary Hamsley, Elisabeth
Hamsley, Joseph Harris, William C. Acton.

1873 - July Term

John T. Davis

1873 - November Term

Theophilus Smoot, Miles Toy, Dallis Ford, N.J.
Miles, Peter Trotter, J.J.B.Barnes, John Jackson,
John G. Chapman, Nelson Lyles, Joshua Swann, Oscar
Kelly, Daniel Rozier, Bernard Matthews, Charles H.
Jameson, R.D.Digges, Joseph H. Mattingly, Jr.,
Julian E. Norris, Frank Jenkins, Dr. R.F.Chapman,
M. Chapman, Paul Edelin, Isaiah Jones, Florence
Frederick, Evelina Stewart, Adrian Posey, Thomas
Jones, Ned Mundell, Robert L. Wedding, Joseph Gray,
John Delaney, George Trures, C.D.Welch, John E.
Bailey, C.C.Perry, Charles A. Neale.

1874 - May Term

Theophilus Smoot, Francis L. Higdon, Thomas M.
Wolfe, William Smoot, F.L.Dent, Samuel Smoot,
J.Edwin Cox, William B. Carpinter, Charles H.
Wills, Thomas B. Delozier, W.E.W.Rowe, Alexander
Haislip, William P. Flowers, William E. Dement,
Thomas Carrico, Samuel Smoot, Zepheniah Mudd,
George W. Carpenter, Jr., A. Judson Groves, J.H.
Roberts, Thomas T. Owens, Henry Edelen, Scott
Hicks, Edward Berry, John Humphries, William T.
Hicks, Darby Chunn, Wilson Wilkerson, Andrew
Jackson, John Thomas Herbert, J.R.Perry, Henry
Richmond, James Richmond, Kate Richmond, Charles
H. Posey, Samuel N. Cox, George P. Jenkins, James
L. Brawner, C.C.Perry, Jubal Barber, William Cox.

Bailiffs and Messengers to Circuit, Orphans' and Commissioners Court

Joseph H. Mattingley, Bailiff; J.B.Mattingley, Messenger; John D. Covell, Bailiff; John H. Jenkins, Bailiff; Samuel Maddox, Bailiff; John D. Covell, Bailiff to County Commissioners; Washington Burch, Bailiff to County Commissioners and Keeper of the Court House; H.T.Rowe, Crier of Orphans' Court.

Crow Bill Certificates

John T. Colton, William Boswell & Co., D.R.Bean, T.A.Smith, P.A.Sasscer, Sasscer & Gibbons, T.R. Farrall, C.Greenbaum, Albert Farrall, William F. Murray, William R. Acton, Albert Farrall, Mason L. McPherson, Townley Robey, Joseph I. Lacey, J.W. Warring, A.T.Monroe, George J. Chappelear, William Wolfe, Perry Rennoe, E.A.Dutton, Myer Greenbaum, Lemuel W. Maddox, Peter Williams, E.L.Huntt, John E.Ware, J.J.Brawner, R.A.Rennoe, William B. Carpenter, Thomas Skinner, Edgar Griswold, Thomas S. Dent, John D. Spalding, Thomas C. Wilkerson, Huntt & Norris.

Collectors of Assessments and Insolvenciess

J.J.Brawner, Washington Page, A.T.Monroe, Townley Robey.

Registration

J.H.Freeman, H.R.Scott, James A. Franklin, James A. Mudd, George W. Carpenter, M. Thompson, H.M. Hannon, Joseph I. Lacey, J.H.Chappelear, T.A. Smith (room rent), Elizabeth Duffy (room rent), C.C. Perry (room rent), C. Greenbaum, T.T.Latimer.

Rent of Election Rooms

C. Greenbaum, C.C.Perry, Elizabeth Duffy, T.A.Smith, C.F.Hayden, S.W.H.McPherson, Thomas H. Murray, D.R.Bean.

Coffins for Paupers

Pratt Maddox, R.S.Corry, Alfred Jenifer, F.L.Dent, George J. Chappelear, Robert Porter, William Swann, John M. Whitty, C.F.Hayden, F.L.Boarman, John R. Murray, Martha E. Wills, Patrick Turner, Joseph Linkins, W.B.Moore, Grandison Alexander.

Coroner's Inquest

Henry H. Bowie

Material for Roads and Bridges

Samuel H. Cox, F. Mason, James L. Hicks, P.A.
Sasscer, James Moore, Henry Mudd, William Hamilton,
Charles S. Williams, J.H.Mitchell, E.W.Rowe,
Mrs. Luckett, John Delozier's heirs, Thomas Y.
Robey, Benjamin D. Tubman, Thomas S. Martin, T.& R.
McDaniel, William H. Claggett, B.W.Moore, William
Wolfe, John Carrington's heirs, Mary C. Pye's heirs,
Mrs. Ann Robey, Nick Stonestreet, Mrs. A. Matthews,
William Boswell, _____Keath , Harris Stonestreet,
William Matthews, Dr. R. Chapman, J.B.Sherriff, G.H.
Berry, _____ Cassin, Sandy Middleton, C.Page,
Margaret Smoot, William B. Matthews, William H.
Higges, Estate of Mrs. Middleton, Mrs. William Wills,
St. Thomas Manor, F. Stone, Pratt Maddox, J.H.D.
Wingate, Mrs. G.H.Simpson, Mrs. T.D.Stone, William
A. Lyon, Robert Johnson, George Lancaster, Robert J.
Lloyd, Alfred Lloyd, Hughes Wills, George Dent, Sr.,
W.W.Ware, Thomas Darnell, Leonard Freeman, W.A.
Posey, John G. Chapman, Mrs. Gough, Mrs. T.D.Stone,
William B. Matthews, John T. Crismond, John F.
Gardiner, R.F.Bowling, Mrs. A. Bowling, Richard L.
Berry, John D. Bowling, Dr. Samuel Mudd, Dr. A.
Carrico, Mrs. R.A.Dickons, George Chappelear, Hosea
Burch, S.A.Canter, Chapman Lyon, Benjamin Adams,
Josias H. Hawkins, Washington Berry, James A. Mudd,
Andrew G. Chapman, Dr. Adams, Ambrose Adams,
Marshall Freeman, J.T.Mudd, Richard T. Wheatly,
M.P.Morton, Thomas Carrico, Thomas Boarman, H.W.
Harned, H.A.Canter, Mrs. A. Morland, Joseph H.
Padgett, Mason L. McPherson, Mrs. Ann Canter, Joseph
T. Ward, Warren Gibbons, Z. Swann, Webster Swann,
T. Middleton Ratcliff, Joseph C. Gray, E.J.Sanders,
William P. Compton, William B. Ferguson, Robert
Ferguson, Edmond Perry, Samuel Hanson, R.S.Hancock,
T.A.Millar, Walter Basting, William H. Mitchell,
Joseph Price, John H. Posey, Alfred T. Willett,
Uzziel Wright, Alexander Wader, Robert H. Sanders,
R.A.Rennoe, Frank Cofer's heirs, M. Cuningham,
John Grinder, E.F.Mason, Thomas M. Ratcliff, R.E.
Ryson, Alonzo Franklin, John S. Greer, William
L. Cooke.

Taxes Erroneously Paid

Dr. Thomas Price, Edgar Brawner.

181

Magistrates' and Constables' Accounts

F.L.Dent, Thomas C. Wilkerson, William F. Hammack,
Samuel Smoot, H.H.Bowie, A.J.Groves, William
Boswell, William L. McDaniel.

Sheriff and Late Sheriff

William L. Cooke, L. A. Martin

Register and Late Register of Wills

M. Thompson, Joseph Stewart.

Clerk and Late Clerk of Circuit Court

B.G.Stonestreet, George A. Huntt

Miscellaneous Items

E. Wells, for printing; E. Wells, for advertising
real estate; James F. Matthews, Attorney to County
Commissioners, use of Washington Page; John R.
Robertson, late Clerk to County Commissioners;
Charles E. Hannon, Clerk to Board of County Commissioners; Dr. Robert Digges, for attending
prisoners; Dr. John T. Digges, for attending
prisoners; Hanson & Robertson, for damages sustained in cutting ditch thro' Hotel lot; Joseph I.
Lacey, store account; John W. Mitchell, for defending criminals; Brent & Matthews, for defending
criminals; Nicholas Stonestreet, account filed;
R.H.Edelen, for defending criminals; Stone &
Mitchell, for defending criminals, D.W.Hawkins, for
defending criminals, Andrew G. Chapman, for defending criminals; William Boswell & Co., for books
and stationery.

W. Frank Brawner married Fannie Burgess at Nanje-
moy Church 23rd inst. by Rev. Robert Prout.
Joseph G. Davis married Eliza R. Monroe Dec. 30 at
rectory by Rev. Dr. Lewin.
Henry Howard died Friday at his residence in
Pomonkey district - 63 years old.
Mrs. Susan D. Shepherd, relict late Alexander
Shepherd died in Washington, D.C. 26th ult at the
residence of her son, ex-Governor A.R.Shepherd.
She was of the well known Robey family in Charles
County. Widowed with four sons and two daughters
in their youth and infancy. Reversal of fortune
deprived her means bequeathed by late husband -
she struggled to educate and properly rear those
left in her care. How well she succeeded!
J.A.Brawner's job in Appraiser's Office, Baltimore
Custom House has been abolished along with five
other clerks.
Horace Wallace, colored, died. He was a most
worthy and excellent roller boy in the Times office for many years. He and his father, Warren,
filled the job for a total of 25 years. "...We
always found Horace polite, prompt and attentive.
He was honest and industrious and we very much
regret his death. He rolled our first side off
on Tuesday last, and seemed then to be in good
health tho complaining a little. But he was
stricken down by an acute attack of pneumonia
and died Wednesday night."

January 8, 1875, Vol. XXXI, No. 37

Richard T. Tubman, mortgagee and J.W.Mitchell,
attorney for the mortgagee, will sell "Part of
Cornwallis Neck" - 480 acres on Potomac River -
2 story dwelling - 2 barns - out-buildings and
wharf known as Pye's Wharf - tenant house on
creek side - between river and Mattawoman Creek.
Mortgage from Charles H. Pye to Mrs. Rosanna
St Clair.
C. Lorenzo Gardiner married Rhoda M. Campbell,
daughter of late William T. Campbell at St.
Thomas' Church Nov. 24 by Rev. Father Murer.
Dr. Thomas A. Carrico unable to serve as President
of the School Board. Col. Samuel Cox and Dr.
T.C.Price, members qualified.
Col. John D. Bowling died at Barnum's Hotel, Bal-
timore Tuesday of acute attack of pneumonia.
Native Bryantown - early mercantile pursuits -
moved to Woodville - built palatial residence -
sons John & Gill Bowling.

W.J.Moore has taken charge of Brawner House and
proposes to dispense hospitality which has made
Moore Hotel in Leonardtown famous. Landlord
Burch remains at hotel as looker-on and a "gentleman of elegant leisure and means." "We wish
good luck to our new, young and good looking
landlord."

George A. Huntt has moved into "old Middleton
property" purchased and refitted by him.

Luther A. Martin has idea "that the nearer he gets
to Court House the nearer he will get to the hun-
gry and thirsty people." He has taken the old
Reeder mansion and opened a first-class restaurant. "Luke has certainly kept a No. 1 table
during the last year. As to his liquors, as we
never indulge, we can't say."

Samuel Cox, Jr., Trustee, sold farm of late John
Delozier for $500. Near Pomfret Church. 128
acres. Purchased by W. McF. Garner, L.A.Martin,
auctioneer.

Sasscer & Gibbons-lumber, general store, Beantown
Station.

Theodore Gross, Oak Grove Store, general goods,
Pomonkey.

January 15, 1875, Vol. XXXI, No. 38

Sheriff Cooke sold "Dent's Marsh Addition" and
"Pope's Creek Landing" 35 acres to Dr. William
R. Wilmer for $200, late property of George Dent.
Also "Part of Struggle & Pheasant Neck" 86 acres
to F. Stone, late property George W. Downing.

Drs. Reeder and Smoot both have pneumonia. Large
territory for Dr. Lancaster, "the only physician,
we believe, who is able to ride, in the Cobb
Neck section, as Dr. Jameson is prevented from
leaving home by rheumatism..."

Robert H. Hatcher seriously hurt while cutting wood.
Dr. William N. Sanders attending him.

Washington Hicks appointed postmaster at White
Plains P.O., vice Mrs. M.A.Rowe, resigned.

L.A.Martin's Restaurant roof caught fire from
burning chimney. Vigilance of inhabitants prevented structure from destruction.

January 22, 1875, Vol. XXXI, No. 39

Wirt Harrison married Miss M.A.Harris at Christ
Church, Port Tobacco on Wednesday, Jan. 20 by
Rev. Dr. Lewin. Bride daughter of late Thomas
Harris, Esq. of Pomonkey.

Prospus Gibbons married Clotilda Franklin at
Bryantown Church Tuesday, Jan 19 by Rev. Father
Voltz.
Alexander Marbury Bryan married Ella Hanson Clagett
at residence of bride's father William H. Clagett
Thursday Jan. 21 by Rev. Dr. Lewin.
Harrison Sewell, colored man, lost mule by slip-
ping on Gambrel Hill into gully. Port Tobacco's
"Mount Misery" very slippery and one of the
County Commissioners gingerly made his way down
grasping at every shrub along the way. Dr.
Stouten W. Dent, one of Judges of Orphans'
Court led his horse down and they both fell.
Dr. A.M. Brooke appointed by Judges of the Circuit
Court to serve on the School Board.

Clerk of Circuit Court - No. Licénses Issued

1874

Marriage (white)	40	Race	4
Marriage (colored)	32	Horses' & Jacks'	10
Traders'	65	Fishing	3
Female Traders'	5	There were recorded	
Ordinary	8	Deeds	138
Retail Liquor	42	Mortgages	59
Exhibition	3	Bills of Sale	56
Oyster house	10	Bonds	22
Oyster Catchers	50	Equity cases doc.	12

Samuel Lunt, deceased, property to be sold "Thorn's
Gut" Fishery on Potomac River comprising beach and
"Thorn's Gut Farm" and lot of several acres at
lower end and houses attached to fishery. John
W. Mitchell, trustee.

January 29, 1875, Vol. XXXI, No. 40

J. Edward Hamilton married Cecilia Miles, daughter
of late Dr. Edward Miles Wed. Jan. 27 by Rev.
Father McAtee.
Charles H. Lane died in D.C. 3 p.m. Wed. Jan. 27 of
pneumonia. He was 64 years old.
J.R.Perry, Harris' Lot, advertises general store.
George Brent and George P. Jenkins, directors State
of Maryland Mutual Fire Insurance Col. in Charles
County. Agents - John T. Colton & William H. Gray.
John Dixon & Co. operate steam mill near Bensville.

February 5, 1875, Vol. XXXI, No. 41

Dr. A.D.Cobey married Sallie C. Price, daughter of
Richard Price at Nanjemoy Church Thurs. Feb. 4th
by Rev. Robert Prout ("Accompanying the above was
a generous slice of cake...")

185

Anna E. Lucas died at her residence on the 30th
ult. of heart disease. She was 50 years old.
"Upon her son, her only child, the support of her
declining years was lavished the love which a
mother ever feels for an obedient and affectionate child..."
Charles Boettner died at his residence in Baltimore on the 27th ult. He was 42 years old. He
was a former resident of Port Tobacco "where he
conducted business as baker and confectioner
during the war."

Orphans' Court Business

T.Y.Robey, executor for Francis Robey passed 1st
and final account.
John S. Chapman, executor for Matilda L.A.Chapman
passed 1st and final account.
Asa Simmons' will admitted to Probate. George
M. Lloyd, executor.

Thomas S. Martin's house in Pomonkey was nearly
consumed by fire.

The Young Debating Society of Port Tobacco Organized

President - William M. Lewin
Vice President - J.W.Shackelford
Secretary - J.R.Lacey
Treasurer - H.H.Boswell
Librarian - S.C.Padgett
Door Keeper - William J. Digges
Assistant Door Keeper - B.E.Padgett

February 12, 1875, Vol. XXXI, No. 42

T.J.Moore (of the "St. Charles Hotel," late the
"Brawner House," Port Tobacco) married Luc A.
Greenwell of St. Mary's County at the Cathedral,
Baltimore at 12 noon on Monday, February 8th by
the Rev. Father Starr.
William T. Davis married Mary E. Scott at Trinity
Glebe on January 12 by Rev. L.H.Jackson.
George F. Canter married Mary Estelle Barnes in
St. James Chapel, Newtown by Rev. L.H.Jackson.
Henry L. Mudd, Esq. married Mary Pauline, eldest
daughter of William H. Gwynn, Esq. (of Thomas)
of Prince George's County at the residence of
the bride's father on 26 Jan. by Rev. Father
Walsh.
James Perry Murdoch died on Sunday, February 7th
of consumption at the residence of his father,

John F. Gardiner granted letters of administration
for the estate of his brother, Thomas I. Gardiner
deceased.
First account of Thomas Y. Robey, statutory guardian of William Robey, passed the court.

February 19, 1875, Vol. XXXI, No. 43

J. T. Richmond, about to return to England is selling his farm of 200 acres for $1500. "The best
and cheapest farm in Maryland." Two good dwelling houses, barn, prize house, stabling for 12
horses, corn house, meat house, cow house, fowl
house, pump of never-failing pure water close to
house--orchard--apply Lancaster's Wharf, Cobb
Neck or James F. Matthews, Esq., Solicitor, Port
Tobacco.
Reverdy A. Rennoe died at his residence "Cherry
Hill" on February 8. He was 47 years old "...He
leaves a widow and four children to mourn their
overwhelming loss...."
Mrs. Wilfred B. Moore died on the 14th inst. at
the residence of her husband.
Edward Spangler died at the residence of Dr. Samuel
A. Mudd on the 14th of February. "...one of the
unfortunate men who suffered imprisonment at Dry
Tortugas, with Dr. Mudd, for his supposed con-
nection with the Lincoln assassination."
Dr. A.D.Cobey, dentist advertises office in Port
Tobacco "over the Grange Hall, in the 'Boswell
Building.'"
Capt. Alfred Nalley's "tough beef" met the train
near Port Tobacco Station head-on - killed a cow
and steer and a freight car was upset and greatly
damaged. Wrecking train came and took car to
Washington for repairs.
George M. Lloyd, executor for Asa Simmons.
A request made for the Charles H. Pye sale of proper-
ty to Richard T. Tubman be ratified.

February 26, 1875, Vol. XXXI, No. 44

Francis Higdon appointed by County Commissioners to
be the Road Supervisor in place of Joseph E.
Sanders, resigned.
Richard Taylor appointed by County Commissioners to
be the Road Supervisor in place of William
Burtles, removed.
R.T.Farrall is preparing to erect a storehouse and
dwelling on the west side of the LaPlata Station.
He purchased the property from Mrs. Amanda
Matthews.

T.J.Moore has erected a double piazza at the St.
    Charles Hotel and "...is quite a handsome im-
    provement..."
Thomas Y. Robey appointed guardian to William Robey
    by the Orphans' Court.
Hawkins family (colored) house was destroyed by
    fire - Hawkins was one of three escapees from the
    Port Tobacco Jail last fall. The house was on
    the farm of Sheriff Cook, near Newtown.
James Burfy, Negro, who escaped from jail with
    Hawkins has been caught in Washington and is now
    in the Maryland Penitentiary.
Houston Morris, "faithful mail-carrier deserves
    praise and sympathies." One horse was killed
    while traveling over "Mount Misery" road and
    another lamed.
George T. Hawkins administrator for Andrew Thomas,
    deceased.
John F. Gardiner administrator for Thomas I.
    Gardiner, deceased.
Calista Lancaster sells property to Benjamin P.
    Donnelly.

March 5, 1875, Vol. XXXI, No. 45

T.R.Farrall, agent for the La Plata Station on the
    Baltimore and Potomac Rail Road declares that "...
    no freight will be delivered to any person at La
    Plata Station until charges on it are paid. I am
    compelled to exact payment thus owing to the
    trouble and vexation attending the collection of
    trifling amounts widely scattered."
T.R.Farrall announces that on 1 May he will move
    "from Store-House I now occupy to my own Store
    on other side of Rail Road..."
J.C.Wenk employed at Chapel Point Mill.
Judge Boswell had a sheep killed by a dog.
J.W.Mitchell reports 10 lambs killed same way.
Henry H. Owens purchased part of "Haberdeventure"
    late William B. Stone owned it. 200 acres for
    $1600. Improved by small dwelling and good barn.

March 12, 1875, Vol. XXXI, No. 46

Peter W. Robey advertises fine jack for sale.
Thomas A. Millar warns against fishing on his
    property on Potomac River - "Nanjemoy Reach"
    several miles of shoreline. "I have shanties
    along the shore that may be obtained at a fair
    rental..."
Rev. H.W.Kinzer returned to Charles Circuit by the
    Baltimore Methodist Church South. Rev. W.H.Seat

and Rev. A.M.Cockey sent to Prince George's
County. Rev. R.A.Reed and Rev. W.Lankford sent
to Charles County by Conference of Colored
Preachers.
Sister Bazella (Edelin of Maryland) died at 80
years of age at the Convent of Visitation. She
was one of the oldest Carmelite nuns, having entered in 1826.
Mr. Harris, Mr. St. Clair and Mr. Burdine, while
hunting along the Mattawoman Creek came across a
beaver "...a rare specimen in these waters,
measured 6' from tip of nose to tip of tail...
they saw four others...dispatched one, 5' long."
Hides were displayed at Glymont before being
taken to Washington.

March 19, 1875, Vol. XXXI, No. 47

Dr. George A. Mudd died at Millwood, Missouri at
the residence of his father. He was the eldest
son of Judge Henry T. Mudd and was born near Port
Tobacco May 17, 1838. The following year his
parents moved to Missouri. In June 1861 he
joined the Missouri State Guard - was wounded at
the Battle of Springfield - received his medical
degree in 1870 and practiced medicine in Panola
County, Texas - struck down with incurable disease, consumption - returned home two weeks ago.

April 23, 1875, Vol. XXXI, No. 52

Allison Hicks, deceased, real estate division.
Perry Rennoe administrator for Reverdy A. Rennoe,
deceased.
E.C.Dutton, William McKenney Burroughs and Samuel
G. Herbert, Road Commissioners, authorized by
County Commissioners to lay off and open Public
Road through lands of George Simmes, Robert
Simmes and Mary Simmes to Hatten's Creek and suf-
ficient land at said creek for Public Landing.
Samuel Cox has sale at Cox Station of farm animals
and all furniture, beds and bedding and cooking
utensils of hotel. (Purpose to close up partnership between Colonel Cox and "mine host Hawkins,
who has so long, and so much to the satisfaction
of his guests, conducted the Hotel." Will be re-
opened under the management "...of Miss Higdon,
a lady in every way calculated, we are told, to
keep a Hotel."
Jere W. Burch died at his residence near Bryantown
Tuesday the 20th inst. He was 67 years old.
Catharine Farrall died at the residence of George

Carrico on Tuesday the 20th inst. She was
60 years old.

George B. Shannon's account of guardian ship of
Charles H. and Mary Ann Shannon was passed by
the Judges of Orphans' Court.

Mr. Harvey and Mr. Milstead appointed Collectors in
1st Collection District. Mr. Harvey declined.
Mr. Milstead appointed for whole district.

J.E.F.Wedding's daughter's dress caught. Quick-
thinking father wrapped a blanket around the
child and saved her.

Hon. Barnes Compton visited the County briefly.

N.T.Cox has stallion "Indian Chief" to be let to
mares. Will stand at following places - leave
home Monday a.m. for E.F.Mason and Green's;
leave for home; Thursday go to J.W.Cox's in Nanjemoy; leave Friday for B. Ratcliffe's near The
Trappe; leave Saturday for John Kendrick's.

May 14, 1875, Vol. XXXII, No. 3

W.P.Ward of Charles County married Sallie C.,
daughter of William Boswell, formerly from this
county on Wednesday, Mary 5 at the residence of
the bride's father in Johnson County, Missouri by
Rev. Abel Leonard. "The happy twain, in company
with Miss Eva, the bride's sister, left on the
eastern bound express train for Maryland the same
evening."

D. Clay Smull married Georgia Neale, daughter of
Dr. Bennet Neale, formerly of Port Tobacco, at
St. Peter's P.E. Church, Baltimore on the 5th
inst. by Rev. Julius E. Grammer.

Louisa A., wife of Joseph Bowling, formerly of
Charles County, died in New Orleans on Friday,
May 7. She was the daughter of the late Judge
Winchester of Louisiana.

S.K.Contee advertises for rent his farm "Elmwood"
excellent dwelling house. Apply P.A.L.Contee or
Josias Hawkins, Esq., Port Tobacco.

Grand Jury
Oliver N. Bryan, Foreman

Thomas R. Halley, W.E.W. Rowe, Thomas P. Gray,
Uzzial Wright, James H. Montgomery, Francis Mc-
Williams, Ambrose Adams, John H. Chappelear,
Nicholas J. Miles, John H. Hancock, James A. Adams,
Thomas S. Martin, Richard Price, Thomas Simms,
William L. McDaniel, John E. Bailey, Richard Barnes,
Jr., G.C.Burch, Peregrine Davis, Thomas A. Millar,
Henry S. Dent, Marshall Chapman.

Petit Jury

Henry Gardiner, Charles E. Hannon, P.A.L.Contee,
Reagan Deakens, James A. Franklin, James A. Keech,
John W. McPherson, Joseph C. Gray, Joseph S.
Boarman, Francis R. Speake, James M. Burch, William
S. Chiles, Albin Price, Thomas B. Berry, Edward D.
Boone, E.F.Mason, Henry Delozier, John Hamilton,
Ernest Hanson, John R. Turner, Augustin W. Neale,
Richard B. Posey, John W. Boarman, Marcellus Burch,
William B. Matthews.

Sister Mary Rose Mudd died at the Convent of Visita-
tion in Frederick the 16th ult. She was 53 years
She was the sister of Dr. George D. Mudd and a nun
for many years.
William B. Carpenter, N.T.Cox and William H. Rowe,
School Trustees for School #3, 2nd Election Dis-
trict.
William T. Hindle, William Fergusson, William Henry
Bruce, School Trustees for School #4, 2nd Election
District.
William A. Lyon, Samuel Swann, Robert Johnson, School
Trustees for School #3, 4th Election District.
J.B.Norris, Lemuel Smoot and Charles C. Perry, School
Trustees for School #1, 5th Election District.
T.R.Farrall in new store with new stock of goods,
policy of "'small profit and a quick return...'
Dick is a live man and always up to time."
C.H.Milton is painting the outside of the St. Charles
Hotel "and when done will present a handsome ap-
pearance."
Henry S. Mitchell's property "Myrtle Grove" 887 acres
to be sold for taxes.

June 4, 1875, Vol. XXXII, No. 5

Henry G. Robertson and J. Hubert Roberts open a new
general store at La Plata.
J. Thomas Colton, R. Payne, and J.H.Reeder, trustees
of school #1, 4th Election District, need teacher.
James B. Owens, carriage and wagon maker, horse shoer
and blacksmith, Port Tobacco "having taken the
shops of John Hamilton..."
A.T.Lloyd married Nannie L. Hamilton, youngest daughter of the late Dr. Patrick H. Hamilton 2nd inst.
at "Milton Hill," residence of the bride's mother,
by Rev. Father McAtee.
George Digges died. "...Though his death was sudden,
we have reason to believe he was not entirely un-
prepared, for on the morning of the day he left his
quiet home, as if he had a premonition of his fate,

191

he sought reconciliation and peace with his God.
.."
Henry Washington, colored, indicted for murder of
Charles Green, colored, arrested, committed to
jail and brought to Charles County to stand trial.

Circuit Court Cases

Francis Farmer vs John H. Chappelear, verdict for
defendant, $150 rent due.
Austin Marbury vs Albert Milstead - stealing corn -
prisoner an old man, no county jail term.
McLane Actor - assault with intent to kill
State vs Alexius Stone, colored, indecent exposure-
not guilty. Digges for State - D.W.Hawkins,
defense.
State vs Stanislaus Pickerell, indicted for stealing
tobacco from Constance Bowling. Not guilty. Digges
for State, D.W.Hawkins for defense.
State vs Joseph Yates - larceny one dozen chickens.
Digges for State, D.W.Hawkins, defense.
John Clements indicted for resisting Deputy Sheriff
Owen Cooke - bailed for appearance next term.

G.S.Griffith, President, Prisoners' Aid Society
toured Port Tobacco jail. He commended the clean-
liness of jail but could not say much else that was
favorable. Urged necessity of re-arrangements so
that prisoners would not be so crowded, and sexes
should be separated.
Leonard Marbury's property "Glymont" 543 acres purchased by "capitalists from Washington City who
design greatly to improve and make it every way
worthy of the large patronage it has always received...a Mr. Cerlton Spaids...proposes to erect
a fine dwelling for himself on hill immediately
above pavilion and improve grounds...price var-
iously reported at $3200...resort for citizens of
Washington, Alexandria, and GeorgeTown...during
season hardly a day or night passes without one or
more excursion parties visiting the spot..."
W.W.Cobey shearing thoroughbred Cotswold sheep at
"Efton Hills."
J.C.Brawner's property "Part of Conjunction" 18
acres to be sold for taxes.

June 11, 1875, Vol. XXXII, No. 6

E.R.Thorp of Virginia married Mary F. Bowie, on
Tursday 25 May "at the Park" by Rev. Robert Prout.

C.A.Gray has for sale or rent his farm near Nan-
jemoy Church "Bush Hill" 500 acres - good
dwelling and tenant house "...churches and school
house convenient."
Maria D. Burch executrix for Jeremiah W. Burch,
deceased.
John R. Murray candidate for sheriffalty.
Thomas S. Dent, Nanjemoy District, had six sheep
killed by lightning.
Mrs. Jameson near Newport had a heifer killed on
same night by lightning.
George B. Lancaster had accident on Gilpin's Hill.
Capt. Pape, superintendent on this end of the
Baltimore and Potomac Rail Road is making a pre-
liminary survey of the wharf at this terminus.
Line now ends in a marsh.

Orphans' Court

Jeremiah W. Burch testamentary letters to Maria
D. Burch.
Edward Milstead appointed guardian to Robert H.
Simmons, minor.
Albert Milstead appointed guardian to Susan
Simmons, minor.
James D. Milstead administrator to Peter Wheeler
ordered to pay to H.W.Hall $334.10.

STATEMENT OF THE EXPENSES OF
CHARLES COUNTY FOR
THE YEAR ENDING ON
June 30, 1875

Judges of the Orphans' Court

Robert Digges, S.W.Dent, Richard Barnes.

County Commissioners

Albert Milstead, P.A.L.Contee, A.W.Marlow, Z. Swann,
A.J.Smoot.

Judges of Elections

N. Stonestreet, James A. Franklin, George M. Barnes,
Samuel Hawkins, Yates Barber, J.B.Sheriff, Lee M.
Southerland, Edward D. Boone, T.E.Gardiner, George P.
Jenkins, Peregrine Davis, D.J.Bragonia, James D.
Milstead, Alexandria Haislip, James M. Harvey, J.N.
Harrison, Samuel T. Swann, John B. McWilliams, John
M. Page, Henry E. Mudd, George F. Bealle, William D.C.
Mitchell, Theodore Dent, P.A.Sasscer, Thomas J.

Boarman, Henry Gardiner, E.D.R.Bean.

Clerks of Elections

John I. Jenkins, James A. Adams, William T. Simmons,
H.H.Bowie, Alpheus Haislip, William P. Flowers,
Peter W. Robey, J.A.Carlin, Washington Page, James
H.M.Dutton, Charles L. Gardiner, William T. Hicks,
W.E.W.Rowe, John W. Halley, Sylvester Mudd, Richard
A. Boone, Henry A. Burch, C.A.Webster.

Grand and Petit Jurors - 1874 - November Term

Hugh Mitchell, William H. Berry, Edward N. Stone-
street, A.H.Robertson, William E. Dement, R.P.Wall,
John T. Davis, Thomas J. Boarman, William Queen,
Samuel Cox, John T. Dutton, E.A.Smith, William F.
Dement, Thomas B. Delozier, Richard W. Bryan, J.B.
Sheriff, Edgar Griswold, John B. Carpenter, John L.
Budd, John F. Gardiner, William Hamilton, George H.
Gardiner, Samuel Hanson, M.P.Gardiner, Thomas F.
Darnell, Walter B. Wood, J.H.Roberts, William P.
Flowers, H.H.Bowie, James B. Latimer, William M.
Jameson, Sylvester Mudd, John I. Jenkins, John A.
Hindle, F.P.Hamilton, John R. Robertson, Charles L.
Gardiner, James H. Morgan, William T. Hindle,
William P. Compton, B.M.Edelen, William H. Price,
Warren O. Willett, Thomas Carrico, Thomas L. Hannon,
William A. Fouke, John H. Freeman.

1875 - May Term

Thomas R. Halley, Oliver N. Bryan, W.E.W.Rowe,
Thomas P. Gray, Uzziel Wright, James H. Montgomery,
Francis McWilliams, Ambrose Adams, John H. Chappelear,
N.J.Miles, John H. Hancock, James A. Adams, Thomas S.
Martin, Richard Price, Thomas Simms, William L. Mc-
Daniel, John E. Bailey, Richard Barnes, Jr., G.E.Burch,
P. Davis, Thomas A. Millar, Henry S. Dent, M.Chapman,
Henry Gardiner, Charles E. Hannon, P.A.L.Contee, Reagan
Deakins, James A. Franklin, James H. Keech, John W.
McPherson, Francis R. Speake, James M. Burch, William
S. Chiles, Albin Price, Thomas B. Berry, Edward D.
Boone, E.F.Mason, Henry Delozier, John Hamilton, Ernest
Hanson, John R. Turner, A.W.Neale, Richard B. Posey,
John W. Boarman, Marcellous Burch, William B. Matthews,
Joseph S. Boarman.

Talismen

George A. Huntt, John R. Murray, William C. Brent,
Ernest Hanson, D.J.Sanders, John H. Hancock, Robert

J. Lloyd, Joseph E. Sanders, John A. Turner,
William R. Acton, B.Z.Tennison, George Digges,
H.G.Robertson, Alexander Ross, Albert Farrall,
John E. Murphy, Francis L. Boarman, L.A.Martin,
A.J.Norris, Albert Milstead, John R. Murray,
William G. Willett.

Witnesses to the Grand Inquest - 1874 - Nov. Term

Samuel Johnson, George Tolson, Samuel Johnson, Jr.,
James A. Keech, A.J.Groves, F. Hanson, Henry Nelson,
Wesley Hanson, V.T.Hayden, John S. Richmond, Joseph
F. Hardesty, Ignatius Moore, James Moore, John W.
Fowler, Francis N. Digges, William Whitty, J.H.
Roberts, George F. Bealle, John S. Richmond,
Edward D. Boone, Samuel Smoot, George D. Mudd, John
H. Chappelear, B.A.Jameson, William J. Knott,
William T. Hicks, Francis P.Hamilton, Thomas W.
Wright, Richard Posey, Richard B. Herbert, George A.
Huntt, Juba Barber, Thomas Barber, Shadrack Bland,
William T. Simmons, J.C.Hayden, John W. Newberry,
John H. Beane, J.A.Anderson, Lemuel Smoot, Daniel
Mullin, Benjamin Wilkerson, Henry Willett, A.N.Gates,
Albert Farrall, Dallas Ford, F.A.Carpenter, Robert
Thomas, F.Frederick, F.Wheeler, Thomas R. Farrall,
Noble E. Barnes, William F. Berry, F. Pennington,
James Scott, Samuel Cox, Jr., Catharine Waters,
Thomas A. Hancock, Ernest Hanson, William F. Hammack,
R.Swann, Jeff Kelly, H.Boarman, J.T.S.Tennison,
Samuel Hawkins, Robert Greenfield, William H. Wade,
John Greenfield, John S. Button, Martha Kelly,
Lucinda Brown, John Butler, Willie King, John Ross,
Thomas F. Hancock, Thomas K. Ching, Elijah Wells,
Samuel Wells, John B. Lyon, A.D.Cobey, T.A.Scott,
James A. Franklin, Thomas Winters, W.Owen Cook,
James H. Gough, Robert Hawkins, Thomas Nevitt, George
J.R.Huntt, Edward L. Smoot, William Moore, Stephen
Hawkins, J.Hawkins, George Wood, William J. Boarman,
Theodore L. Robey, McLane Acton.

1875 - May Term

Lewellyn Jenkins, A.Judson Groves, Henry A. Burch,
T.J.Moore, Thomas R. Farrall, J.C.Hayden, Elizabeth
Duffy, William T. Simmons, Z.V.Posey, B.F.Burch, John
W. Clements, Thomas M. Welch, William B. Carpenter,
Hanson Driver, Dennis Hawkins, R.B.Herbert, Richard
Posey, F.L.Dent, E.N.Stonestreet, Frank Coats, John
W. Newberry, Albert Carrico, Joseph Stone, Noble E.
Barnes, William F. Hammack, William T. Hicks, Lemuel
Smoot, James A. Franklin, Charles J. Sidler, C.A.
Bowling, W. Owen Cook, Joseph S. Lancaster, W. Moore,
R.V.Welch, B.G.Stonestreet, Stephen Hawkins, Robert

Simms, George H. Cooksey, Robert G. Tucker, George
Chapman, Benjamin Padgett, James Church.

Witnesses in State Cases - 1874 - July Term

Robert Thomas, F. Frederick, George Worrick,
F.M.Lancaster.

1874 - November Term

John S. Richmond, James H. Luckett, Theophilus
Smoot, Peter Trotter, Thomas Farrall, Thomas T. Owen,
Henry Edelin, George Worrick, F.M.Lancaster, Charles
J. Carey, John H. Hancock, Samuel N. Cox, Charles H.
Wills, George Waller, B.W.B.McPherson, Benjamin D.
Tubman, Robert A. Chapman, John A. Wood, George A.
Adams, Samuel Smoot, Joseph L. Watson, William E.
Williams, William W. Thomas, Joseph F. Thomas,
George Tolson, Henry Nelson, Ignatius Moore, George
D. Mudd, Robert Thomas, Samuel A. Mudd, James Slater,
William Yates, William T. Hicks, George D. Mudd,
F. Frederick, Ernest Hanson, F.A.Carpenter, Frank
Wheeler, John T. Crismond, Thomas Croft, Daniel
Mullin, Catharine Waters, B.A.Jameson, Jeff Simms,
John Adams, Bell Adams, Frank Kelly, George Digges,
Jackson Howard, John G. Chapman, A.W.Neal, Robert
Digges, Sr., John A. Maddox, Albert Farrall,
F. Pennington, Jeff Kelly, Samuel Cox, Jr., Lucinda
Brown, John Young, Martha Kelly, Frank Kelly, Nelly
Swann, John Butler, Willie King, Samuel Hawkins,
Wilford Jackson, Washington Brown, B.A.Jameson,
Abraham Queenan, James H. Bailey, William J. Molly-
horn, John E. Bailey, C.C.Perry, Charles A. Neale,
Richard Posey, Lemuel W. Maddox, Walter M. Millar,
Robert Hawkins.

1875 - May Term

Theophilus Smoot, Albert Milstead, J.J.Barnes,
George W. Wheeler, J.S.Franklin, William Jordan, Fred
Dorsey, Ned Jones, James Willis, Peter Trotter, John
H. Moreland, J.H.Roberts, Albert Farrall, Robert
Hawkins, James H. Gough, Frank Barber, Edward Herbert,
B.Frank Blandford, Charles W. Willett, Marshall Chap-
man, Dennis Hawkins, Benjamin Kelly, J.H.Matingly, Jr.,
George Hawkins, J. Alexander Ross, Richard Young,
Edmond Jacks, Thomas R. Farrall, William Johnson,
Henry Jones, Vincent Jacks, Benjamin Padgett, John W.
Albrittain, Jr., Henry A. Burch, L.W.Burch, George
D. Mudd, T.E.Gardiner, Thomas J. Hunter, George J.
Chappelear, James Bowling, J.H.Langley, George

196

Chapman, F.L.Dent, B.M.Edelen, Frank Bowling,
Henry Robertson, George W. Berry, Thomas R.
Farrall, Dennis Bond, Nick Matthews, Humphrey
Millar, John Combs, W. Owen Cook, William E. Dement,
William M. Ward, Thomas Taylor, William Moore,
Stephen Hawkins, John Hawkins, George Wood, C.
Bowling, William G. Willett, Marcus Pickrell, John
Clements, McCartney Monroe, William Pickrell,
William T. Hicks, Samuel Dent.

Bailiffs and Messengers

John D. Covell, John H. Jenkins, J.B.Mattingley,
Samuel Maddox, H. Turner Rowe, Washington Burch.

Crow Bills Certificates

P.A.Sasscer, Albert Farrall, George S. Simpson,
F.S.Dent, George Berry, N. Nutwell, Nicholas Stone-
street, Alfred T. Monroe, Robert S. Corry, William
B. Carpenter, Thomas R. Farrall, John W. Warring,
Thomas Skinner, Thomas H. Murray, Timothy A. Smith,
Uzziel Wright, Meyer Greenbaum, Lemuel W. Maddox,
Townly Robey, Peter Williams, William L. Robey,
George J. Chappelear, W.E.W.Rowe, Albin Price,
R.D.P.Ratcliffe, E.A.Dutton, Coleman Greenbaum,
Aquilia W. Marlow, William R. Acton, John H.
Chappelear, Jere T. Mudd, J. Thomas Colton, Henry
C. Robey.

Collectors of Assessmants and Insolvencies

Alfred T. Monroe, Washington Page, John J. Brawner,
John T. Dutton, William B. Carpenter, Francis
McWilliams, John A. Marlow, George J. Chappelear.

Registration

Joseph I. Lacey, Robert E. Rison, Timothy A. Smith,
Washington Page, John H. Hancock, William Turner,
James A. Mudd, Henry M. Hannon, John H. Freeman,
Elizabeth Duffy, C. Greenbaum, T.A.Smith, William
A. Hancock, Charles C. Perry.

Rent of Election Rooms

Coleman Greenbaum, Timothy A. Smith, Charles C.
Perry, Elizabeth Duffy, Samuel W.H.McPherson,
John H. Chappelear.

Coffins for Paupers

Joseph H. Padgett, for making coffin and burying pauper, Joseph H. Milstead, same, George Carpenter, for burying a pauper, Alexander Haislip, for making coffin and burying pauper, George Chappelear, same, C.M.Bond, for making six coffins, Philip Gilham and John Wade, for making coffin and burying pauper, John S. Gardiner, same.

Coroner's Inquest

Henry Bowie, James A. Franklin, Bailiff.

Materials for Roads and Bridges

Samuel H. Cox, Cecilia Miles, Edgar Brawner, Hyland Brawner, Richard McDaniel, Elizabeth Myers, Francis Rozier, John Carrington's heirs, William Carrington's heirs, John H. Cox, Samuel B. Sexton, James M.Moore, Thomas Y. Robey, John H. Murray, William E. Dement, Mary R. Robey, William Wolfe, Wilson Wilkerson, Marcellus Thompson, William N. Sanders, Noel B. Hannon, John W. Thomas, John W. Warring, Arthur Shaw, Mary Jane Johnson, George W. Gardiner, Dominic Mudd, Thomas B. Berry, Joseph C. Gray, Mrs. Lowe, Francis R. Burgess, William T. Hindle, Ella Rison, Joseph Price, Rev. Robert Prout, R. Rennoe, Peter Williams, E. Lloyd, J.T.Sanders, John B. Carpenter, Alexander Franklin, Peter Trotter.

Miscellaneous Items

E. Wells, John S. Button & Co., James F. Matthews, Attorney to County Commissioners, Charles E. Hannon, Clerk to County Commissioners, John W. Mitchell, Richard H. Edelen, D.W.Hawkins, A. Campbell, Henrietta McWilliams, John H. Jenkins, John H. Chappelear, William Boswell.

July 2, 1875, Vol. XXXII, No. 9

This is the first issue to be printed on Times' new
  Cottrell and Babcock press. "...We have it in con-
  templation to otherwise improve the Times, when we
  get better fixed and settled in our new office..."
William A. Middleton administrator T. Columbus
  Middleton, deceased.
J.W.Mitchell, F.W.Weems, and A.J.Smoot, Committee
  to attend Democratic State Central Committee.
B.W.Moore, Robert Pearson, G.R.McDaniel, W.O.Willett

S.D.Roby, John H. Cox, H.O.Page, William Wolfe,
John Dixon, R.H.Willett make appeal to County
Commissioners to open and make public a Road
leading from the Road known as the White Plains
Road, thence through lands of John T. Gipson,
S.B.Sexton, Thomas I. Robey, etc. to mail road
leading from Port Tobacco to Piney Church.
John W. Owen's house struck by lightning - slight
damage. William B. Carpenter had tree struck.
Tobacco prize attached to tree "was shivered...
negro man plowing close by stunned."
Orlando King and Abraham King, colored, upon oath
of William T. Howard charging them with assault,
committed to jail by Justice Boswell.
Peter Douglass, colored, one of three men escaped
from Port Tobacco jail last fall has been re-
captured and is in jail again. Indicted for
stealing books from DeSales Mudd, Bryantown.
Dudly Digges, daputy clerk, injured when thrown
from sulky.
Grace Bean, colored, burned in accident while filling lighted kerosene lamp. She is in employ of
Walter Marr on farm of John W. Mitchell, Esq.
Dr. Pearson Chapman was at the farm at the time.

Exchange Base Ball Club Organized

President - J.M.Carpenter
Vice President - George Price
Secretary - Albin Price
Treasurer - P.W.Owen
Captain 1st Nine - J.W.Carpenter
Captain 2nd Nine - A.R.Carpenter

Capt. Samuel Cox rents hotel at station to Capt.
Ridgeway, conductor on passenger train and takes
possession with family at once. He will continue
his duties as conductor.

July 16, 1875, Vol. XXXII, No. 11

J.C.Hayden and wife, complainants vs A.J. Smoot,
administrator for James R. Tompkins, J.B.
Harrison and wife, defendants - offer for sale
"Fair View" or "Tompkins' Purchase" 270 acres.
John F. Semmes, deceased.
William H. Baxter married Lizzette V. Ratcliffe at
"Wellington," residence of bride's father on
Wednesday, July 7, by Rev. Samuel Saunders.
Misses Neale open boarding school for young ladies
near St. Thomas' Church. Formerly kept school at
their home "Mount Air."

199

James F. Matthews, candidate for State's Attorney.
William M. Burch, candidate for Sheriffalty.
James H. Morgan, P.A.L.Contee, William McK.
   Burroughs, John H.D.Wingate, Charles C. Perry.
   Commissioners will sell real estate of A.B.
   Simms, deceased, "Bachelor's Hope" 175 acres on
   Cobb Neck - comfortable dwelling.

Democratic Conservative
County Convention

President - John W. Mitchell
Vice President - J.W.Jenkins and Dr. A.J.Smoot
Secretaries - T.R.Farrall and D.I.Sanders
Delegates to State Convention nominated:
   Dr. Thomas C. Price, Dr. Peter W. Hawkins, George
   A. Huntt, Col. Samuel Cox, Dr. Thomas A. Carrico,
   and Vivian Brent, Esq. Elected: Price, Hawkins,
   and Huntt.
Delegates to Convention

1st District - John T. Davis, William Boswell,
George A. Huntt, P. Davis, William P. Compton,
Henry G. Robertson, William B. Matthews, A.G.
Chapman, J.W.Mitchell, T.R.Farrall.

2nd District - A.H.Robertson, Richard Price, Pliny
Bowie, J.J.Brawner, Joseph A. Gray, William B.
Fergusson, F.A.Hanson, H.H.Bowie, C.W.Millar,
E.A.Smith.

3rd District - Joseph Price, Thomas Haislip,
William H. Gray, T.C.Price, W.F.Hammack, John F.
Cobey, W.S.Chiles, Thomas E. Speake, Alexander
Haislip, Thomas Skinner.

4th District - George M. Lloyd, S.W.Dent, E.L.
Smoot, G.W.Thompson, Samuel Cox, Jr., C.C.Digges,
W.C.Nevett, Samuel Cox, Sr., J.L.Budd,
C.L.Carpenter.

5th District - A.J.Smoot, W.Simpson, C.A.Posey,
J.B.Norris, E.C.Dutton, F.Freeman, George Simpson,
H.Lignon, C.H.Sheirbourn, Thomas Wood.

6th District - Hugh Mitchell, William E. Dement,
S.H.Mitchell, John H. Cox, R.A.Murray, D.I.Sanders,
J.H.Hancock, E.J.Sanders, B.F.Blandford, A.W.S.Hicks.

7th District - T.R.Halley, Richard W. Bryan, A.T.
Monroe, J.W.Jenkins, O.N.Bryan, S.A.Miles. W.Little,

A.J.Norris, E.H.Brawner, J.S.M.Thomas.

8th District - W.M.Burch, J.T.Ward, E.V.Edelen,
Alexander Smoot, W.M.Jameson, H.F.Montgomery,
W.J.Boarman, F.L.Dent, R.Farrall, T.A.Carrico.

9th District - E.D.R.Bean, William Turner, A.Adams,
H.A.Canter, C.A.Webster, R.P.Wall, J.T.Wall,
R.Lamar, R.Robey, W.Gibbons.

Robert Rodey's house near Piney Church was struck
    by lightning. Little damage.

July 23, 1875, Vol. XXXII, No. 12

William Boswell, William P. Compton and Samuel Cox,
    Jr. Committee of Crescentia Grange announce they
    will hold a Home Market in Port Tobacco the first
    Tuesday of each month.
Mr. Dows, "Rosemary Lawn" will offer 25 Lincoln-
    shire long wool ram lambs for sale at Home Market
    in Port Tobacco.

Circuit Court Cases

State vs Peter Douglas, colored, for stealing books
    from DeSales Mudd, acquitted.
Samuel Cox vs Dennis B. McMahon - defendant moved to
    quash proceedings. In favor of claimant.

William H. Wade has new roof on his house.
George A. Huntt makes repairs on his hotel.
Editor Wells says "...In contemplation to give our
    present office building some needed repairs..."

George Washington Base Ball Club
Organized

President - J.T.Herbert
Vice President - R.H.Herbert
Treasurer - Robert C. Johnson
Secretary - John F. Boswell
Captain 1st Nine - J. Richard Cox
Captain 2nd Nine - Noble A. Thompson
Players - Juveniles - William Smoot, William Barnes,
Houston Morris, William Digges, William Morris,
H. Heber Boswell, Michael Fahey, Hensy Barnes,
James Shackelford.
Players - Foresters - John Gray, James Price,
George Gray, Joseph Cocking, Harris Stonestreet,
Gustavus Gray, Robert Young, Frank Gray,
_____ Mattingley.

Mrs. Mary E. Smoot, wife of Keeper of Light House,
Upper Cedar Point, has been appointed Assistant
Keeper "An excellent appoint, we have no doubt."

August 6, 1875, Vol. XXXII, No. 14

Dr. Edward Miles, deceased, property "The Farm
Called Mount Acacia" 300 acres on Mattawoman
Creek and Potomac River, ½ mile below Glymont -
"small but comfortable dwelling house, barn,
stable, granary, 2 tenement houses, etc." Also,
all that portion of the Farm called "Willow Glen,"
that is contained within the two fields that lie
next to public road and the lands of S.H.Cox and
E. Hyland Brawner...large and well-arranged dwelling house...lies in Mattawoman Valley..." Whole
tract contains about 500 acres. R.H.Edelen, trust.
Rev. Robert Prout, rector Durham Parish married
Bettie Cobey at "Efton Hills," home of bride's
mother by Rev. Dr. Lewin.
Mary H. Tompkins died in Washington City July 27,
5 a.m. She was 19 years, 13 days. "The richest
gems, the fairest flowers, Are chosen to adorn
the heavenly bowers."
Annie Hampton, beloved wife of Dr. John W. Hawkins
of Cockeysville, formerly of Charles County,
died in Cockeysville. She was the daughter of
Rev. S.S.Shriver of Alleghany County, Pennsylvania. She was 20 years old.
Virginia Bartle Lancaster died of consumption at
her late residence near Newport July 22. She
was 46 years old.
Misses Neale boarding school Terms:
Board, tuition, washing and mending per ann.$125
Music   25
French   10
One-half the above amounts are required semi-
annually in advance.
C.C.Digges is thanked by Editor for basket of apples
"...the kindly remembrance of the poor Printer by
the donor did our heart good."
Mrs. Lacey thanked for cantaloupe "of the nutmeg
variety...Blessed are they who remember the Printer."

August 13, 1875, Vol. XXXI, No. 15

Mary D. Adams died Saturday, Aug. 7th at her residence near Middletown. She was 83 years old.
"...active but retired life...rarely going from
home unless it was at the call of duty to admin-
ister to the sick and afflicted..."

C. Greenbaum, Hill-Top, is closing his country
  store business, general merchandise and household and kitchen furniture.
Miss Nellie Lewin "under direction of her father,
  Rev. Dr. Lewin, would like to take a few scholars
  to educate, with her sisters, at the Rectory.
  10 months, 1st Monday in September - last Friday
  in June

Elementary English branches $25.00
Higher English branches   40.00
(Latin and rudiments of French taught, at no
  extra charge)
Music (per quarter)   8.00
Drawing (per quarter)   5.00
Use of instrument   2.00

Literary Association

Constitution and by laws adopted. Officers elected:
    President - William Boswell
    Vice President - William M. Brent
    Secretary - D.I.Sanders
    Amanuensis - Wallace Mitchell
    Corresponding Secretary - Samuel N. Cox
    Treasurer - T. Yates Robey
    Librarian - T.J.Moore
    Committee on Questions - Eugene Digges, A.W.
      Neale, P. Wilmer
    Committee on Library - Messrs Mitchell, Cox and
      Robey.
    This group is to be not only a debating society
    but also a Circulating Library. A series of en-
    tertainments is contemplated to raise funds to
    start a library.
J.W.Warring's kitchen in Pomonkey was struck by
    lightning. Two negro boys sleeping there were
    stunned. Dr. Ruel K. Compton treated burned boy
    by applying cold water to body and use of stimu-
    lants. Skillful treatment saved boy's life.
Mr. Morgan of 5th District hired negro Hanson Small-
    wood to feed wheat threshing machine. Had to
    warn Smallwood about his bad feeding and laziness.
    Machine taken to son-in-law, Yates Barber, to
    thresh his wheat. Mr. Morgan rode over there and
    warned negro to properly feed machine. Smallwood
    insulted Morgan and he proceeded to hit him with
    handle of a cedar rake. Smallwood pulled him off
    his horse onto ground with such force Morgan's
    arm broke at the shoulder. Drs. Lancaster and
    Smoot sent for. Morgan too weak to even let
    doctors properly bandage arm.

Rough and Ready Base Ball Club

Near Pisgah, club organized last Saturday.
  President - N.T.Cox
  Vice President - E.J.Milstead
  Secretary - T.P.Simmons
  Captain First Nine - J.A.Franklin
  Captain Second Nine - J. A. Bowie

August 20, 1875, Vol. XXXII, No. 16

Philip Albert died "At Old House Hill" July 25,
   short illness, son of James R. Lawson and Sarah
   M. Higdon, 6 years, 9 months, 6 days "...the
   light of the house was dimmed when he was
   removed..."
Franz Boetner died, native of Prussia, at the home
   of his daughter, Mrs. A. Quenzel, Port Tobacco,
   Saturday, August 14. 70 years old.
Asa B. Fargo and Henrietta K, his wife, property
   "Hickory Level," "Eagles' Nest" and "Bendit's
   Rest" 223 acres to be sold at Court House door
   in Port Tobacco. Purchased from Dr. Thomas C.
   Price. Sarah L. Miller, administrator John
   Miller. In Nanjemoy, 3-4 miles from Nanjemoy
   Stores where all Potomac steamers make landings-
   comfortable dwelling, usual out-buildings.
Samuel W.H.McPherson appointed by Governor to be
   Registrar of 7th District, vacancy caused by
   death of Hyland M. Hannon.
J.H.Kinnamon thanked for "fine head of Flat Dutch
   cabbage - weighed 6#.
Francis Price, 18 years, drowned at wharf at Sandy
   Point on Potomac. Son of William H. Price, Esq.
Robert Davis shot by Charles J. Sidler after dis-
   pute about a coat between Davis and Mrs. Sidler.
   Davis' employer William B. Carpenter. Davis
   under care of Dr. A.H.Robertson. Sidler ar-
   rested and committed to jail.
Base ball game - Umpire - Percival Padgett;
   Scorers - Messrs S.C.Padgett and William M. Lewin.
   Bob Young played "remarkably well...he will be-
   come quite expert, provided always he lives
   long enough."
W.F.McGarner's candle on mantelpiece affected by
   lightning.

August 27, 1875, Vol. XXXII, No. 17

James L. Brawner, candidate for County Surveyor.

Hezekiah Franklin, deceased, property "Franklin's
Beginning" 100 acres, 2 small dwellings to be
sold at William B. Carpenter's store. Henry H.
Bowie, administrator.
William G. Robertson of Montgomery County married
Nellie B. Digges, daughter of late Judge Francis
Digges, of Charles County, in Washington City at
St. Peter's Church September 1 by Rev. Father
Boyle.
Samuel Judson Clements died of pneumonia at the
residence of his father near Duffield. He was
the son of Judson and Susan Ann Clements and
was 22 years of age.
Robert Digges, candidate Judge Orphans' Court.
W.O.Willett, Charles Stewart and Theodore Lyon
trustees of School #6, 6th E.D. need teacher.
Col. W.H.S.Taylor buried near spot where he was
born, beside his kindred Gov. William Stone.
Rev. Mr. Murer replaced at St. Thomas by Rev. Mr.
Wiget who was there many years ago.
John T. Davis (Agent for Washington Paving Co.)
has contract "to pave the flooring in all the
rooms on the first story of the Court House.
The material to be used is called 'artificial
stone flagging' and is said to be very durable."

Beantown Station

Situated on Baltimore and Potomac Rail Road about
two miles from old Beantown. It has 25-50 inhabitants. Messrs Sasscer and Gibbons are whole-
sale and retail dealers in dry goods. Pliny
Bealle keeps the hotel - patronized by both
white and colored visitors. Peter Trotter and
Son run blacksmith shop. Willie Trotter has
charge of shop.

September 24, 1875, Vol. XXXII, No. 21

Thomas Hawkins, Times chief engineer, had hog
stolen. Hugh Roberts had hog in same pen and it
mysteriously disappeared.
Ignatius Smallwood jailed after assaulting George
Spalding. Spalding and B. Mudd jointly own farm
near Newport. Justice Smoot fined Smallwood $50
and costs and was jailed when unable to pay.

4th District Registration List

Newly registered - James M. Bean, Ernest Day,
James L. Hill, Walter Smoot, William H. Sweetney,
F.H.Wheatly.
Transferred to - J.T.Boswell, Thomas H. Cooksey,
Thomas S. Jamison, Julian E. Norris, C.O.A.Oliver,
N.T.Philips.
Stricken off - transferred from - Joseph Clark,
Samuel Hawkins, William J. Knott.

October 1, 1875, Vol. XXXII, No. 22

Laura V. Thompson property "Barton's Addition" to
be sold for taxes.
C.W.Herganroeder advertises for sale warehouse in
Hughesville, 160 x 40' including 12 acres of land
"previously used for a tobacco curing warehouse."

Republican Convention

Dr. George D. Mudd called to chair. Following is
ticket -
Daniel W. Hawkins and Dr. F.M.Lancaster -Delegates
to House of Delegates
Eugene Digges - State's Attorney
George P. Jenkins, James M. Harvey, W.E.W.Rowe -
Judges Orphans' Court
William H. Wade - Sheriff
C.W.Sturdevant, Sylvester Mudd, J. Reverdy Carlin,
Thomas L. Hannon, George J. Chappelear - County
Commissioners
Committees to attend to Registration and to correct
Registration lists -
1st District - Albin Wade, white; Washington Burch,
colored
2nd District - William B. Carpenter, white; Juba
Barber, colored
3rd District - Noble Barnes, white; John Dunning,
colored
4th District - J.R.Carlin, white; Christopher Blair,
colored
5th District - William J. Higges, white; John
Barnes, colored
6th District - J.B.Sheriff, white; Darby Chunn,
colored
7th District - T.L.Hannon, white, Walter Swann,
colored
8th District - Enoch Jones, white; Caleb Reeves,
colored
9th District - George J. Chappelear, white,
Sylvester Thomas, colored.

"After a brief address by George P. Jenkins, Mr.
Digges and Dr. Wilmer, the piebald Convention ad-
journed at a late hour."

October 8, 1875, Vol. XXXII, No. 23

Comptroller's List of State Officers Whose Accounts are in Arrears

	Prin.	Int.	Total
Thomas J. Stewart, late Sh.	$1,058.00	$565.31	1623.31
William M. Morris " "	565.00	236.03	801.03
John R. Murray " "	210.31	49.00	259.31
William B. Carpenter " Coll 1874	515.12	15.62	530.74
J.A.Marlow Late Coll. 1874	240.39	7.20	247.59

October 15, 1875, Vol. XXXII, No. 24

Judges of Election

1st E.D.-Nicholas Stonestreet, Samuel Hawkins,
        Peregrine Davis;
2nd E.D.-James A. Franklin, D.J.Bragonia, James
        D. Milstead;
3rd E.D.-George M. Barnes, Alexander Haislip,
        Uzzial Wright;
4th E.D.-Samuel T. Swann, Joseph N. Harrison,
        C.C.Digges;
5th E.D.-Yates Barber, John B. McWilliams,
        Thomas Simms;
6th E.D.-Henry E. Mudd, Charles L. Gardiner,
        George F. Bealle;
7th E.D.-L.M.Southerland, William D. Mitchell,
        Theodore Dent;
8th E.D.-E.D.Boone, Thomas J. Boarman, P.A.Sasscer;
9th E.D.-Thomas E. Gardiner, E.D.R.Beane, Henry
        Gardiner.

Bernard Bridgett, near Centreville found a colored
   male child in a fence corner in a wood adjacent to
   his cornfield. Child now in possession of two old
   colored persons.
Robert Fergusson, Jr. was run over by a wagon load of
   lumber while going down Mount Hill "...this most
   dangerous road. We do not believe there is another
   civilized community which would have submitted so
   long to such an outrage."
W.H.S.Taylor's grave will be scene of solemn burial
   services of the Masonic Order.

John H. Bean married Alice R. Berry Tuesday, October 12 at St. Paul's Chapel, Piney, by Rev. Dr. Lewin.

John H. Bocock, Prince George's County, married Mary A. Hancock of Charles County on Tuesday, October 12 at Cox's Station by Rev. Dr. Lewin.

William Walter, infant son of William and Mary Sheirburn died at "Milton Hill," the residence of his grandmother on the 6th inst. He was 2 months and 25 days old.

Jere Herbert died at his residence in St. Inigoes' district, St. Mary's County the 5th inst. He was 77 years old and formerly from Charles County.

"Mount Tirzah" scene of tournament and ball to benefit William and Mary Parish.

Spencer Purser left Port Tobacco and went to California. On the way he taught school among the Mormons, whom he left in utter disgust..."

Barnard and Clark property, 1st Collection District, fishery, 10 acres sold for taxes. J.J.Brawner.

October 22, 1875, Vol. XXXII, No. 25

Archy Gray gave picnic at his farm near Port Tobacco. Democratic candidates invited.

R.A.Rennoe, deceased, personal property sold.

Col. W.H.S.Taylor rites - Worshipful Master - Henry G. Robertson; Past Master - John S. Button, Edgar Griswold and George Taylor; Senior and Junior Wardens - Dr. A.D.Cobey and J.H.Roberts; Secretary and Treasurer - B.D.Everett and John G. Chapman; Senior and Junior Deacons - J.J.Brawner and W.A.Fowke; Stewards - W.E.W.Rowe and James L. Brawner; Tiler - William Wolfe.

October 29, 1875, Vol. XXXII, No. 26

B.W.Spalding, White Plains, sells farm stock.

Charles E. Wade married Kate Youngman "At Pomphret Church..." Tuesday, October 26 by Rev. Father McAtee.

William C. Hardy married Mary F.E.Rowe at St. Paul's Chapel, Piney, Oct. 26 by Rev. Dr. Lewin.

Ola Blanchard died October 4 at Boyd's Hole, Va. She was the infant daughter of William H. and Philomenia J. Posey, formerly of Charles County. She was 14 months, 10 days old.

Mrs. Ann E. Brown died at the residence of her son-in law, John P. Marshall in Picawaxen Sunday last. She was 63 years old.

Perry Rennoe administrator, Reverdy Rennoe, deceased, sale of personal property.

Registration Lists
corrected in Oct. 1875

First District - Newly Registered
James Beans, Ned Brown, John H. Butler,
F.M.Brooke, Alexander Campbell, Richard H. Cooke,
George H. Cooke, William H. Coats, James M. Dyer,
Col. William N. Dorsett, Nathan Edelen, Fredrick
Farrall, Elias Farrall, Charles H. Farrall,
Wesley Franklin, Thomas Franklin, James R.
Garner, Thomas Gray, William E. Hill, William
Hanson, William Hawkins, Samuel Hawkins, Thomas
Luckett, John A. Lee, Walter Marr, James Marr,
Charles H. Milton, Richard E. Murdock, John H.
Mundle, T. Jackson Moore, Richard C. Moore, J.R.
Monroe, John Newman, James B. Owens, Lemuel B.
Owens, B.F.Oliver, Charles J. Pye, James L.
Padgett, Enoch Rollins, Samuel Smith, Richard
Smoot, John Smith, Alexius Stone, John H.
Thomas, Morgan Thompson, T. Beal Welch.
                Stricken Off
Creed Callwell, Charles H. Cross, William
Glascoe, John Holt, Zachariah Johnson, Alfred
Jenifer, Joseph Lee, Ticton Matthews, Richard F.
Mattingly, Henry Norris, John W. Swann, Madison
Thomas, Joseph Wallace, John A. Wink.

Second District - Newly Registered
Wesley Bowie, John S. Baxter, John Bowie, James
L. Carter, Henry Chapman, John A. Clements,
Walter H. Clements, Francis Cater, Charles H.
Cross, John F. Gilroy, Dennis Hawkins, Wesley
Jones, John F. Johnson, Thomas Jones, Joseph
Lee, Victor Matthews, Aloysius Matthews,
George W. Mckeel, Joseph H. Penn, Hezekiah Robey,
James H. Rison, Joseph Scott, Joseph S. Simmons,
Roszell Skinner, Herbert Short, Ferdinand Small,
Sylvester Skinner, Patrick Slattery, John A. Wenk,
Andrew Welch, Richard A. Wright.
                Stricken Off
J.B.T.Burgess, Dennis Brown, Francis Briscoe,
Jerome Dixon, Wesley Franklin, Thomas Franklin,
Mitchell Johnson, John W. Marbury, F.M.Nelson,
Charles J. Pye, Joseph E. Sanders, John Smith,
Charles H. Thomas, Noble Willis.

Third District - Newly Registered
James Butler, Dennis Brown, Ethelbert Bowie,
Joseph S. Franklin, Joseph Flowers, Nace Hanson,
John W. Hart, Gus. R. Ingraham, James Johnson,
Francis Johnson, Mitchell Johnson, Robert A.
Murdock, Lewis McDade, Thomas W. Price, Amos

Rison, Samuel Small, William T. Simmons, George
C. Simmons, William A. Southerland, Noble
Shelten, William S. Stewart, James Lit
Thompson, Noble Willis, Jubez Wright.
Stricken Off
Francis Cater, William Clements (dead), John F.
Gilroy, John F. Johnson, Patrick Slattery,
Richard A. Wright.

Fourth District - Newly Registered
Walter Adams, Stephen Boarman, F.A.H.Bush, Jesse
Clark, Thomas H. Cing, T.A.Dobbins, R.S.Garner,
William J. Hawkins, Robert Hawkins, B.T.Lyon,
Walter Middleton, Lewis T. Matthews, Marrion
Ouzts, P.B.Swann, William T. Swann, James L.
Thomas, R.O.Turner, George L. Taylor.
Transferred To
Creed Callvell, Joseph Campbell, John F. Dorey,
R.K.Dorey, S.W.Dyson, A.M.Freeman, John Holt,
Andrew Jackson, Henry Marshall, Hugh C. Nevitt,
Francis Nevitt, Henry Norris, Edward Proctor,
Joseph E. Sanders, William A. Swann, Charles H.
Thomas.
Stricken Off
John C. Bush, George W. Burk, Michael Courtney,
George H. Dorsey, Thomas B. Gough, John M.
Lancaster, A.P.Lloyd, Richard Thomas, John M.
Whitty.
Transferred From
R.H.Cook, John H. Davis, Thomas Luckett.

Fifth District - Newly Registered
Joseph A. Butler, Thomas M. Colbert, Stanny
Chisley, M.C.Hawkins, Thomas D. Hayden, Jr.,
Josias Jenkins, James Price, Peter Sweetning,
Gusta Short, William T. Stoddert, William
Frederick Short, William Short.
Stricken Off
Transferred
Henry Marshall.
Removed
Francis Bush, John E. Hopp, John M. Page,
David Smoot

Sixth District - Newly Registered
John W. Albrittain, W.W.Acton, Joseph Ayears,
Thomas Bloise, Washington Brown, Charles
Cambel, Charles Chapman, Charles H. Cambel,
Ignatius Digges, David Duckett, Richard
Farmer, Jr., James Forest, Jr., Washington
Hicks, Oscar Hill, John Johnson, Alfred Jenifer,
Charles B. King, Thomas R. McPherson, James A.

Murray, C.M.Martin, Charles E. Matthews,
William T. Moore, William E. Marlow, William
Miller, George A. Miller, Frank Miles, John R.
Nevett, Richard C. Oliver, S.B.Padgett, Peter W.
Robey, Francis P. Slattery, Joseph A. Wathen,
R.O.Wade, Daniel W. Wink, Henry L. Wood, Henry
Washington, Hilleary Young.

Stricken Off

Rogers Grindford, James King, Alexander Mason,
Gusty Mackle, William F. Thomas.

Transferred

John A. Booth, Charles Brawner, James Beans,
George H. Cook, John G. Clark, J.A.Clements,
Gusty Duckett, Alfred Duckett, Elias R. Farrall,
Charles H. Farrall, Thomas Grey, William E. Hill,
Joseph W. Hawkins, George Jameson, B.T.Jenkins,
Pliny Martin, Walter Marr, James Marr, Benjamin
F. Oliver, Joseph V. Padgett, J.T.Thompson,
T.B.Welch.

Seventh District - Newly Registered

William Brady, William P. Barker, J.A.Clements,
W.H.Dixon, Jerome Dixon, James N. Green,
Edmund Green, Thomas Gray, Samuel Johnson, John
W. Johnson, Scott Jackson, J. Webb Little, John
W. Marbury, Richard F. Mattingly, F.M.Nelson,
Charles H. Newman, Charles H. Pye, William Henry
Queen, William C. Robinson, Buck Ransom,
S.B.Smith, R.T.Tubman, John T. Thompson.

Stricken Off

William Abell, Matthew Cole, George W. Coombs,
Samuel Day, Alfred Dyson, Henry L. Etcherson,
James Forest, Richard Farmer, Thomas Gray, John
Johnson, Frank Miles, Thomas R. McPherson, John
R. Nevitt, Henry Offer, Joseph Benjamin Swann,
Henry L. Wood.

Eighth District - Newly Registered

Stephen Burch, Louis Butler, Ignatius Burch,
Patrick Butler, Charles H. Butler, James T.
Canter, Henry Chapman, Jr., John Godfrey Clarke,
Marcellus O. Dyson, Alfred Duckett, James
Duglass, Gusty Duckett, Robert Duckett, Josias
Duckett, Robert Leonard Dorsey, Samuel Duckett,
George H. Golden, Milton O. Hunter, Henry J.
Hawkins, John Haily, Richard E. Hughes, William
Joseph Jameson, Joseph Janifer, Benjamin T.
Jenkins, Zachariah Johnson, W.J.Knott, James
Langley of Henry, George C. Oliver, John Francis
Proctor, James V. Padgett, Robert Thomas, David
Thomas, William Thomas, Dory Thomas, Sandy

Washington, George H. Washington, Dominick Wade,
William H. Wood, James D. Washington, J. Allison
Wilmer.

Stricken Off
Transferred

Thomas Bloice, A.M.Freeman, Washington Hicks,
Andrew Jackson, Hanson Makle, William Mudd,
James A. Murray, Peter W. Robey, George W.
Runtzell, Joseph W. Taylor.

Erased

John S. Wade.

List of Grand Jurors
John S. Chapman, Foreman

Walter B. Wood, Thomas C. Wilkerson, John F.
Thompson, James H.M.Dutton, John F. Cobey, William
P. Flowers, George Dent, William L. Berry, Francis
P. Hamilton, James B. Latimer, Henry H. Bowie,
Alfred G. Lloyd, Warren O. Willett, John T. Higdon,
Edward L. Huntt, Alexander M. Freeman, John T.
Dutton, Addison Marbury, Charles C. Perry, Thomas
M. Posey, William McK. Burroughs, James A. Mudd.

Petit Jurors

Thomas J. Speake, William Hamilton, John L. Budd,
Benoni W. Hardy, E.N.Stonestreet, Washington A.
Posey, Samuel Cox, William H. Price, John H.D.
Wingate, William A. Fowke, Robert J. Lloyd,
J. Reverdy Carlin, Hugh Mitchell, Samuel Carrington,
Francis Carpenter, Samuel N. Cox, Frederick L.
Dent, William W. Cobey, Richard P. Wall, Thomas H.
Murray, Francis R. Burgess, John H. Cox, John J.
Hughes, Philip Harrison, William H. Gray.

Judges of Election Appointed

2nd E.D.-Ernest Hanson in place of James D. Milstead
3rd E.D.-E.W.Sturdevant in place of Uzzial Wright
6th E.D.-Thomas B. Berry in place of E.D.R.Bean
8th E.D.-Warner Gibbons in place of Geo. F. Bealle

Tournament and Ball at Port Tobacco

Chief Marshal - John T. Davis
Aids - J.E.Hamilton and Col. James S. Ammon
Heralds - E.H.Brawner, N.J.Miles and F.P.Jenkins
Judges - Col. Samuel Cox, P. Davis, T.J.Moore, Hugh
        Mitchell and Dr. George D. Mudd.
"A Ball at night, at the St. Charles Hotel, will
also come off and doubtless be well attended by the

beauty and grace of old Charles..."

List of Democratic Delegates
to the County Convention in P.T.

First District - John W. Mitchell, George A. Huntt,
John H. Jenkins, William Boswell, A.G.Chapman,
P.Davis, Dr. Robert Digges, John G. Chapman,
V. Brent, William P. Compton.
Second District - Charles H. Wills, J.J.Hughes,
J.J.Brawner, J.D.Milstead, J.B.Carpenter, H.H.
Bowie, W.A.Fowke, William B. Ferguson, Joseph A.
Gray, Benton Barnes.
Third District - Dr. T.C.Price, W.S.Chiles,
Thomas M. Posey, W.H.Gray, Alexander Haislip,
Joseph Price, Samuel W. Adams, Thomas Skinner,
R.H.Posey, Francis Dunnington.
Fourth District - W.B.Wood, George Dent, Sr.,
Samuel Cox, Sr., John T. Crismond, J.G.Gough,
John T. Colton, W.A.Posey, George Spalding,
Samuel Cox, Jr., Richard Cox.
Fifth District - C.H.Posey, C.C.Perry, B.G.Harris,
William Sheriburn, E.C.Dutton, Lemuel Smoot,
Dr. A.J.Smoot, Philip Harrison, J.H.D.Wingate,
J.E.Norris.
Sixth District - William F. Dement, D.I.Sanders,
T.T.Hancock, Hugh Mitchell, William E. Dement,
Dominic Mudd, F.B.Green, William Wolfe, J.H.Cox,
B.W.Spalding.
Seventh District - Thomas R. Halley, John W.
Jenkins, O.N.Bryan, S.A.Miles, A.J.Norris, A.T.
Monroe, William H. Cox, H.S.Mitchell, J.W.Halley,
H.M.Thomas.
Eighth District - Dr. P.W.Hawkins, Josias Hawkins,
J.F.Gardiner, M.L.McPherson, B.M.Edelen, Dr. T.A.
Carrico, Dr. E.V.Edelen, H.A.Turner, William H.
Berry, Townley Robey.
Ninth District - George W. Berry, William Cross,
R.P.Wall, J.W.Lamar, Richard Lamar, H.A.Lyon,
Rufus Robey, J.H.Luckett, John T. Wall, E.D.R.Bean.

Henry Kelly, colored, imprisoned for horse stealing
in Charles County 6 or 7 years ago in Penitentiary.
After serving five years he was pardoned and released. Now, he has been caught, tried, convicted and sentenced to seven years in the Penitentiary for same offense, committed this time in
Prince George's County.

November 5, 1875, Vol. XXXII, No. 27

Washington Hicks marries Mollie A. Wheeler of Iowa

at Waugh Chapel, Washington, D.C. September 30
by Rev. Richard Norris.

Mary Eliza, beloved wife of Rev. L.H.Jackson, Rector of Trinity Parish, died at the Rectory on October 23rd. She was 46 years old.

Mrs. Ann E. Brown died at the residence of her son-in-law, John P. Marshall, 25th ult. She was 66 years old. "...Deceased was a member of the Episcopal Church...In her last sickness, when told that her sands of life were nearly run, that her hour of departure was near at hand, she was enabled to exclaim: 'O death, where is thy sting? O, grave, where is thy victory?..."

V.H.Neale advertises a dark bay horse for sale.

B.L.Higdon warns trespassers from his farm "Locust Grove."

E.W.Sturdevant has public sale of personal property at "Chinquapin Farm" in Nanjemoy.

B.W.Spalding advertises private sale of farm stock. White Plains P.O.

A.C.Wenk advertises corn meal, hogshead siding, hoops, lumber and 100,000 bricks at Chapman's Mill.

John Dixon and J. Henry Murray warn trespassers.

A.J.Groves, Constable, will sell at auction for James H. Rison, deceased, property "Foxhill" by writ issued by William Dunnington. Richard Posey suit.

Rev. Robert Prout, rector, Durham Parish for 53 years. Recently visited by Dean of Washington Convocation. Dean Lewin was assisted by Rev. Charles D. Andrews, rector of Christ Church, Washington, D.C. where Rev. Prout was baptized.

Samuel Cox, because of health reasons, is giving up his merchandising business and will rent storehouse, barn, hay scales, etc. at Cox's Station.

Elizabeth C.C.Ware warns trespassers on "Oak Grove" and "Brentfield."

R. Cutler Fergusson warns trespassers on "Causin's Manor."

November 12, 1875, Vol. XXXII, No. 27

Mrs. Mary Ann Spalding died of paralysis at her residence in Washington City Oct. 22. She was 67 years old and the widow of the late George Rufus Spalding of Charles County, also the beloved daughter of Michael Cleary, Ocoquan, Virginia. "A true christian, a firm friend, a most devoted wife, mother and sister..."

Mary E. Larner property in 1st Collection District "Part of Montrose" 153 acres sold for taxes.

Edward Lloyd and John William Golden warn trespassers "...upon our respective Farms or Marshes..."
Circuit Court November Term to begin. Editor asks
friends to visit the Times office. "Recollect it
is now located on High Street, nearly opposite
the Post office..."
Outgoing Judges of Orphans' Court lauded for their
long and dedicated service to the County: Judge
Dent, Judge Robert Digges and The Hon. Richard
Barnes, Chief Justice.

Port Tobacco Tournament and Ball

R.C.Moore - Knight of St. Charles
LaVega Burch - Knight of Preference
R. Dudley Digges - Knight of Ivanho
Reed Wills - Knight of Potomac
Henry Mattingley - Knight of La Plata
Robert Murphy - Knight of Greenland
Camilus Howard - Knight of Cox's Station
Edwin Posey - Knight of Mount Tirzah
John R. Martin - Knight of Port Tobacco
Henry Hawkins - Knight of Eagles

Queen of Love and Beauty - Bessie Stone, crowned by
Knight of Mount Tirzah
1st Maid of Honor - Kate Wills, crowned by Knight of
La Plata
2nd Maid of Honor - Dotie Digges, crowned by Knight
of Potomac
3rd Maid of Honor - Bessie Wills, crowned by Knight
of Preference

November 19, 1875, Vol. XXXII, No. 28

Eugene Digges, State's Attorney, Charles County,
married Mary Iglehart, 2nd daughter of James A.
Iglehart of Anne Arundel County November 11th at
White Marsh, Prince George's County by Rev.
B.F.Wiget.
James A. Swann, deceased, property, house and lot in
Port Tobacco to be sold "so long used by said
Swann as an Oyster House and Restaurant, and small
farm known as part of 'May Day' 12 acres arable,
balance in wood and timber and is improved by a
small tenement."

Circuit Court Cases

A.J.Groves vs Peter Williams - tenant arrears in
rent-property sold, Williams bought to amount of
his debt-dispute over amount Groves should receive. Verdict against Groves.

State vs McLane Acton-assault with intent to kill
  William Moore, colored. Jury trial.
State vs Henry Washington, indicted for murder.

William H. Wade, newly elected sheriff presented
  bond to Orphans' Court for $25,000.00. Sureties
  are: M.O.Wade, Richard Wade, N.Stonestreet,
  D.W.Hawkins, B.G.Stonestreet, M.Thompson,
  J.H.Roberts and William L. Cooke.

November 26, 1875, Vol. XXXII, No. 29

Licenses for Sale of Liquor
Our Grand Jury of the present Term of Court, have
recommended the granting of license to the follow-
ing named persons, for the sale of spiritous or
fermented liquors, for one year from 1st of May
next.
John T. Colton. . . . . Allen's Fresh
E.A.Dutton. . . . . Duttonsville
James Rufus Perry . . . . Harris' Lot
Thaddeus Mudd . . . . Beantown
Turner Bros. . . . . Bryantown
John H. Chappelear. . . . . Bryantown
Thomas H. Murray. . . . . Bryantown
Benjamin Gross. . . . . Pomonkey
Theodore Gross. . . . .
J.M.Latimer & Son . . . . Newport
J.S.Lancaster, Lancaster's Wharf & on schooner
Chappelear & Bro. . . . . Hughesville
Thomas S. Dent. . . . . Mill Brook
Joseph Stein. . . . . Hill Top
Albin Price . . . . Exchange
J. Henry Turner . . . . Benedict
Thomas Skinner. . . . . Doncaster
William B. Carpenter. . . . . . . Mount Pisgah
Richard B. Posey. . . . .
Miss Elizabeth Duffey . . . . . . Duffield
John R. Edwards . . . . Benedict
Joseph H. Nutwell . . . . Hughesville
Richard Payne . . . . Allen's Fresh
George A. Scheckell . . . . Glymont
Coleman Greenebaum. . . . . Stilltown (Hilltop)
Rodier & Baum . . . . Marshall Hall
George A. Huntt . . . . Port Tobacco
M. Greenebaum . . . . Pisgah
G.T.Simpson . . . . Simpson Trap
Huntt & Norris. . Allen's Fresh & Centreville
Thomas J. Boarman . . . . Hughesville
Weems & Smith . . . . Newtown
Alfred Farrall. . . . . Newtown
W.W.Padgett . . . . Port Tobacco
Richard A. Garner . . . . Pye's Wharf

```
M.C.Herbert . . . . . . . . . . Newport
G.B.Shannon . . . . . . . . . .
J.H.Padgett . . . . . . . . . . Gallant Green
William H. Wade . . . . . . . . Port Tobaccc
C.D.Spaids. . . . . . . . . . . Glymont
J. Roberts & Co . . . . . . . . Port Tobacco
T.R.Farrall . . . . . . . . . . La Plata
S. Cox. . . . . . . . . . . . . Cox Station
Chiles & Harvey . . . . . . . . Liverpool Point
A.F.Bealle. . . . . . . . . . . Beantown Station
Peter Dill. . . . . . . . . . . Dill's Wharf
A.J.Walker. . . . . . . . . . . Jacksonville
E.C.Dutton. . . . . . . . . . . Tomkinsville
R.S.Corry . . . . . . . . . . . Newport
J.W.Fowler. . . . . . . . . . . Chapel Point
Bean & Lyon . . . . . . . . . . Patuxent City
Huntt & Ward. . . . . . . . . . Bensville
Flora Gross . . . . . . . . . . Pomonkey
Isaac Gross . . . . . . . . . . Port Tobacco
Thomas F. Nicholson . . . . . . Benedict
T. Jackson Moore. . . . . . . . Port Tobacco
J.L.Lacey . . . . . . . . . . . Port Tobacco
L.A.Martin. . . . . . . . . . . Port Tobacco
James Little. . . . . . . . . . Marshall Hall
Lemuel W. Maddox. . . . . . . . Bayne
```

F.W.Stone, Port Tobacco P.O. has lost 1 ox and
   1 heifer "From the Hill-Top marshes..."
James T. Padgett married Martha Maria Albrittain
   in Christ Church, Port Tobacco by Rev. Dr. Lewin
   on Monday last.
Henry G. Robertson married Annie Stone, daughter
   of Hon. F. Stone in Christ Church, Port Tobacco,
   Wednesday last by Rev. Dr. Lewin.
Thomas Edwin Speake married Miss Buena Vista,
   daughter of the late Dr. George Clagett of Prince
   George's County at Nanjemoy Church, Durham Parish on the 16th inst.
State vs McLane Acton-jury-not guilty.
State vs Henry Washington-judges-not guilty.
State vs John Clements indicted for resisting arrest
   by Sheriff Cooke-acquitted.
F.P.Hamilton's horse which was reported stolen, was
   found dead in a marsh where it had strayed and
   become mired.

December 3, 1875, Vol. XXXII, No. 30

John S. Richmond advertises auction sale of farm
   animals, tools, household furniture.
John T. Crismond advertises real estate sale of
   land below public road from Newport to Allen's

Fresh-2 tenant house-barns, etc.
John W. Wheatley married Fannie C. Robey st St.
    Peter's Church, Washington City 25th November.
Judges of Orphans' Court met - Mr. Harvey declined
    Chief Judgeship-defer to Judge Jenkins-granted
    letters of administration to M.M.Haviland upon
    estate of Lelia Haviland and to William J. Molly-
    horn on the estate of Joseph Herbert-admitted to
    probate the will of Hannah Ann Gregory.
County Commissioners met - George J. Chappelear
    elected President - Charles E. Hannon appointed
    Clerk - Nicholas Stonestreet appointed attorney -
    Washington Burch, colored, appointed Bailiff.
Joseph Lancaster in business of shucking oysters on
    his vessel and then put on train at Pope's Creek
    for Baltimore - Parties there will pay 56¢
    a gallon.

December 24, 1875, Vol. XXXII, No. 32

Daniel Haviland and Lillias Haviland, deceased,
    property sold near Bryantown - furniture, farm
    implements, etc. Joseph H. Haviland and Merrit
    M. Haviland, executors.
Francis Nevitt married Roberta Burch in Christ
    Church of William and Mary Parish on Dec. 15th
    by Rev. John M. Todd. She is the daughter of
    the late John A. Burroughs, Esq. (A descrip-
    tion of the wedding appeared for the first time
    in this newspaper. It was submitted by one of
    the guests.)
Richard Swann "a worthy colored man" living near
    Cox's Station lost house and two children to
    fire, also furniture, 1000# pork, part of to-
    bacco crop, 15 bbls corn and a dog.

December 31, 1875, Vol. XXXII, No. 33

James E. Wingate and others vs William Boswell,
    administrator and heirs of James A. Swann.
Notley J. Dutton, formerly of Charles County,
    married Belle McLaughlin of Baltimore 22 Dec.
    by Rev. Thomas L. Poulson.

INDEX

Note: Property names appear in this index under the heading, "Tract".

BARBOUR, Ben 27 Jacob 27 Robert 27
BARKER, W P 33 William P 211 Wm P 25
BARKLEY, W H 14 Walter H 5 33
BARNARD, 208
BARNED, ---- 99
BARNES, Beal T 30 Benton 69 93 104 142 144 177 213 Charles 23 49 Charles W 54 Eleanor 164 George M 23 166 193 207 Hannah 117 Hanson 23 Hendley 174 Henly 161 Hensy 201 Hillery 23 J J 196 J J B 178 179 James E 30 John 25 173 206 John H 25 John I B 28 Joseph E 30 Louis 28 Mary Estelle 186 N E 151 Noble 206 Noble E 179 195 R 58 R Jr 106 118 145 Rezin 62 Richard 2 9 18 57 92 144 177 193 215 Richard Jr 20 94 95 190 194 Richard Sr 71 73 T Benton 117 Walter 49 Walter M 11 William 201
BARNS, Ferdinand 27 Henley 27 Henry 27 James 27 John 27 Truman 27
BARRIS, Leon 33
BASTIN, Lorenzo 27 Pearson 27
BASTING, Walter 181
BATEMAN, Benjamin 62 James 167 179 James T 11 53 60 147 Joseph F 33 Mary E 37 Mr 126 Notley 154 Notley H 37 Richard 38
BATEMEN, James 97
BATTLE, Alfred 32
BATTLES, Alfred 150
BAUM, 216
BAXTER, Henry 34 Isam 61 J S 33 John S 25 173 209 Lizzette V 199 Philomenia Jane 78 W 148 William 147 William H 94 96 199
BEAL, John 23
BEALE, George F 104
BEALL, A 59 B F 33 B Franklin 27 Francis 174 Geo F 10 George F 9 46 166 J 16 John Henry 173 Nathan 33 Rachel A 163 Thomas 25 173 Thornton 16 25 Wesley 173

BEALLE, A F 217 Ann 58 Geo F 212 George F 57 58 93 98 145 146 177 193 195 207 J W F 161 John G 147 Pliny 205
BEALLY, Hanson 11
BEAN, 217 Alice R 208 D R 180 E D R 10 13 17 18 20 60-62 69 72 97 98 147 150 158 166 194 201 212 213 Edward D R 1 155 Francis 23 Grace 199 H H 17 39 40 53-55 76 89 150 Harriet 85 Henry H 81 Hezekiah H 99 James 169 James M 81 206 John 11 23 John H 85 208 Thomas O 68 81 W H 85 W N 21 118 153 William E 85 William N 146 158
BEANE, E D R 207 John H 195
BEANS, Francis H 28 James 32 209 211 Jim 32 Peter 32 Sam 32
BEATLEY, John H 25
BEAUFORT, Jerry 30
BELL, Alfred 25 Cato 30 H 97 Hanson 30 95 96 Hillery 30 John 30 John Henry 25 Philip 30 Robert G 174 Thornton 149 Walbert 30 74 Wesley 25
BELT, 165 Frederick 32
BERKLEY, William N 80
BERNARD, Z 166
BERRY, Alice R 208 C M 150 Clara D 78 Edward 179 G H 181 Geo W 10 George 118 197 George F 45 George W 17 30 47 141 158 175 197 213 Henry 23 Julian 78 L Brook 175 Maria 16 N E 154 Samuel 77 Samuel H 75 Samuel T 11 12 16 20 57 149 161 Thomas B 3 4 9 57 59 93 104 144 145 161 177 191 194 198 212 Thomas B Jr 11 Thomas Jr 12 W L 97 Washington 36 181 William 67 99 William F 22 195 William H 20 62 69 93 101 102 177 194 213 William L 16 46 58 62 99 150 177 212
BEST, John 34
BISCOE, Christopher C 28
BISHOP, 91 John H 137
BLACKISTON, James H 28 John 28
BLACKISTONE, John F 34 John H 34 Peter 34

BRAGONIER, Daniel J 166
BRANCH, Sandy 27 William 27
BRANSON, Alfred 33
BRANSTON, Louis 33
BRATTON, Thomas 27
BRAWNER, Amanda E D 165
Charles 11 32 211 E H 138 160
201 212 E Hyland 170 202 Edgar
138 150 158 178 181 198 Fannie
183 Francis 30 Henry A 66
Highland 62 Hyland 198 J A 105
123 183 J Alexander 122 J C 192
J J 180 200 208 213 J L 58
James L 12 21 52 67 70 77 99
105 111 141 146 148 165 171
179 204 208 John 23 John J 85
122 148 171 197 John R 30
Jordan 33 Joseph 32 Josey 12
Jourdan 113 Maggie J 170 Mattie
66 Mr 56 Mrs 165 Mrs J E 150
Swaney 32 W Frank 183 William
28 William F 66 148 William H
70 73 78 William L 173
BRENT, 182 George 3 104 109 185
Henry 116 Ida D 116 James 36
Judge 38 151 V 3 23 78 83 213
Vivian 8 12 14 22 59 63 82 96
100 105 146 150 168 171 200 W
C 59 65 104 116 133 William C 1
6 13 19 61 97 98 103 148 194
William M 203 Wm C 58 59
BRIDGETT, Bernard 207 Frank 12
Thomas 99 Thomas S 81
BRISCO, Thomas 33
BRISCOE, Addison 30 E 170 150
Francis 25 209 George 34 Gusty
34 Henry 28 John T 28 Lewis 32
Nace 36 Patrick 34 Philip T 28
Richard 28 T M 149 Theobold 58
Thomas 27 William 32
BROOK, A M 146 George 33 James
O 28
BROOKE, A M 149 185 Baker 135 F
M 209
BROOKS, Basil 25 173 Bill 138
Charles 36 Dennis 11 32 Jacob
36 59 John 23 32 Moses 36
BROTHERTON, Morris C 88 Sarah
M 88
BROWN, Ann E 208 214 Anthony
23 59 Basil 25 C G 60

BROWN (Continued)
Charles 27 32 88 Charles Francis
23 Charles H 30 Charles Henry
31 Dennis 27 209 Dominic 30
Edward 34 Eliza 11 Francis 30
Frank 12 G L 82 G T 118 175
George 25 33 96 George H 23
George W 33 Gustavus 21 89
Gusty 30 Gusty T 30 Harrison 23
Henry 23 25 30 Isaac 27 113
James 25 30 33 113 James H 30
34 James R 30 Jane 59 81 John
28 95 96 John H 34 John R 28
30 Lucinda 195 196 Ned 209
Patrick 32 175 Phil 32 Robert
171 Thomas 23 33 34 Wallace 33
Washington 28 34 196 210 Wil-
liam 23 33 61 115 Wm Henry 32
BRUCE, Andrew 15 H 44 W H 39
William 122 William Henry 191
BRYAN, A M 105 107 Alexander
Marbury 185 Ella Hanson 185 F
W 50 G R 33 107 George B 60
George R 61 81 94 96 J B 59 O N
40 41 67 72 85 139 171 177 179
200 213 Oliver N 6 39 46 58 157
160 194 R W 98 160 Richard W 1
7 17 46 58 61 94 95 101 114 123
155 194 200
BRYANT, G H 54 Oliver N 62
BUCKNER, Andrew 34
BUDD, Henry L Sr 69 J L 200 John
L 18 21 58 63 73 75 98 146 156
178 194 212
BUMBERY, James 33
BURCH, 117 A M 94 96 Amelia
Josephine 84 B F 10 17 46 97 98
121 178 195 Benjamin F 23 58
94 95 C Eugene 34 C L 17 20
Catharine D 8 43 Charles G 28
Charles L 6 10 14 17 D F 137 G
C 1 10 13 20 46 51 61 94-98 118
146 155 158 178 179 190 G E
194 George C 58 Gonzaga C 140
H A 91 Henry A 45 68 177 194-
196 Hosea 17 181 Hy A 9 Ignati-
us 211 J M 10 94 96 J W 10
James M 58 69 93 99 145 191
194 James W 9 21 Jere W 9 12
21 57 58 93 94 96 104 118 145
158 177 189 Jeremiah W 193

BURCH (Continued)
John A 28 103 178 Josea 34 L
169 L W 196 Landlord 184
Lavega 215 Marcellous 194
Marcellus 158 178 191 Maria D
193 Richard H 178 Robert L 6
Roberta 218 Samuel 23 Stephen
178 211 Susan R 45 Thomas A
34 151 174 W M 118 201 Wash-
ington 23 154 178 180 197 206
218 William 23 94 William J 94
96 William M 10 46 48 58 61 84
94-96 98 146 200 Wm M 96
BURDINE, Mr 189
BURFY, James 171 188
BURGESS, Benton 62 164 F C 39
59 67 F R 44 F Richard 157
Fannie 183 Francis R 198 212
Hannah O 44 J B T 209 John 16
John B 124 John B F 149 Lizzie
157 N 95 96 Richard 59 149
Thomas A 39 101 114 124
Washington 30
BURK, George W 210
BURKE, Richard 179 William 146
147
BURKS, William P 76
BURROUGHS, B B 115 Edward 30
Eliza C 44 Eliza T 85 Esther 125
J A 18 James 36 John A 62 83
85 102 218 John W 30 Lewis 30
Mary 115 McKennie William 85 E
E 167 Mrs McK 125 126 Rebecca
D 140 Robert 30 Sallie 51 W McK
124 William McK 51 121 200 212
William McKenney 162 189
BURTLES, William 187 William E
156
BUSH, F A H 210 Francis 28 210
Henry 28 John 21 John C 4 5 19
28 95 96 210 Josias 28 William 28
BUTLER, 115 Aaron 32 113 Alexius
25 174 Austin 30 Benjamin 36 C
J 33 Charles 23 Charles H 113
211 Charles Henry 36 Charles J
57 93 Clem 15 Cornelius 33 Dury
34 Emanuel 32 Fitzjames 23 Geo
11 George 32 36 George A 30
George Henry 23 H 12 Harrison
32 Harry 34 Henry 25 27 28 33
Henson 32 Ignatius 30 Jacob 23

BUTLER (Continued)
James 27 209 James Mad 34
James R 34 James W 30 Joe 32
John 33 34 195 196 John F 34
John H 30 209 John Henry 36
John R 36 John S 27 John T 28
113 Joseph 36 Joseph A 210
Leonard 25 M 12 Madison 23
Miley 34 Patrick 211 Reubin 149
Richard 23 174 Richard C 30
Richard Thos 34 S A 33 Sandy A
125 156 Smith 114 Stephen 34 T
Smith 34 Thomas 23 30 Thomas
H 34 W 59 Walter 27 Washington
28 William 27 28 36 146 147
William H 33 Wm 27 Wm Alex 34
Wm Joseph 25
BUTTON, John S 6 40 52 66 77 81
111 171 195 198 208 Mr 124
168 Sarah Jane 81
CALBERT, James H 32 Richard 32
CALLAN, Charles C 101
CALLVELL, Creed 210
CALLWELL, Creed 28 209
CALVERT, Abraham 28 Hanson 30
John T 30 Joseph A 28 R 59
Robert 4 Rufus 30 Thomas 4 34
William 30
CAMBEL, Charles 210
CAMERON, Moses 24 113
CAMPBELL, A 198 Alexander 209
Alexius Jr 28 Charles 28 Charles
Jr 28 George F 28 Isaac 45 Jas
Wm 25 Joseph 28 210 Math 30
Rhoda M 183 Wash'ton 28 Wil-
liam 28 William T 183
CANAN, James A 151
CANTER, A E 179 Ann 181 Frances
O 154 George F 34 186 H 91 H A
51 181 201 Henry 99 Henry A 17
James T 176 211 Jane 99 Mary
Estelle 186 Robert 150 S A 181
CAREY, Charles 179 Charles J 196
Egbert 70 73 122 M M 179
CARLIN, J A 194 J R 10 21 40 57 59
75 118 146 206 J Reverdy 1 98
206 212 Justice 114 Reverdy A
149 Sarah E 21
CARLSON, R 13
CARPENTER, 18 153 A R 199 C L
118 200 Catharine E 133

CARPENTER (Continued)
Charles L 46 58 145 Charles T 73
D W 61 F 118 F A 62 99 195 196
Francis 93 94 95 212 Francis A
98 G J 58 George 7 25 153 198
George M 114 George W 1 7 19
20 59 61 63 67 98 103 137 148
155 158 161 180 George W Jr 61
179 J B 49 67 213 J M 199 J
Wesley 173 James D 45 James F
145 John B 23 60 69 93 97 99
148 149 194 198 John H 16 Kate
43 69 Marbury 43 133 Mary E
114 William B 13 16 69 97 98
114 148 160 180 191 195 197
199 204-207 216

CARPINTER, Bettie 154 J D 154
William B 179

CARR, Levin 32 33 175

CARRICO, A 169 181 Albert 195 G
169 George 189 190 George W 17
T A 12 17 61 67 83 97 133 201
213 Thomas 16 17 20 57 68 94
95 98 99 149 150 155 166 172
179 181 194 Thomas A 2 12 17
59 62 78 80 99 183 200

CARRINGTON, F C 151 Jane S 37
John 62 84 101 155 181 198
John W 101 150 151 Mary E 101
155 Samuel 38 69 93 212 William 14 175 198

CARROLL, Anthony 12 27 Oswald
33 William 27

CARTER, Francis H 34 Henry 33
James 28 James L 209 Moses 27
Thomas 28 174 William 33

CARTWRIGHT, John E 28

CARY, Egbert 91 James 24

CASH, John W 141 John William
156 175 Robert L 30

CASSIN, ---- 181 J R 149

CATER, Francis 27 209 210

CAUSIN, G B 46

CAWOOD, H R V 33 85 Lawrence 28
S H 33

CHAPALEAR, G J 59 George 59
George J 57 60 68 94 96

CHAPELEAR, J H 93 John A 91

CHAPMAN, 55 A G 14 18 20 39 55
60 105 121 153 157 166 200 213
A G 140 Alexius 34 Andres G 39

CHAPMAN (Continued)
Andrew G 15 17 56 63 71 73 76
100 105 133 150 158 181 182
Caleb 32 Charles 33 Edward 30
Ellen 7 67 G 59 General 157
George 179 196 197 George Jr
175 George Pearson 7 Helen M
66 Helen Mary 76 Henry 11 209
Henry Jr 211 J G 21 22 46 57 68
75 81 104 106 170 172 John C
94 John G 15 20 22 23 62 67 83
95 149 157 162 171 179 181 196
208 213 John S 50 144 186 212
John W 33 34 M 10 58 59 179
194 Marcellus 28 Margaret
Harwood 66 Marshall 7 15 59 67
69 94 95 190 196 Matilda L A
186 Matthew 33 Nathan 32 P 14
57 Pearson 6 20 50 57 76 87 199
R 181 R A 160 R F 94 96 179
Raymond 152 Robert A 196
Sigismunda M 6 Simon 35 76
Susan 81 82 Susan P A 83 T
Raymond 175 Warring 30
Washington 25 William H 113
Wm H 36 Wm Henry 32

CHAPPALEAR, Geo J 11 Geo 17 18
George J 17 George R 17 John 11

CHAPPALIER, George 17

CHAPPELEAR, 71 152 216 George
181 198 George J 11 118 145
150 160 180 196 197 206 218 J
H 180 James W 178 John H 36
103 137 145 148 177-179 190
192 194 195 197 198 216

CHASE, Baptist 34 Edward 25
George 33 Gusty 24 Ignatius 28
John 33 Josias 36 Raymond 36

CHES, John Henry 24

CHESLEY, George 34 Rev Mr 44

CHEW, Michael 176

CHILDS, 99

CHILES, 217 W I 8 W S 200 213
William H 76 77 William J 69 72
78 155 159 161 174 William L 66
William S 67 161 191 194

CHING, Robert C 141 T K 10 67
Thomas K 82 133 146 157 158
195 Thos K 11 62

CHIPLEY, E S 3 James 60 James T
50 Mary 50

227

228

EDELEN (Continued)
E V 83 94 96 99 133 201 213
Edward 20 Edward V 12 Eliza-
beth 20 Francis H 9 Geo Richard
35 George 109 H 12 Harrison 12
35 Henry 179 John 29 179 John
Robert 175 Laura 168 Lawrence
28 Leonard B 20 Leonard C 2 68
Louisa 5 Maria 168 Mary F 5
Millard 12 Mrs C 62 Nathan 209
Phil V 176 R H 4 7 8 14 21 59 60
66 67 77 78 82 105 106 122 125
153 163 164 168 182 202 R W 2
Richard H 63 100 106 147 164
198 Sarah 62 109 Sarah H R 9 W
T 62 William F 68 Wm Harrison
35 Wm Joseph 35
EDELIN, Baker 66 Bazella 189
Henry 196 John Henry 24 Paul
24 179
EDGERLY, Daniel W 108 Malvine S
108
EDISON, Henry 33
EDWARD, John Sr 29 Lewis 175
EDWARDS, John E 157 John R 216
Lewis 32 58 113 Mary E 157
EILBECK, William 89
ELKAHAN, Lyon 16
ELKINS, William H 60
ELZEAR, Thomas 113
EMPSON, William 135
ETCHERSON, Henry L 211 W L 33
EVERETT, B D 208 D D 145 J W 93
145 Joanna C 77 P D 33 177
FAHEY, Michael 201
FANTZ, Cap 103
FARGO, Asa B 174 204 Henrietta K
204
FARMER, Francis 35 192 Hanson
24 113 141 Ignatius 25 Richard
32 211 Richard Jr 210 Samuel
29 W H 97
FARRAL, Charles H 209 Dick 191
Elias 209 R 201 Stanislaus 115
FARRALL, Albert 35 39 60 97 148
180 195 196 197 Alfred 216
Caroline 18 Catharine 189
Charles 64 Charles H 211 Elias R
211 Fredrick 209 J William 174
James T 150 Joseph 24 Josie
Clara 115 Michael 6 Mr 123

FARRALL (Continued)
Nathan H 113 Nathan Henry 24
R 67 R T 13 34 187 Rich 10
Richard 17 20 21 58 152 178
Stanislaus 17 T B 12 T R 15 118
180 188 191 200 217 Thomas
196 Thomas B 94 Thomas L 29
Thomas R 22 36 61 72 95 97 98
117 140 146 148 168 195-197
William 17
FARRAN, John 11
FARROLL, Charles 5 Elizabeth 5
Jane 5
FEARSON, John 37 51 W T 70
FENDALL, Adelene 11 Ben 59 J C
12 John 89 Phil Rd 89
FENDELL, Chapelier 24 Geo Othos
M 24 Nathaniel 24 Oscar Levi 24
Walter 24
FENWICK, Hillery 29 James C 29
Washington 24 William 93
FERGUSON, Robert 181 William B
181 213
FERGUSSON, Charles Jr 84 Jennie
6 John H 32 Katie S 170 R 18 R
C 18 119 167 R Cutler 214 R Jr
56 Robert 15 18 41 Robert Cutler
170 Robert Jr 207 W B 57 Wil-
liam 191 William B 15 20 69 93
157 169 200 Wm Albert 32
FFENDALL, Josias 134 135
FIELDS, Jane 60
FINICK, John 24 Louis 24 William
24
FLAHERTY, Anthony 60
FLARITY, Anthony 33 John 33
FLETCHER, James 33
FLOWERS, J C 12 Joseph 27 209 W
P 1 115 William 13 William P 10
16 46 57 58 61 70 93 99 145 146
155 177-179 194 212
FLOYD, Olivia 12 Sarah 18 98 149
157
FOLEY, Rev Mr 152
FORBES, George 32 75 77 George
Sr 89 Nace 32 Richard 35 58 59
175 176
FORD, Adam 35 113 176 Calvin 30
Clem 11 24 Dallas 29 195 Dallis
179 David 36 Ford 55 Francis 33
113 George 36 Henry 27 36

HAISLIP (Continued)
207 213 Alexandria 193 Alpheus
87 194 James 61 Thomas 200
Walter A 149
HALL, George 26 Grandison 26
Henry H 24 John 89 Richard 4
William 35
HALLEY, 67 171 Charles 35 J T 14
105 J W 213 James T 115 John
M 107 John W 14 158 178 194
Mollie C 115 Nathaniel 107 R T
11 93 R Turner 105 Richard T 11
59 T R 200 Thomas B 57 Thomas
R 9 12 16 67 71 73 92 98 107
133 140 144 160 178 190 194
213 Winfield 33 98 Z W 105 107
HALLY, Thomas R 177
HAMERSLEY, Glovia 149 J 12 John
10 Mrs G 102
HAMERSLY, John 69
HAMESLY, Joseph 30 William J 30
HAMILTON, 55 C H 42 Cecilia 185 F
P 10 57 97 109 155 167 169 194
217 Francis 19 Francis P 19 20
57 60 111 145 177 195 212
Frank P 92 H W 16 Henry 17 J E
212 J Edward 185 J L 16 17 60
James E 14 John 3 7 15 62 66
99 104 139 145 149 158 168 191
194 John E Jr 22 L L 67 Margaret A 112 142 Mary Emily 101 Mr
3 45 Mrs 152 Nannie L 191 P H
46 Patrick H 191 Priscilla 19 W
11 William 9 10 18 57 93 104
142 145 147 148 177 181 194
212 William N 161 Wm 12
HAMMACK, Emmet 154 Homer B
154 W F 200 William F 164 178
182 195
HAMMERSLEY, Hanson 36 John 9
HAMPTON, Annie 202
HAMSLEY, Elisabeth 179 Mary 179
HANCOCK, A A 35 F 16 J H 59 67
200 John 16 145 155 John H 48
61 94 95 98 148 158 164 178
179 190 194 196 197 Jos H 59
Mary A 208 Mary Henrietta 107
R S 181 Sarah J 39 T T 63 107
213 Thos A 19 195 Thos F 195
Thomas T 175 William A 197
HANNON, Charles E 9 57 93 104

HANNON (Continued)
142 144-146 156 177 182 191
194 198 218 H M 180 Henry M 1
13 61 98 103 137 148 155 164
197 Hyland M 204 Mrs J A 17 N
B 150 Noel B 9 198 T L 14 67
118 206 Thomas L 146 153 194
206
HANSON, 182 Daniel 27 Earnest 1
104 Ernest 16 107 118 142 144
145 146 177 191 194-196 212 F
195 F A 145 177 200 F Alvan 77
H Ernest 18 H Maud 77 Harrison
32 33 Henry 26 Ignatius 24 Israel
26 J D 2 38 59 101 James 24
Jennie R 77 Jere 29 John D 173
John Jr 29 46 John Sr 29 John
W 29 Maggie 90 Nace 209 R W
149 Robert W 15 S 65 Sam 89
Samuel 3 15 20 23 41 49 57 62
67 69 71 73 92 93 109 144 145
177 181 194 Thomas 96 Walter
89 Wesley 195 William 209 Wm
Henry 35
HARBIN, Mr 45 R H 98 146 Richard
11 12 Robert H 147 148 W 60
HARDESTY, Joseph F 195 Richard T
26
HARDINER, George H 155
HARDING, William L 12 20 57 58 93
95 158 161 178 Wm L 10
HARDY, B W 14 69 93 178 Benja-
min 61 Benoni W 158 212
Charles C 16 21 158 Francis Mrs
22 John F 20 57 Mary F E 208
William C 208 Wm Clinton 32
HARMAN, D H 108 David H 108
Elizabeth A 108
HARNED, H W 99 181
HARNEY, Patrick 176
HARRIS, B G 95-97 162 167 179
213 H R 46 67 Henry R 46 58 62
90 102 121 149 James 30
Joseph 179 M A 184 Mr 189 Mrs
H R 66 Mrs T 150 Nannie C 90 R
G 59 77 Rev Mr 66 Thomas 184
HARRISON, George 27 J B 199 J N
193 John B 161 Joseph N 166
207 Joseph R 67 M A 184 P 149
Philip 118 124 145 146 212 213
Phillip 177 Richard 89 176

HARRISON (Continued)
Richardson 176 Walter 45 Wirt
141 184
HART, C H 27 Charles 166 John 27
John W 209 Richard W 173 T R
61
HARTY, James 30
HARVEY, 99 217 Alice 97 Ann 149
James 166 James M 66 115 193
206 Mr 190 218 William P 72 99
HATCH, John 135
HATCHER, Robert H 184
HATTON, Peter D 62
HAVILAND, D P 20 53 Daniel 218
Daniel P 46 64 E W 91 J H 51
James 99 Joseph H 71 72 106
218 Lelia 218 Lillias 218 M M
218 Merrit M 218
HAWKINS, 67 140 188 189 200
Andrew 29 Benjamin 35 141
Charles 35 Charles B 33 D M 58
D W 20 96 182 192 198 216
Daniel 30 32 Daniel W 2 14 22
63 64 73 100 150 206 Daniel
Webster 167 Delvey 26 173
Dennis 24 195 196 209 Emily
157 Family 188 Francis 35 Geo
Henry 24 George 26 33 196
George T 188 H 15 Harry 26
Henry 112 142 176 215 Henry H
35 Henry J 175 211 Hillery 29 36
Hollin 24 Hugh 29 J 58 59 195 J
H 20 33 J H Jr 169 Jane Y 39
Jas Sam'l 35 John 24 36 197
John A 29 John Daniel 24 John
H 29 John L 119 John W 50 202
Joseph 33 Joseph W 211 Joseph
Wm 32 Josias 9 17 20 43 46 57
67 71 73 82 88 92 140 144 152
160 171 177 190 213 Josias H
17 20 22 39 99 150 177 181
Littleton 33 Lizzie 157 Luke W B
1 15 16 M C 210 Margaret 149
Matthew 29 Mr 168 Mrs Augusta
R 119 Mrs Luke 139 Nannie 169
P W 20 67 72 155 213 Peter W
17 140 200 Philip 122 Richard
24 Richard E 36 Robert 29 195
196 210 Samuel 10 15 35 145
166 193 195 196 206 207 209
Samuel J 24 Smith 36

HAWKINS (Continued)
Stephen 36 59 195 197 T Y 176
Thomas 24 205 Warren 29 Wil-
liam 209 William B 29 William J
210 William Jr 29 William Sr 29
HAYDEN, A 30 53 149 Aloysius 59
B 149 B G 149 C F 153 180
Charles 31 141 Charles F 80 81
148 J C 147 149 161 179 195
199 L 149 L T 149 Louis M 29
Lucetta 154 Lucretis 96 Luke 31
M 149 Martin 152 Sallie 51 T D
30 149 Taylor 147 Thomas D Jr
210 V T 141 195 Z T 30 Zachari-
ah 31 171
HEARD, Edmund 32 Hillery 8
Michael 32 171 Washington R 32
HEMISLY, John Paptist 24
HEMSLEY, Hendly 26
HEMSLY, Alfred 32
HENDERSON, Daniel 26 J H 165
Jas R A 27
HENKLE, Eli J 168
HENNEKEN, Horace 24
HENRY, James 33 Joseph 32
HENSEN, Daniel 113
HENSON, Frederick 113 Lemuel 32
Samuel 26 Thomas 27 Thomas Jr
113
HERBERT, Edward 196 Francis E
30 J T 201 Jere 61 123 208 Jere
T 16 John L 82 John Thomas
179 Joseph 218 Joseph T 101
147 178 M C 217 Maggie 123 R B
195 R H 201 Richard B 195
Samuel G 189
HERGANROEDER, C W 206
HICK, Alison 118
HICKMAN, E B 147 R B 147
HICKS, A W S 200 Allison 165 189 J
L 14 149 James L 156 181 Levi
70 73 87 Mollie A 213 R 14 Scott
179 W L 10 W T 11 14 Washing-
ton 184 210 212 213 William 94
96 153 William F 179 William T
60 179 194 195 196 197
HIGDON, B L 15 18 20 22 57 69 93
102 125 142 146 162 170 177
214 B Leonard 10 Ben 58 59
Benjamin 29 Bettie 59 Bettie A 3
C C 58 Charles 24 Chs 11

236

237

MARR (Continued)
211 Walter M 33 Webster 34
MARSHALL, Benjamin 35 37 Bruce
M 32 Charles H 37 Cope 35
Dennis 35 Eleanor 5 66 Frederick
31 George 26 Hanson 31 113
Henry 11 31 210 James 31 John
H 31 35 John Horace 176 John P
208 214 John W 31 Joseph G 31
Nicholas 32 Thomas 24 35
Washington 34 Wm Francis 32
MARTEALL, Thomas 113
MARTIN, Benjamin 32 C M 211
Henry 32 J E 107 L A 11 57 61
75 178 182 184 195 217 John R
215 L G 50 Luke 126 184 Luther
11 Luther A 12 58 59 60 66 71
73 74 94 96 99 148 184 Michael
24 94 95 147 Pliny 211 R 169 R
M 107 Rev Mr 44 T Lawrence 66
Thoams S 150 Thomas 94 96
Thomas S 16 62 99 105 178 181
186 190 194 William 30
MASON, 16 149 Alexander 32 211
Alexius 26 Cutler 158 E F 16 18
21 58 62 94 95 149 177 181 190
191 194 F 181 James 147 153
158 James A 24 James H 35 Jim
158 John 157 John H 175 John
Henry 24 M A 95 96 Madison 24
Martha F 119 Mary A 94 96
Richard 35 Thomas 154
MASSEY, James 34 125 156 Sarah
125 156 William D 82
MATHANY, R L 70
MATINGLY, J H Jr 196
MATTHEWS, 182 Alexander 37
Aloysius 209 Amanda 15 138
187 Basil 24 Bearnard 178
Bernard 11 179 Charles E 211
Dick 32 E Harriet 3 F 137 Fran-
cis 29 George 32 George H 32
Harriet 11 Henry 29 138 Henson
32 Hillery 34 Hollis 32 J F 67 77
102 123 James 26 James F 54
56 92 133 141 156 163 182 187
198 200 James H 29 Jas Francis
32 Jennie R 76 John 6 29 35 164
King 24 Lewis T 210 M 97
Martha F 102 Mary 87 98 Matthew
26 113 Mrs A 181 Mrs M R 17

MATTHEWS (Continued)
Nicholas 24 29 32 Nick 197
Thomas 3 34 76 113 Ticton 209
V 60 Victor 94 95 96 173 209 W
B 16 William 29 38 181 William
B 6 16 22 39 40 41 46 58 59 77
92 93 95 98 114 170 177 181
191 194 200 William H 15 18
William I 29 Wm B 26 62
MATTINGLEY, ---- 201 Eleanor 43 F
149 Gregory 173 Henry 215 J B
148 180 197 J Benjamin 97
James F 25 John T 26 113
Joseph H 13 60 93 97 146 148
180 Joseph H Jr 178 179 Lizzie 6
Richard F 65 Rose 65 Sarah M
88 Thomas 43
MATTINGLY, Gregory 174 J H 103
138 John T 123 Joseph H 139
Richard F 209 211
MCALPIN, George 54
MCATEE, F 43 49 65 74 88 101 115
157 171 Rev Father 39 114 170
185 191 208
MCCARTHY, Rev Father 166
MCCARTY, Ann 82 Daniel 82
MCCLEAVE, Robert H 86
MCDADE, Lewis 209
MCDANIEL, D R 16 98 G R 198
George R 17 Margaret 59 Mr 3 R
96 181 Richard 16 87 97 198
Sally 5 T 181 T R 96 98 Thomas
162 W L 10 97 118 William 146
William L 4 9 46 51 57 58 88 93-
95 145 177 178 182 190 194
MCELROY, David 173
MCGARNER, W F 10 204
MCKEE, John 37 Robert H 86
MCKEEL, George W 209
MCKIM, Rev Mr 78
MCLAUGHLIN, Belle 218 Wm J 82
MCMAHON, Dennis B 201 John V L
56 M 94 96 Michael 29
MCMANUS, Rev Father 115
MCNANTZ, Alice 165
MCPHERSON, B W B 5 12 19 20 57
62 93 95 160 196 Francis 26
Frank 113 Grandison 32 J W 10
12 145 John 32 45 John W 4 9
21 57 58 93 104 144 177 178
191 194 Kate 137 M L 10 17 20

MCPHERSON (Continued)
213 Mason 18 Mason L 9 17 46
58 61 62 99 148 150 158 178
180 181 S H W 93 S W H 69 74
97 158 180 S W M 61 Samuel
147 Samuel W 13 137 Samuel W
H 197 204 Spencer 31 142
Thomas R 210 211 W 97 W B 97
Walter 87 William 46 Wilson 32
MCWILLIAMS, Ellen 58 F 67 71
Francis 80 94 96 158 160 190
194 197 Frank 97 Henrietta 63
198 John B 166 193 207 Lewis
59 Louis 37
MEADE, James 37
MEDLEY, F O 16 98 Francis O 20
57 George 37
MERRICK, Senator 110 William M
48 William T 22
MERRY, Wm H 10
MESSICK, Benjamin L 37
METTAM, Joseph 141
MIDDLETON, A L 12 Anna L 65
Anthony 29 Benjamin 29 Dory 37
Elizabeth A 120 121 Francis 29
31 Francis Sr 29 Hillery 27 J C
15 23 50 65 94 96 J F S 10 34
67 68 J P S 97 Jane 100 Jas H A
29 John 24 John Donatius 86
John F 35 Mrs 181 Mrs E A 18
62 98 168 Richard H 31 Sandy
16 181 T Columbus 198 Thadde-
us Beverly 65 Walter 210 William
A 198
MIKESELL, Jesse 108 Mary E 108
MILBURN, George Henry 24 John A
24
MILES, Ambrose 26 B F 34 C 149
Cecie 139 Cecil 107 Cecilia 125
167 185 198 Cecilia A 65 170
Charles 23 Dr 54 E 98 150
Edward 32 54 65 166 168 170
185 202 Frank 24 211 Frederick
34 George 29 Henry 24 Henry 35
John 24 Louis 24 M J 81 98
Maggie 139 Maggie J 170 Mamie
154 Mary E 41 N G 194 N J 94
96 147 179 212 N V 75 Nicholas
17 154 Nicholas J 149 190
Richard E 35 Richard Edw 35 S
A 61 166 168 200 213

MILES (Continued)
Sidney 107 Sydney A 138 W H
138 William 35 William Benjamin
141 William Thomas 41
MILLAR, C W 200 Henry 15 Humphrey 197 Jane H 16 Mary 101
Maynard N 68 Mrs Col 37 T A
181 Thomas A 2 16 19 20 39 57
65 69 93 109 151 161 188 190
194 W 15 Walter M 196
MILLARD, Benjamin 24 Ignatius 24
MILLER, 10 David 31 George A 35
176 211 Humphrey 24 J W 10
Jane H 5 John 32 204 John Ed
35 Robert 26 Sarah L 204 William 211
MILLS, Caleb 35 George 35 113 L 59
MILSTEAD, A 58 59 67 A B 178
Albert 1 14 16 46 58 97 147 148
177 178 192 193 195 196 Alice
Virginia 77 Allen B 1 147 155
173 E J 204 Edward 193 George
S 113 Hannibal 27 74 Henry A 98
99 Hillery 27 J D 213 James D
12 111 118 123 124 165 166 193
207 212 Joseph H 198 Josias
173 Josias H 26 Lydia 16 Mr 190
Thomas 83 Thomas I 170 W W
16 60 Walter 78 William 67 William O 61
MILTON, C H 109 191 Charles H
109 153 209 Harry B 109 J D
109
MINER, Jerry 24
MITCHELL, 182 Bettie F 4 Cassie
152 Cecilia W 157 E DeC 85
Elizabeth A 56 Eugene DeC 34 H
S 213 Henry S 7 20 191 High
149 Hugh 4 18 41 64 69 74 118
145 157 167 172 194 200 212
213 J H 4 139 181 J W 14 16 20
53 69 72 133 164 183 188 198
200 James A 74 John H 4 22 38
62 66 68 78 149 150 157 168
169 John W 5 7 8 41 55 59 63 65
67 80 100 101 133 138 139 150
John W 154 163 164 168 182
198-200 213 Joseph 27 Lillie T C
22 Mary R 74 157 Mr 203 R W 69
Richard 24 Richard S 34 S H 200
Thomas 28 W 14 18 Wallace 203

MITCHELL (Continued)
Walter 4 15 18 50 149 William D
207 William D C 193 William
DeC 166 William H 16 19 181
MOLISON, James 37
MOLLISON, J 93 James 57
MOLLYHORN, Mr 3 Sarah J 87
William J 58 196 218
MONROE, A T 93 180 200 213
Alfred T 57 148 197 Eliza R 183
G O 97 George 26 147 H D 118 J
H 17 John H 80 L McC 87 97 98
Levi McC 95 96 McCartney 97 197
Mrs John 150
MONTGOMERY, Anderson 107 B F
62 B J 34 F 118 Francis 17 137
H F 201 Henry 27 J A 118 J H 11
17 147 J H Sr 37 James 26 27
James H 17 60 62 123 146 158
172 190 194 Jane 107 John 26
Juliana 5 Lenn 27 Martha Ann
107 Martin 27 Nace 107 Richard
J 12 Susan 107
MOORE, A T 85 145 B W 148 181
198 Benj L 35 George L 16
George S 150 H A 118 Ignatius
35 178 195 196 J D 27 James 12
97 181 195 James B 32 James M
133 198 James S 16 150 Jordan
35 L M 16 Luc A 186 Marcus 27
Miranda 12 Mrs Wilfred B 187 R
C 215 Rev Mr 135 Richard C 209
Sallie 5 T J 186 188 195 203 212
T Jackson 209 217 W 195 W B
17 180 W H 93 151 W J 184
Wilfred B 13 62 William 97 195
197 216 William B 62 William H
2 12 15-18 49 60 98 106 137
148 178 William T 211 William
Wilson 175 Wilson 34 Wilson L
113 Wm H 10 17 Wm T 32
MORAN, Ellen F 7 Marshall 17 Mary
M 7 165 Samuel C 165 Thomas K
11 12 17 59
MORELAND, J A 97 John H 196
MORGAN, 203 J H 46 James H 46
58 59 62 194 200 Jas M 10 John
H 36 Mr 203 Z R 165
MORLAND, Mrs A 181
MORRIS, Caroline C 49 George 99
174 Grandison 27 Houston 188

MORRIS (Continued)
201 John 49 M C 170 Mary S 82
Mr 116 Stephen 24 Thomas 24
William 170 201 William M 14 15
18 52 70 77 86 169 170 171 207
MORTAN, Bettie 125
MORTON, Ellen H 5 John C 109 M
P 181 Thomas 35
MOULDEN, John 29
MUDD, Ambrose 34 B 205 Catharine 5 DeSales 199 201 Dominic
16 98 198 213 Dominick 161 Dr
187 E M 12 22 Edward McC 35
Emily 106 Fannie T 172 G D 20
98 G L 12 Geo D 11 George 47
George A 189 George D 2 12 14
20 22 63 94 96 158 191 195 196
206 212 George F 35 George L 22
H L 118 Henry 150 181 Henry E
16 166 193 207 Henry L 62 186
Henry L Sr 93 Henry T 189 J A
93 J R 84 153 J T 4 11 58 77
111 118 142 155 169 181 James
A 9 21 57 58 69 93 99 103 104
106 137 139 140 145 148 155
158 164 178 180 181 197 212
Jere T 11 13 17 18 20 39 41 46
51 58 61 63 95 98 125 146 148
197 Jeremiah T 140 John E 175
Marian 22 Mary Pauline 186
Mary Rose 191 R V 163 Mr 153
Mrs Samuel A 22 S A 155 S M 59
61 Samuel 62 150 156 181
Samuel A 35 187 196 Spalding
205 Susan 11 Sylvester 10 13 22
94 95 96 140 169 194 206 Syl-
vester A 11 Sylvester B 35 Sylves-
ter M 58 60 81 T Jere 94
Thaddeus 35 216 Theophilus 27
Virginia 169 Walter 27 William
27 212 William A 12 88 Zepheni-
ah 179
MUGLETON, F 97
MULHOLLAND, Charles 142
MULLEN, Daniel 171
MULLIKIN, Clem 32
MULLIN, Daniel 195 196
MUNDELL, Ned 179
MUNDLE, Edward 26 John H 209
MUNROE, John 37
MUNSON, Ralph 32

MURDOCH, J P 93 James Perry 24
186 John 67 174 Mrs John 2 R L
59 Richard L 52 60 W 59 Wesley
59 William H 174
MURDOCK, John 16 Richard E 209
Robert A 209 Wm W 27
MURER, Rev Father 183 Rev Mr 171
205
MURPHY, C C 148 Cincinnatus 17 F
D 67 Francis A 141 James 61
Jane 141 John E 195 Joseph 11
Joseph L 72 Nathan 61 P A 62
101 173 175 P C 173 175 P H 169
Patrick 94 95 Robert 215 William
35 61 96 William B 61
MURRAY, A R A 13 17 53 62 83 101
102 122 Adeline A 53 Ann 17 96
97 101 102 Edward 147 Edward
M 178 Edwin M 176 Francis G
142 George 175 H 67 J H 98 J
Henry 214 J R 59 84 85 James A
32 210-212 John B 63 John H
198 John R 2 3 10 14 15 17 20
67 69 70 99 100 133 140 145
146 178 180 193-195 207 Jos L
11 Joseph 32 147 152 M 97
Matilda 96 R A 15 94 95 200 S
97 Samuel 96 Thomas H 147 148
178 180 197 212 216 Wm F 180
MURRER, Rev Father 121
MURRY, George 31 Thomas 29
MUSCHELL, Geo H 58 George H 46
MUSCHETT, Anthony 32 Brooke 32
Geo H 10 George H 15 P H 4 10
24 Wm M 32
MYERS, E 150 Elizabeth 198
NALLEY, Alfred 4 15 187 U 65
Uzzial 16 109
NASH, C 115
NEAL, A W 196 Augustin W 133
Bennett 14 James H 101
NEALE, A W 3 22 46 58 93 95 165
167 194 203 Augustin W 191
Augustine W 76 B 68 77 Bennet
57 63 145 190 Bennett 2 9 93 95
96 C 169 C A 75 167 Charles A
117 178 179 196 Charles H 179
E Clarence 117 Francis 51 98
112 142 Francis T 31 Frank 51
Georgia 190 H A 11 95 96 Henry
A 12 94 95 96 Hillery 34 J H 155

NEALE (Continued)
James H 9 16 46 58 67 93 95
110 111 141 159 Jennie 56
Jennie R 76 John W 147 Lemuel
34 Lewis 32 Mary Alice 117
Misses 199 202 Robert 44 V H
169 214
NEAVE, Samuel R 71
NELSON, F M 173 209 211 Henry
35 195 196 Mitchell 161 Richard
F 161 Violetta B 161
NEVETT, John R 211 W C 200
NEVISON, James 89
NEVITT, Cox 94 96 Francis 210 218
Hugh C 210 J 60 John 95 96
John P 29 141 John R 211 John
W 57 Mary G 78 R G 78 Robert
218 Thomas 195 William 75 104
145 William Jr 118 146 165
William Sr 57 93-95 142 145 177
NEWBERRY, John 38 John W 178
195
NEWBURY, J W 12
NEWMAN, 87 Charles 87 Charles H
211 Francis 27 H 31 Henry 149
James 26 173 Jesse 27 John 209
Josephine 149 M 31 Mary 97
Mary B 80 Rev Dr 78 Thomas 60
147 Thomas R 80
NEWTON, Frank 37 George A 37
NICHOLSON, F 59 Thomas F 147
217
NORMAN, R C 98 99
NORRIS, 74 148 180 216 A J 12 15
47 59 60 151 170 195 201 213
Andrew J 60 63 94 95 Columbus
32 Elizabeth C 170 George 29 98
George W 31 77 Henry 29 173
209 210 J B 149 191 200 J B Jr
162 J E 213 James 24 James E
149 John B Jr 80 Joseph 77
Julian E 85 178 179 206 Richard
214 Thomas W 170 Washington
74 William E 95 William J Jr 162
William L 96
NUTWELL, Joseph H 216 N 197
O'BRIEN, William N 27
O'BRYAN, Elender 76 Ellen 5
OFELLOW, Charles 31
OFFER, Henry 34 211
OLIVER, B F 209 Benjamin F 32

OLIVER (Continued)
124 211 C O A 206 Catharine A
82 Charles H 82 George 17
George C 211 George H 35
George P 12 James 97 James O
44 Mary 77 R B 97 Richard A 26
77 Richard C 211 Robert 17 66
138 146 Sarah A 138 W G 11
OSBOURNE, Elizabeth 5
OUZTS, Marrion 210
OWEN, Alberta E 152 Francis 173 H
H 125 John W 199 Lemuel B 26
P W 199 T T 15 38 Thomas T 154
161 179 196 W W 15 38
OWENS, Henry H 188 James 94 95
120 147 148 James B 191 209
James F 163 John E 27 Lemuel
B 209 Mrs 117 Thomas T 179
William 15
PACA, William 45
PADGETT, A R 83 Adelaide R 52 B E
186 Benjamin 196 C L 59 Elisha
60 H T 32 J H 17 57 217 J T 83
163 J V 137 James L 209 James
T 175 217 James V 211 John 16
John E 65 Joseph 11 Joseph B
50 Joseph H 48 59 60 62 94 95
100 181 198 Joseph V 211 Lilla L
5 Logan 60 Margaret A 65
Martha Maria 217 Minnie Turner
137 Mr 101 102 Mrs Joseph H
48 Percival 163 204 Roberta 137
S B 211 S C 186 204 Thomas A
59 W A 62 97 101 W W 10 18 60
62 64 97 99 101 145 146 216
William A 23 42
PAGE, C 181 H C 3 11 12 18 59 69
142 H Clagett 11 62 H O 199 J M
162 John M 102 166 193 210
Mary 150 W 169 Washington 31
85 148 158 159 161 162 164 180
182 194 197 Washington Jr 167
PAPE, Capt 193
PARISH, Mary 62 William 62
PARKER, George T 52 James A 52
John F 52 165 Joseph 47 52 104
109 111
PASSAGE, George 26 73
PASSEY, W A 62
PATTERSON, Ignatius 24
PAYNE, Alice A 122 160 Daniel J 40

PAYNE (Continued)
George C 29 James H 29 R 43 62
67 95 148 154 191 Richard 7 10
13 58 94 95 97 98 216 Savanah
34 William T 29
PEARSON, Robert 198
PEDLUPA, J B 51
PENN, Alexander 138 141 Joseph H
209 Oscar 24 95 96 Stephen 11
Stpehen 32
PENNEY, Mary E 97
PENNINGTON, Capt 137 F 195 196
Franklin 113 173 Sallie B 137
Sarah 112 143
PENNY, John 12 27 32 87 97 147
Mary E 147 Sarah 147 Thomas
26 W A 35 William 16 26
PERRY, C C 13 58 59 60 77 94 95
96 97 121 148 149 179 180 196
213 Charles 103 Charles C 1 13
16 19 61 98 102 145 146 148
177 178 191 197 200 212
Clements 27 Edmond 177 181
Edmund 10 15 16 23 62 70 78
120 146 Edward 27 G C 60 61 95
J R 31 149 179 185 James R 166
James Rufus 216 R D 166 Rufus
58 59 77 94 95 96 97 Thomas D
142 175 William 26 William S
149
PHILIPS, N T 206
PICKERAL, Caleb 97
PICKERELL, Aloysia L 114 Mary E 5
Stanislaus 192
PICKRELL, Marcus 197 William 197
PIERCE, Henry 24
PINCKNEY, William 51 William 68
PIPER, John 135
PLATER, James H 29 John 6 Louis
29 Mary 59
PLOWDEN, Ferdinand 24 Jerry 31
John H 31 Joseph 31 Michael 32
Robert H 31 175
PORTER, R 56 Robert 56 180
POSEY, 67 A B 175 Adrian 178 179
Ann 66 C A 200 C H 102 122 213
Catharine 109 Charles H 147
150 155 179 E 169 E A 121
Edwin 215 Elizabeth E 114 Ellen
C 76 Francis 121 Francis A 168
Frank 27 George R 12 149

POSEY (Continued)
Henry H 16 149 Hugh P 114
Ignatius 27 John H 109 149 181
John W 11 Joseph 27 Lawrence
66 74 106 Lemuel 27 Mrs Lawrence 106 Ola Blanchard 208
Philomenia J 208 Philomenia
Jane 78 R B 102 145 R H 213 R
K 62 Richard 2 151 195 196 214
Richard B 9 21 41 47 49 56-58
93 104 142 144 149 177 178 191
194 216 Roger 149 Samuel 9
Sandy 27 Susannah W 154 T M
10 Thomas 9 46 57-59 76 93 104
142 144 145 149 177 178
Thomas M 7 67 140 145 158 168
212 213 Thomas R 174 W A 10
11 17 37 57 69 104 112 121 140
142 181 213 Wady 5 Washington
A 9 16 93 120 144 145 148 177
212 William D 174 William H 27
78 208 Z V 195 Zachariah V 172
POULSON, Thomas L 218
POWERS, James L 25 173
PRICE, 90 200 A 95 Albin 11 12 59
67 72 79 80 94-96 146 147 158
165 178 191 194 197 199 216 Dr
54 F 103 Francis 10 16 69 93
146 158 173 174 178 204 George
199 J A 16 20 46 61 67 72 154
James 26 201 210 John A 13 20
55 58-61 94 95 97 98 173 John
F 54 Joseph 9 10 16 47 57 67 85
93-95 98-100 104 140 145 150
158 178 181 198 200 213 R Jr
61 Richard 10 20 57 93 145 149
178 185 190 194 200 Sallie C
185 T C 85 140 183 200 213 T W
99 Thomas 181 Thomas C 67 90
151 200 204 Thomas W 209
Valentine 27 William H 16 21 94
95 149 194 204 212
PRIOR, Henry 31
PROCTOR, A 94 96 Alexander 35
Charles H 37 Chs 35 E 94 96
Edward 35 210 George A 113
George W 29 Gusty 35 H Thomas
35 Henry 35 113 Hillery 31
James W 29 Jenifer 17 John 35
John A 31 John Francis 211
John H 35 Joseph 34 Joseph I 32

PROCTOR (Continued)
Miley 35 Peter 29 Rob't 35 Robert
Henry 176 Thomas 35 53 W
Henry 35 William B 34 William N
29 Willie 35
PROUT, Bettie 202 R 154 Rev 214
Rev R 154 Robert 16 51 90 157
169 183 185 192 198 202 214
PUGH, 91
PURSER, Spencer 208
PYE, Brent 44 Charles A 92 124
Charles H 13 14 19 111 114 118
183 187 211 Charles Henry 24
Charles J 209 Henry 29 James L
29 John 84 Mary C 181 Mary
Edmonia 125 Mary M 124 Mrs
Charles J 84 Mrs E M 17 Sylves-
ter 29 141 Washington 24 Wil-
liam 29
QUEEN, Charles 12 Frank 27 Henry
26 John 26 29 32 71 Joseph 35
176 Raphael 34 Samuel 26 Wil-
liam 20 22 125 155 159 167 194
William Henry 211 William M 20
QUEENAN, Abraham 196 Andrew
29 Henry 29 Isaac 29 James 29
Thomas A 141 William 174 Wil-
liam L 29
QUENZEL, J 121 Julius 4 60 Mrs A
204
QUINN, Patrick 178
RADCLIFF, R D P 60 148
RADCLIFFE, R D P 101
RADIE, Edward Jr 115 Josie Clara
115
RAILEY, Samuel J 29
RAMMACK, William F 195
RANDALL, John H 173 Walter J 113
RANDELL, Mary Jane 156
RANDOLPH, John 34
RANSOM, Buck 211 Daniel 37
James H 26 173 William 34
RATCLIFF, T Middleton 181 Thomas
M 171 181
RATCLIFFE, Lizzette V 199 R D P 13
197
REDGIT, John 27
REDMUND, Caroline 37
REED, Charlotte 163 E 21 Harrison
34 Marion 35 Marion C 113 R A
189 Robert 24 Samuel D 35

REEDER, Calvert 37 Dr 184 Grandison 26 J H 67 154 191 John H 16 43 149 John Wesley 37 M 59 Richard R 46

REESE, Charles 147 Charles E 147 Charles P 146

REEVES, Caleb 17 35 206 Cecilia 5 E C 12

RENNOE, Mr 3 Perry 180 189 208 R 198 R A 11 21 72 74 149 180 181 208 Reverdy 208 Reverdy A 16 60 97 99 187 189

RENWICK, Albert 84

REUBEN, John W 34

REYBOLD, 157

RHODES, Linda 139

RICHARDS, A 137 George S 24 28 Georgie 80 Isham 24 Jane S A 81 John F 28 John Francis 24

RICHARDSON, F 14 J F 14 James 81 R G W 35 Stephen 26 Vincent 26 W G 12 Wesley 27 Wm 27

RICHMOND, Henry 179 J L 171 J T 187 James 179 John S 146 195 196 217 Kate 179

RIDGEWAY, Capt 199

RILEY, James 27

RISON, Alexander 16 149 Amos 209 210 Ella 198 Gerard 85 149 173 Gerrard 16 James 173 James H 209 214 R E 67 Robert E 3 72 93 164 179 197

ROBBINS, B F 58 94 95 Benjamin F 146

ROBER, Peter W 188

ROBERT, Hexander 181 J Thomas 125 Robert 34

ROBERTS, Henrietta 107 Henry 12 24 Hugh 205 J 217 J H 1 11 12-16 37 57-60 93-96 144 146 154 172 179 194-196 208 216 J Hubert 5 23 40 52 77 123 145 171 191 Lilla L 123 Maria Josephine 123

ROBERTSON, 182 A H 7 21 64 88 93 194 200 204 A H Jr 173 Alex H 20 57 Alex Jr 26 Alexander 139 Alexander A 69 Alexander H 9 15 46 177 Annie 217 E F L 165 Eleanor 62 98 Eleanore 16 George 34 H G 172 195

ROBERTSON (Continued)
H Gerard 40 Henry 31 197 Henry G 4 6 11 52 58 77 94 95 170 171 191 200 208 217 J P 111 142 J R 13 60 62 64 100 103 117 John H 31 49 John R 14 15 16 63 76 97 100 148 150 182 194 Mary 5 Nellie B 205 Verlinda S 46 William G 205

ROBEY, 114 171 201 Aloysius 11 Ann 181 Annie 156 C E 175 Charles 114 Charles C 49 54 Columbus 162 Elizabeth A 108 Eva T 108 Family 183 Fannie C 218 Francis 16 65 186 Franklin A 32 142 George W 108 168 H 94-96 H C 17 H Clay 122 H W 168 Henry 175 Henry C 61 197 Hezekiah 27 209 James J 108 James M 108 John A 108 John H 12 17 108 111 142 John L 13 John N 17 111 L S 99 176 L T 38 Leonard Smallwood 155 Louisa 162 Lucien 12 Malvine S 108 Mary C 43 Mary E 108 Mary R 198 Mary S 108 Mr 203 P W 56 Peter W 10 13 57 93 145 151 165 177 194 211 212 Rufus 1 10 13 46 57-59 61 68 91 93 94 96 98 145 213 S H 118 Samuel C 16 175 Samuel H 43 Sarah J 111 142 Sophia 108 T B 155 T Y 10 59 60 172 186 T Yates 67 69 146 203 T Yates Jr 24 T Yates Sr 86 Teresa R A 121 Theodore L 62 Thoedore L 195 Thomas I 199 Thomas V 65 Thomas Y 9 10 13 181 187 188 198 Townley 1 3 13 20 57 58 61 69 72 85 93 97 98 118 145 146 148 156 158 160 180 213 Townly 18 58 67 178 197 W L 167 W T 118 William 188 William L 153 197

ROBINSON, Mrs E 99 William C 211

ROBY, Eleanor A 5 Georgie 80 Isaiah 157 S D 199 Somerset D 80 T Yates 93 146

ROCHE, William 59

RODEY, Robert 201

RODIER, 216

ROLLINGS, Aloysius 29

ROLLINS, 102 Enoch 209 William R
113
ROLSON, Frank 97
ROSE, Mary B 80
ROSS, Alexander 15 195 Henry 29 J
Alexander 196 Jerry 24 Jesse 27
John 35 195 John Henry 24
Joseph 27 96 William 26
ROW, George N 39
ROWE, C H 61 Charles H 34 38 139
E W 181 George N 1 13 14 21 52
60 89 97 99 102 120 138 148
163 175 H T 180 H Turner 148
197 Lizzie S 139 Mary F E 208
Mary Matilda 139 Mrs M A 184
Turner 172 W E W 3 10 20 57 65
78 93 104 118 137 145 160 171
179 190 194 197 206 208 Wil-
liam H 191
ROZIER, Clem 16 59 147 Daniel
179 F 98 Francis 198 Francis W
39 James M 31 Richard 34 Wil-
liam 34
RUNTZELL, George W 212
RUSSELL, Victor W 39 William 97
RUSSELS, J C 149
RUSTIN, George 29 141
RYE, Willis 61
RYLAND, J H 49 111 142
RYSON, R E 181 Robert 155
SAINTCLAIR, George H 88 91 Mr
189 Rosanna 183
SAMUEL, T 40
SANDERS, Alexander 109 D I 10 41
67 105 120 133 138 158 169 178
200 203 213 D Ignatius 14 43 66
80 D J 194 Dr 15 E J 15 181 200
Edward 149 Edward J 62 115
149 Fannie 115 Ignatius 63 J T
198 James 174 Joseph E 9 21 58
68 69 93 156 187 195 209 210
Joseph Norris 25 Mary 68 Mary A
80 107 Mr 118 Robert 115 Sally
M 149 Wm N 18 62 67 184 198
SANDY, Albert 111 Alice Virginia 77
J A 27 Jane F 111 Thomas E 175
Thomas Edwin 77
SASSCER, 13 17 60 61 180 184
Ellen A 102 Maggie Mayo 102 Mr
205 P A 12 16 68 69 85 93 94 96
97 118 121 145 165 180 181 193

SASSCER (Continued)
197 207 Philemon A 166 Philip
22 102 Philip A 17 20 57 61 99
100 133 140 146 148 150
SAUNDERS, James 27 Samuel 199
SAVOY, Ananais 27 Charles 35 36
113 Cornelius 36 John 36 John
A 37 Miley 36
SAXTON, William 84
SCHECKELL, George A 216
SCOOT, Amelia 5 S B 34
SCOTT, Adelaide R 83 H R 6 31 97
149 161 175 180 Henry 32 Henry
R 103 137 141 147 148 155 159
Isaac 27 James 195 James Henry
24 Joseph 7 209 Llewellyn 174 M
A 138 M C 97 Mary A 165 Mary C
147 Mary E 186 Matthew 4 Mrs
40 Mrs M A 1 106 R D 166
Robert 27 Silas 27 T A 195
Thomas H 3 21 58-60 97 William
32 William J 7 8
SCROGGIN, W Francis 26
SCROGGINS, Charles H 154 H 16
William F 154
SEAT, W H 162 188
SEIBOLD, 117
SEMBLY, Alexander 37 George 36
George R 35 Joseph 176
SEMMES, Charles 15 Charles H 59
E B 18 John F 161 199 L E 38 M
L 38 Mark L 163 Mary Jane 22
Robert 12 35 58 59 62 Susannah
59 Thomas 62 142 145 Zepheni-
ah 18
SEWALL, George 60 147 George H
35
SEWELL, Alfred 176 Frank 25
George 25 Harrison 25 185 John
36
SEXTON, S B 199 Samuel B 198
SHACKELFORD, J W 163 186
James 97 201
SHADE, Henry 29 Lemuel 31
Thomas H 29
SHADRICK, Lewis 17 36
SHANKS, George 31 William 31
SHANNON, Charles H 190 G B 17
217 George B 18 50 75 190
George H 16 18 Jane F D 50
Mary Ann 190 Rachel 5

SHARP, Horatio 89
SHAW, Arthur 198 C A F 162
   Charles A F 125 Charles F 102
   Howard 56 Innocenes B 5 William 45
SHECKELS, George A 146 George H 147
SHEIRBOURN, 10 C H 59 200
   Charles H 16 97 Chs H 11 W 149
   W L 145 William 31 58 William L
   84 93 104 142 Wm L 75 Wm M
   61
SHEIRBURN, 2 Mary 208 Mary R
   178 William 208 William L 69
   177 William Walter 208
SHELTEN, Noble 210
SHELTON, Alonzo 26 113 John 27
SHEPHERD, A R 183 Alexander 183
   Susan D 183
SHERIBURN, William 213
SHERIFF, J B 1 11 12 16 57 67 72
   98 107 145 149 166 193 194 206
   Joshua B 10 89 J R 93 Samuel
   86 89 107
SHERRIFF, J B 178 181
SHIVEL, Patrick H 32
SHIVERAL, Henry 26 Richard 27
SHORT, Bettie 122 Charles 26 E 59
   Edward 29 George H 31 141
   Gusta 210 Henry 29 Herbert 209
   James 26 29 Jesse 27 John 29
   34 John Thomas 26 Joseph 29
   Marcellus 26 Robert 29 William
   25 210 William A 32 Wm Frederick 210 William H 31 Wm S 29
SHORTER, James R 36 John 175
   John Alex 32 Thomas S 35
   Thomas W 37 William 36
SHORTS, Washington 36
SHOW, Fannie 99
SHREVE, James H Sr 21
SHRIVER, S S 202
SIDLER, 204 Charles J 59 113 195
   204 Mrs 204 Richard W 113
SIMMES, George 189 John Davy 23
   Louisa E 9 Mark L 9 Mary 189
   Robert 189 Thomas 25
SIMMIS, George N 179 Robert 179
SIMMONS, Ann A 83 Asa 186 187
   Benjamin 83 Charles 26 Frank
   27 George C 210 George T 174

SIMMONS (Continued)
   Ida M 114 James 26 John F 27
   Joseph S 209 Noel R 114 Richard
   G 173 Robert H 193 Susan 193 T
   P 204 W T 179 Wesley 171 William 13 16 60 83 148 William T
   194 195 210
SIMMS, A B 200 Alexander 25 171
   Benedict 29 Charles H 24
   Charles Henry 25 Clem A 31
   Francis 35 Francis A 113 Jeff
   196 John 37 Peter 37 R 67
   Robert 72 195 196 Samuel 36
   Thomas 167 177 190 194 207
   William 35 William Henry 25
   William Sr 36
SIMPSON, 91 A 93 Alonzo 12 27
   Amanda C 68 G T 160 216
   George 200 George H 9 17 20 57
   62 66 68 George S 146 197
   George T 6 57 93 145 147 148
   178 J R 17 J S 148 J W 31 J W T
   98 James 27 John W 44 Mary J
   E 44 Mrs G H 181 N W 149
   Richard T 29 Thomas D 16 62
   116 149 170 W 200 W F 149 Web
   58 59
SIMS, Alonzo 162
SINCLAIR, Ann 82
SINGFIELD, Humphrey 31 Samuel
   31
SKEKELL, George A 87
SKINNER, Edward 37 113 176
   Elizabeth 101 103 George W 27
   James E 37 113 176 John
   Hanson 175 Richard E 37 113
   Roszell 209 Sylvester 209
   Thomas 13 16 60 74 97 147 148
   180 197 200 213 216
SLATER, Coates 56 Coats 34 James
   37 196
SLATTARY, Patrick 175
SLATTERY, Francis P 211 Patrick
   32 209 210
SLIVILL, John 31
SLY, Alton 31 John Edward 25 John
   H 31
SLYE, A B 118 123 B 12 Edward 29
   George Robert 25 Henry 35 Mary
   A 106 Moses 15 29
SMALL, Ferdinand 209 Jos Henson

THOMAS (Continued)
Francis H 29 Frank 36 George 12
26 29 37 H A 34 H M 107 160
213 Henry 25 31 32 34 37 175
Hillery 29 Isaac 28 J F 94 96 J R
161 J S M 201 J T 160 J W 41 56
150 James 25 141 James F 177
James L 210 James T 9 93 104
145 James W 31 Jere 37 Jesse
25 John 25 29 168 John A 31
John E 29 John H 29 209 John
Jr 29 113 John T 57 John Vincent 25 John W 31 67 198 John
Walter 37 Joseph 26 Joseph F 11
59 94 96 124 196 Joseph Wm 26
Lorenzo 29 Madison 25 209
Mamie 154 Marshall 138 Miley
37 Mitchell 27 Neely 36 Orlander
113 Orlando 29 Perry 58 Philip
32 33 87 96-98 R H 31 Richard
25 37 59 113 178 210 Robert 26
36 195 196 211 S W 31 Samuel
25 29 Sylvester 37 206 Thomas
26 29 Tolison 59 60 Tom 33 W
58 59 Walter 50 Washington 29
36 William 29 33 34 37 211
William F 211 William H 29 William Joseph 113 William W 31
196 Wm Henry 29
THOMPSON, A 17 Benjamin 31
Chandler 25 Charles 29 32
Clarinda V H 43 Congey 26
Francis 37 G W 200 George 135
George W 151 Henry 29 57 93
Henry A 17 48 83 88 J C 86 J F
13 16 118 J T 211 James 28 33
113 James A 29 James Lit 210
Jesse 27 John 7 John C 29 86
John F 146 158 178 212 John T
32 211 Laura V 206 Lucinda 83
M 180 182 216 Marcellus 1 7 13
18 19 59 61 98 103 137 141 148
198 Morgan 209 Noble 64 Noble
A 201 Rezin I 29 Rose 65 Samp-
son 28 Sydney 26 173 Thomas B
29 W J A 13 William 25 29 32 37
William B 173 William R 43 Wm
H 29
THORP, E R 192 Mary F 192
TIBBS, James 27
TILLMAN, William 31

TINKER, Hanson 26
TIPPET, William 16
TODD, J M 48 90 154 John K 74
John M 6 51 74 218
TOLSON, Adam 27 Alex 31 Eliza
147 F A 91 111 142 George 195
196 Joseph 28 Linsey 27 Moses
31 Philip 25 Toney 31 Walter 27
Wesley 28
TOLTON, Leck 31
TOMPKIN, J R 12
TOMPKINS, Elizabeth 78 101 111
142 J R 16 141 James R 78 101
111 119 142 157 199 Mary H
202
TOPP, J T 85
TOWLES, J 81 114 John 65 Rev
Father 81
TOWNSEND, Rev Mr 115
TOWNSHEND, Joshua C 37
TOY, Miles 179 Miley 29 36
TOYER, Dennis 27 Valentine 28
TRACT, Annapolis 117 Apple Grove
109 Bachelor's Hope 200 Bag-
got's Boot 157 Barton's Addition
206 Belmont 118 Bendit's Rest
204 Berry's Plains 118 Boar-
man's Rest 53 103 Boswell Build-
ing 187 Brawner House 56 186
Brentfield 91 110 214 Brentwood
38 Briars 102 Bromont 38 46
Broomfield 49 Bunker Hill 168
Burch's Reserve 105 Bush Hill
193 Calvert's Hope 8 53 103
Canal Hotel 126 Carrick 101
Carter's Inheritance 50 Causin's
Manor 214 Cedar Grove 65 68
107 Cedar Hill 169 Cedar Point
Farm 76 Chandler's Hope 72 170
Charlesboro 151 Cherry Grove 48
74 Chinquapin Farm 214 Clifton
39 76 81 Cold Streams 107
Cornwallace's Neck 111 Crain's
Low Ground 66 Cuttle Manor 118
119 Decker's Delight 37 Deep
Point 7 Dent's Levels 101 Dent's
Marsh Addition 184 Dent's
Resurvey 21 Dolley's Purchase
168 Double Trouble 2 Double
Trouble Enlarged 2 Eagles' Nest
204 Edelen's Discovery 20

250

TRACT (Continued)

Tompkin's Purchase 161 Tompkins' Purchas 199 Tompkinsville 101 Tranquility 19 Trappe 3 Tryall 50 Tulip Hill Farm 101 Two Sisters 165 Uncle Peter's 68 Upper Goose Bay 154 Walnut Grove 109 Walnut Landing 65 Ward's Addition 121 Ware 50 Waverley 38 Waverly 47 55 82 172 Wellington 171 199 Westwood 44 121 Westwood Manor 166 White Hall 168 Whitehall 107 Wicomico House 7 Widow's Place 153 Widow's Pleasure 153 Wilderness 49 Woodbury Harbor 7 Woodbury Hope 65 Wycomoco Fields 102 Yatten 18

TRAVIS, George 26 John 26

TROTTER, Peter 12 17 60 67 147 178 179 196 198 205 William 147 Willie 205

TRURES, George 179

TUBMAN, B D 12 101 105 114 150 151 160 Benjamin D 9 12 17 20 57 62 93 104 144 145 147 177 181 196 G W 10 George W 10 Mrs B D 160 Peter 28 R T 13 67 101 105 151 170 211 Richard T 56 61 72 97 120 183 187 William 25 173

TUCKER, E 94 95 96 Mary V 124 R V 94 96 R Y 95 96 Robert 85 Robert G 196 Thomas W 124 Thomas Wilson 152 W A 150 Wilson 152

TURNER, Amelia 43 101 Aquila 5 Arthur 134 Bros 216 C S 17 Charles A 29 E D 167 E Dudley 18 F H 57 G H 173 Gerard B 29 H A 213 Henry 101 155 Henry A 22 36 43 178 J A 17 J Henry 179 216 J Hy 176 J R 17 18 J Samuel 175 J T 17 18 James H 28 John 36 75 John A 111 195 John H 17 John N 17 John R 9 45 69 70 73 74 93 191 194 John W 113 Joseph S 121 Littleton 29 Matthew 37 Nannie 5 Nathan 28 P H 93 Pad 27 Patrick 180 Penny 59 R O 210 Richard 29

TURNER (Continued)

Robert H 141 Rose 140 Samuel 22 Samuel Henry 101 Sandy 26 T P 155 Teresa R A 121 Thomas 17 29 Thomas L 29 Thomas P 29 69 74 Thomas S 29 140 Violetta G 18 39 William 67 68 94 95 109 155 164 177 197 201 William Lewin 101 Wm 10

TYLER, David 31 James 28 John 32

UNDERWOOD, G W 17 33

VALL, James 36

VELLAGER, Rev Father 77

VICINANZA, C 50 64 Rev C 43

VINCENT, Alexander 28 William 25 31

VOLTZ, Rev Father 185

WADE, 37 Albert 178 Albin 206 Benjamin 37 140 C A 12 C E 22 59 Capt 163 Charles B 59 Charles E 59 147 208 D 59 Dominic 36 Dominick 212 Fielder 113 Fielder J 37 Frank 37 Hillery H 37 John 94 96 198 John B 37 John S 212 Kate 208 M O 216 Marcellus 37 Oscar 14 R 14 R O 67 211 R Oscar 137 Richard 163 216 William H 153 195 201 206 216 217

WAGAMAN, Mattie 66

WAITES, Walter 26

WAKER, James 135

WALKER, 135 A J 149 217 Alexander 36 C 96 97 C W 160 162 Lucy B 22 Steward 26

WALL, 37 J 169 J T 201 John T 213 R P 10 20 22 68 69 93 104 145 178 194 201 213 Richard P 9 41 57 72 81 106 140 160 212

WALLACE, Edward 25 Francis 25 Henry 34 Horace 25 183 Jesse 28 John 25 Joseph 18 25 209 Noble 25 Warren 183 Wilson 25

WALLER, George 26 196

WALLIS, Josephine 11

WALLS, Richard P 89

WALSH, Rev Father 186

WALTERS, John 28

WARD, 140 217 Alexander 28 Daily 28 J T 12 13 58 98 201 J T W 10 James 94 96 John 26

WOODS, George H 36
WORRALL, William 40
WORRICK, George 179 196 George
  W 31
WORTON, William 175
WRIGHT, Isaac 34 Jubez 210 Rich-
  ard A 209 210 T W 61 138
  Thomas 72 87 Thomas W 59 60
  61 80 96 103 146 147 151 178
  179 195 U 21 Uzzial 61 73 87
  190 207 212 Uzziel 181 194 197
YATES, C 97 Francis 30 31 James H
  30 John Was'n 25 Joseph 30 192
  Maria 11 Rezin 30 William 31

YATES (Continued)
  149 196
YEATS, Henry 36 William 36
YOUNG, 37 Aaron 36 Abram 36
  Alexander 36 Bob 204 Calvert 30
  Frank 36 Geo Henry 33 Hilleary
  211 Hillery 36 Jacob 26 John 30
  97 196 Joseph 33 97 Louisa 179
  R 111 Richard 196 Robert 62 201
  Samuel 25 Samuel J 25 Stephen
  30 Thomas 30 174 Washington
  31 Wesley 30 William 28 36
YOUNGMAN, Kate 208
ZIMMERMAN, Valentine 102